LEGENDARY LOCALS

OF

EDGECOMBE AND NASH COUNTIES

NORTH CAROLINA

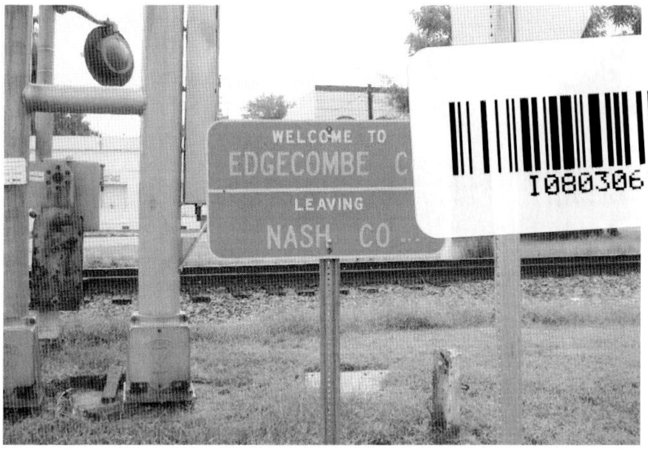

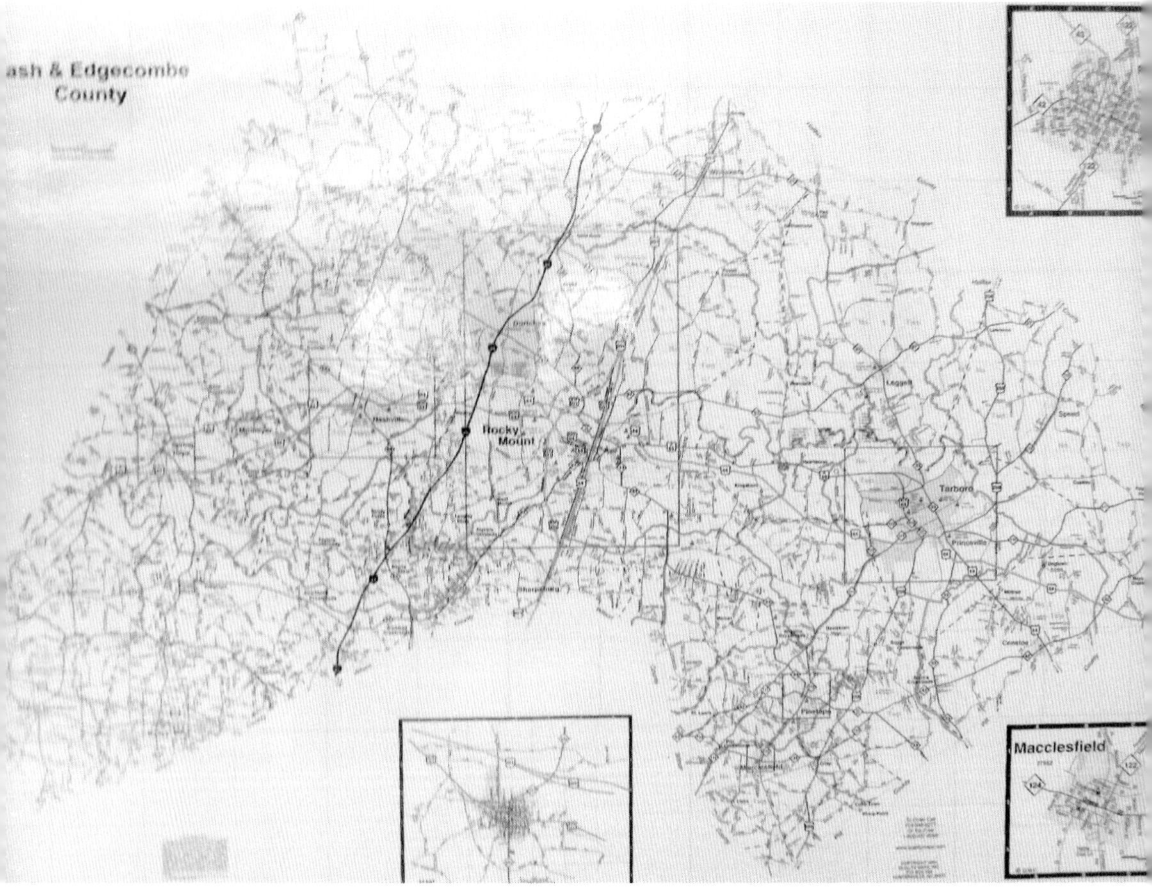

Twin Counties
The "Twin Counties" are displayed in a map in the local history room of Braswell Memorial Library. (Photograph by the author.)

Page 1: Edgecombe and Nash Counties Sign
This county line sign at the railroad tracks shows that it is just an artificial line that separates the counties. (Photograph by Daniel Chasse.)

LEGENDARY LOCALS

OF

EDGECOMBE AND NASH COUNTIES

NORTH CAROLINA

MONIKA S. FLEMING

LEGENDARY LOCALS

ISBN 978-1-4671-0044-1

Legendary Locals is an imprint of Arcadia Publishing
Charleston, South Carolina

Printed in the United States of America

Library of Congress Control Number: 2012946162

For all general information, please contact Arcadia Publishing:
Telephone 843-853-2070
Fax 843-853-0044
E-mail sales@arcadiapublishing.com
For customer service and orders:
Toll-Free 1-888-313-2665

Visit us on the Internet at www.arcadiapublishing.com

Dedication

This book is dedicated to the many volunteers of the Twin County Hall of Fame, Edgecombe County Veterans' Military Museum, Blount-Bridgers House, and Spring Hope Museum, and local history librarians Traci Thompson and Pam Edmondson. These people help honor the legends and keep their stories for future generations.

On the Cover: From left to right:
(TOP ROW) George Higgs, blues musician (Courtesy Twin County Museum and Hall of Fame, portrait by Susan Fecho, page 49); Anne Cobb, music teacher (Courtesy Cobb family, page 58); Benjamin Bunn, Rocky Mount Mayor (Braswell Memorial Library, page 74); Charles Johnson, radio station owner and announcer (Courtesy Johnson family, page 36); Robert "Bob" Melton, founder Melton's Barbecue Restaurant (Courtesy Melton family, page 20).
(MIDDLE ROW) George Howard, judge and business leader (Courtesy Blount-Bridgers House Museum, page 35); Milton Bullock, musician (Courtesy Twin County Museum and Hall of Fame, page 48); Evelyn Wilson, educator (Courtesy Evelyn Wilson, page 62); Dred Wimberly, North Carolina senator (Courtesy Wimberly family, page 74); Cyrus Edson, educator (Photograph by Roberta King, page 58).
(BOTTOM ROW) Mary "Jackie" Sumner Blount, community (Courtesy Blount-Bridgers House Museum, page 35); Milton S. Brown, businessman and photographer (Courtesy Edgecombe County Memorial Library, page 33); Blake Williams, local veteran killed in Iraq (Courtesy the Willliams family, page 112); Rosa Broadie, educator and community advocate (Courtesy Rosa Broadie, page 57); Buck Leonard, Baseball Hall of Fame (Courtesy Twin County Museum and Hall of Fame, portrait by Susan Fecho, page 122).

CONTENTS

ACKNOWLEDGMENTS

The Twin County Museum and Hall of Fame (TCHOF) was created at the beginning of the 21st century by a group of individuals interested in preserving the history of the region and recognizing those who made the area what it is. Since 2004, select citizens of the Twin Counties have been inducted into the Hall of Fame and presented with a portrait by local artist Susan Fecho. The portraits are on display at the current home of the museum, the Rocky Mount Amtrak station. All the inductees have been included in this book and are identified parenthetically with the abbreviation "TCHOF" and their year of induction.

While all board members are dedicated to this project, president John Mebane and former president and Rocky Mount City Council member Chris Miller have been a tremendous help with the gathering of information and photographs for this work. Not everyone in this book has been inducted into the TCHOF, but each one has made an impact on the Twin Counties. Thanks to all of those who contributed information and photographs. Many of the organizations acknowledged here are referenced throughout the text; please note that, in the interest of space, several have been assigned abbreviations, which appear throughout the photographic credits in this book. Thanks to the North Carolina Division of Archives and History (NCDAH); the Barringer Studio, which operated in Rocky Mount from 1942 to the 1980s (Barringer); George Banks, keeper of the records at Edgecombe County Veterans' Military Museum (ECVMM); Carol Banks of the Blount-Bridgers House Museum (BBH); Traci Thompson of Braswell Memorial Library (Braswell); Pam Edmondson of Edgecombe County Memorial Library (ECML); Mary Tom Bass, Edgecombe Community College Public Information Officer (ECC); Kathy Winslow of North Carolina Wesleyan College Library (NC Wesleyan); Dewand Taylor, battalion chief of Rocky Mount Fire Department (RMFD); Anne Anderson of the Country Doctor Museum; Gay Sturgeon of the Spring Hope Historical Association; Mike Caldwell; Rusty and Mary Ann Holderness; Rudy Love; Joe Pitt; Steve Raper; Terry Smith; Mike Stokes; Tom Suiter; Noelle Talley; Jon Wiggs; Tiffany Frary and Erin Vosgien, my editors at Arcadia; and Martin Fleming, my husband and assistant researcher.

INTRODUCTION

Settlers migrated south from Virginia and west from the coast to settle the Tar River Basin in northeastern North Carolina's coastal plain during the first quarter of the 18th century. Most came to start small family farms. In the first 50 years of settlement, agriculture was the primary economic base for the region, which is situated along the fall line and is geographically part of the Piedmont and the coastal plain of the state. As the population grew, Edgecombe County, chartered in 1741, was divided into new counties with their own county seats. The northern area became Halifax in 1758, and with it went the original county seat, Enfield, leaving Edgecombe with no courthouse or seat of local government. Tarboro was chartered in 1760, becoming the county seat four years later. Situated at a bend in the Tar River, it would be the commercial leader of this area for the next century.

A few years later, in the midst of the American Revolution, Edgecombe County was again divided, this time with the eastern section remaining Edgecombe and the western half taking the name Nash in honor of North Carolina patriot Francis Nash, who died at the Battle of Germantown. A new county seat, Nashville, was established for the western county. Thus, the "Twin Counties," as they are often called, came into being with the birth of Nash County in 1777. For the next century, they grew and developed together, using resources found along the Tar River, especially the tar, pitch, and lumber provided by the pine forests. New technology brought textile mills, railroads, and communications to the area that would change the land, shape the people, and sometimes bring about a rivalry between the citizens of the two counties. After the War of 1812 ended and prosperity grew, three men took a chance and built the second textile mill in the state on the falls of the Tar River, in an area that would eventually become Rocky Mount. In 1840, the longest railroad (at that time) in the United States came through the area. The railroad brought more people to the region, and agriculture was no longer the only source of income as the occupations of merchant, craftsman, and factory worker became more commonplace.

Because of the rich agricultural production, the Twin Counties had a large slave population and a number of free black craftsmen. During the Civil War, hundreds of local men fought for the Confederacy, and some escaped slaves served in the union. At the war's end, there was an economic upheaval as the former slaves now worked for wages and developed their own communities.

Rocky Mount was officially incorporated in 1867 with a population of just under 700. It was situated in both counties and, by the turn of the 20th century, had surpassed both county seats in population. Today, it is the bridge that keeps the counties connected. A 1910 chamber of commerce publication described the area this way:

> Rocky Mount is the metropolis of the two counties. Half in Nash and half in Edgecombe [with] the Atlantic Coast Line (ACL) Railroad being the dividing line between the counties, Rocky Mount occupies a commanding position in both, by reason of wealth, intelligence and population. The two counties are rich in historical fame, as well as in their soil, and the diversity of their industries. They have produced some of the ablest and noblest sons of North Carolina, men who have made and written the state's history in War and Peace. And the sons of Nash and Edgecombe today are taking a large part in the political and industrial, as well as the moral and social development of the commonwealth. The weight of these twin-counties is always felt in legislation, and the voice of their people carries a potent influence in the councils of the political parties of the state. (*Rocky Mount: Gateway to Eastern North Carolina,* page 16).

Just a century later, little has changed. Rocky Mount, with a population just under 60,000, is the largest city in the Twin Counties, which have a total combined population of over 152,000. Other towns formed and grew in both counties because of the railroad and factories. The Tar River, which had been the commercial draw to the area in the 1700s, was no longer the artery of transportation. First, the railroad challenged and eventually replaced the river. The coming of the automobile, highways, and, eventually, the interstate corridors of Highway 301 and Interstate 95 provided access for both business and people to locate in the Twin Counties.

As Rocky Mount became home to the ACL Railroad repair shops, the city saw over 100 trains a day traveling through the Twin Counties, with one-third of those being passenger lines. Although rail travel is no longer the most common form of transportation, Amtrak still has at least six passenger trains a day at the Rocky Mount station going west (to Raleigh and beyond) and traveling the Carolinian north–south line between Florida and New York.

Agriculture continued to prosper, especially the cotton and tobacco markets in the 1890s, but now industry, in the form of textile mills and other business ventures from banking to communication, spread through the area.

As the Twin Counties grew, local citizens worked to create communities that were good, healthy environments for families. This led to the development of the state's first county health department and the first city-owned milk plant in the southeast. Several hospitals have been established during the past century to provide the latest in medical care.

Numerous schools of all grade levels, both private and public, were established, including an African American junior college at the beginning of the 20th century. As the area developed, some individuals saw the need to preserve the past and established organizations and museums to set up historic districts and community centers. Creative writers, artists, and musicians abound in the Twin Counties, and other more athletically inclined individuals have participated in the Olympics and played on professional teams in the National Football League (NFL), Major League Baseball (MLB), and the National Basketball Association (NBA).

Since the founding of the United States, citizens have served in local, state, and national government. The Twin Counties have produced three North Carolina governors, three lieutenant governors, one state attorney general, two state supreme court justices, and numerous congressmen and state legislators, including several African Americans.

Throughout the 20th century, the sons and daughters of both counties served in all branches of the armed forces during military conflicts, including during both World Wars. Hundreds of individuals are recognized in the Edgecombe County Veterans' Military Museum. Some gave their lives in fighting for their nation but most returned home to raise families and contribute to the quality of life in the Twin Counties. The selection of individuals in this book are just the highlights of the many area citizens who have given their time and skills to make the Twin Counties a good place to live.

CHAPTER ONE

Business

Small farms and large plantations provided work for 90 percent of the population, both black and white, until the coming of the railroad. The ability to export crops to other markets and import various goods led to the development of more towns, more stores, and new ventures. Rocky Mount Mills was the first of half-a-dozen textile mills that would locate in the area. Businessman David Pender took his D & P Grocery Store to Virginia and created the Big Star Supermarket chain. The Atlantic Coast Line Railroad repair shops created thousands of jobs and relocated an entire community of railroad workers from South Carolina to Rocky Mount. In Tarboro, Carolina Telephone & Telegraph Company formed in 1896 and became the major telecommunications provider for the eastern third of the state for the next 80 years. Jewish merchants moved to Tarboro and other towns along the railroad to open general merchandise shops and several specialty clothing stores that would last for decades. A few businesses have been in the area for a century or longer, such as Bulluck's Furniture in Rocky Mount, Simmons Furniture, Carlisle Funeral Home, and Marrow-Pitt Hardware. At the rise of the Progressive Era, Planters and Peoples Banks were established, along with several branches of the North Carolina Bank. In the 1920s, a new bank in Whitakers was described as the finest bank between Richmond and Miami. Automobile dealerships have come and gone, but Bullucks Chevrolet in Rocky Mount has been selling and servicing cars since 1920. After World War II, Long Manufacturing opened to produce farm equipment, and Robert Barnhill began a construction firm that was one of the largest in the southeast. The food industry has had an impact on the local economy, from farmer's markets to family diners (some started by Greek immigrants after World War I). Both Tarboro and Rocky Mount had bottling companies for the new beverages Coca-Cola and Pepsi Cola. A group of businessmen took a chance on a new fast-food enterprise in 1960, and the flame-cooked burger of Hardee's began in Rocky Mount. Today, Sara Lee Bakery processes frozen desserts in Tarboro, while the Cheesecake Factory makes cakes in Rocky Mount.

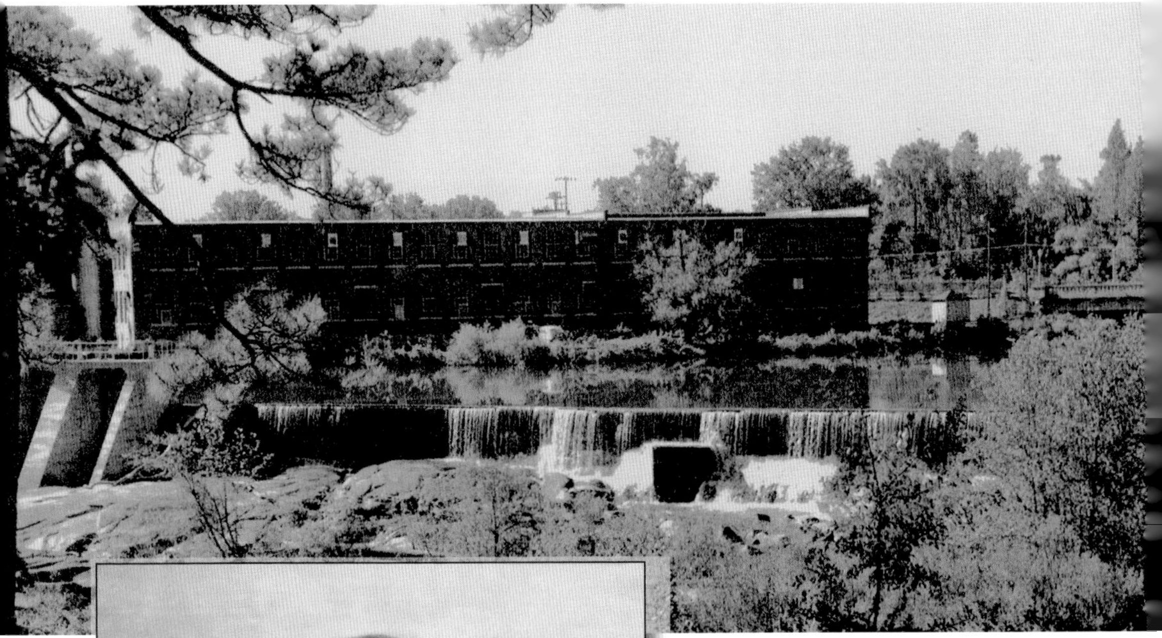

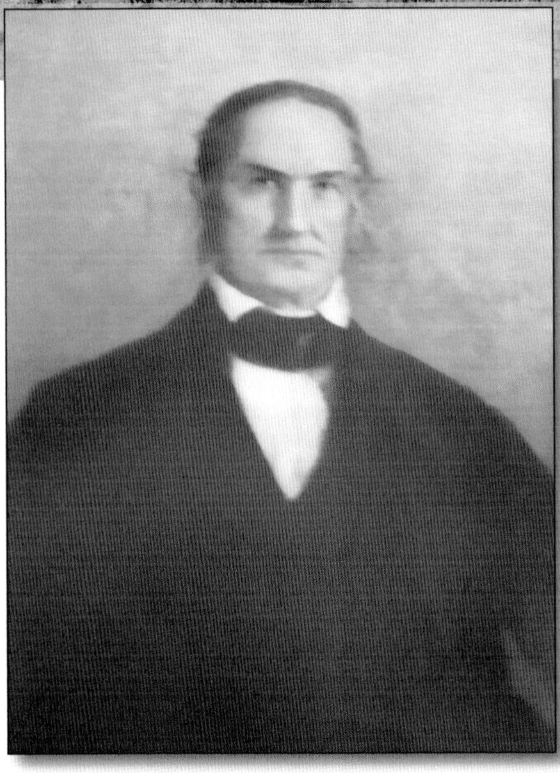

Rocky Mount Mills and James Smith Battle

Joel Battle partnered with Peter Evans and Henry Donaldson and built a mill at the falls of the Tar River in 1818, the second textile mill established in North Carolina. Eventually, Joel bought out his partners before selling it to his cousin James Smith Battle in the 1820s. James Smith Battle expanded the mill to include a gristmill and a saw mill. James also was involved in the building of the Wilmington & Weldon Railroad which, when completed in 1840, was the longest railroad in the world. Initially operated by slaves, the 40,000 spindles were eventually worked by women. The mill burned twice and was rebuilt, continuing operations until closing in 1996. (Above, photograph by Barringer; left, portrait by Thomas Sulley, courtesy BBH.)

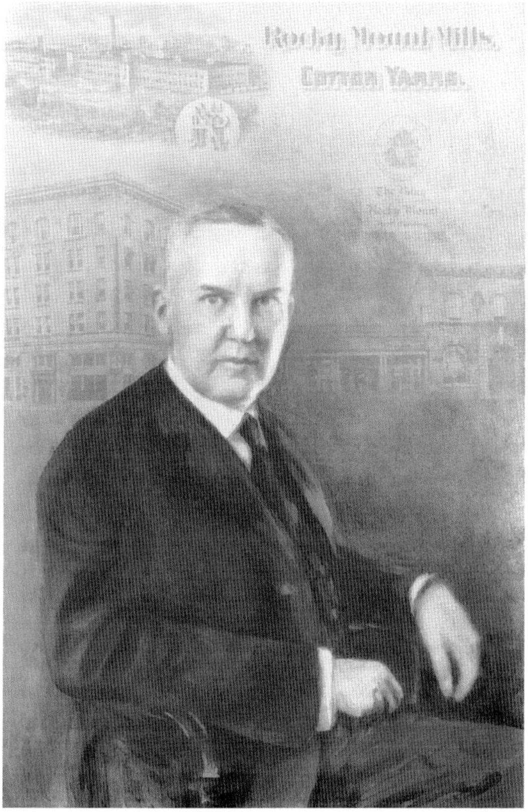

Thomas Hall Battle

Often called the "Father of Rocky Mount," Thomas Hall Battle (TCHOF 2004) was not just a business leader but was also a community builder. The great-grandson of Joel Battle, the founder of Rocky Mount Mills, Thomas was the son of Kemp Plummer Battle, one-time president of the University of North Carolina at Chapel Hill (UNC). Thomas graduated from the university and passed the bar in 1882. He practiced law in Tarboro before settling in Rocky Mount as the attorney for the mill. He was elected mayor of Rocky Mount in 1886 and served in that position for 10 years. At the same time, he moved up through the offices at the mill, becoming treasurer, then stockholder, then chief executive officer, and finally, president and chairman of the board. Thomas was a community builder, serving on various boards and leading them to improve conditions in Rocky Mount. When he first moved to the young village in 1884, it had no bank. He founded the National Bank of Rocky Mount and soon divided his day, working at both the bank and at the mill. He was also president of the first trust company, the Rocky Mount Savings & Trust Company, and of the Rocky Mount Homestead & Loan Association. He established the Village of Rocky Mount Mills, which was housing for the mill workers. He served on the board of aldermen from 1896 to 1917. With other citizens, he chartered the Board of Rocky Mount Graded Schools and served as the chairman for 34 years. During the era of segregation, he sponsored bonds to build schools for both the white and the African American children. In 1919, the second such bond passed, becoming the first bond in the state intended solely for the education of African Americans. Battle led a campaign with the woman's club to have a community library. When the Thomas Hackney Braswell Library was established in 1922, Battle was the president of the library board of trustees for 12 years. He worked with the ACL Railroad to bring the Emerson Shops to Rocky Mount and later contributed both funds and support for housing for railroad workers to keep the railroad expansion in the 1920s. His efforts were not limited to Rocky Mount. He helped create the North Carolina Bankers Association and became its first president in 1896. Battle died in January 1936, at the age of 75. (Portrait by Susan Fecho.)

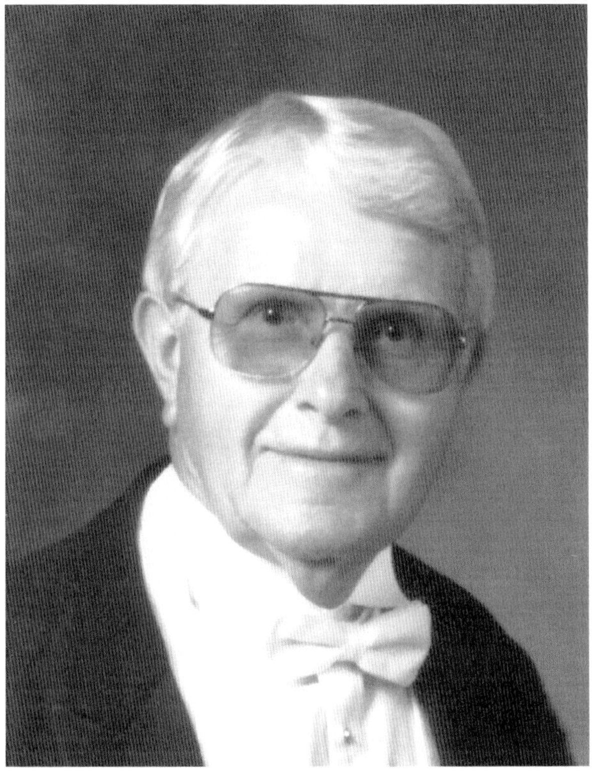

Robert Barnhill Sr.
A graduate of Conetoe High School, Robert Barnhill Sr. (TCHOF 2005) established one of the major construction firms in the state. Barnhill Contracting Company, ranked 23rd of North Carolina's top-100 privately owned businesses, has built highways in Virginia, Maryland, and Delaware. Recognized as "Entrepreneur of the Year" for the construction industry in 1993, Barnhill died in 2000. He was inducted into the North Carolina Transportation Hall of Fame in 2005. (Courtesy Barnhill family.)

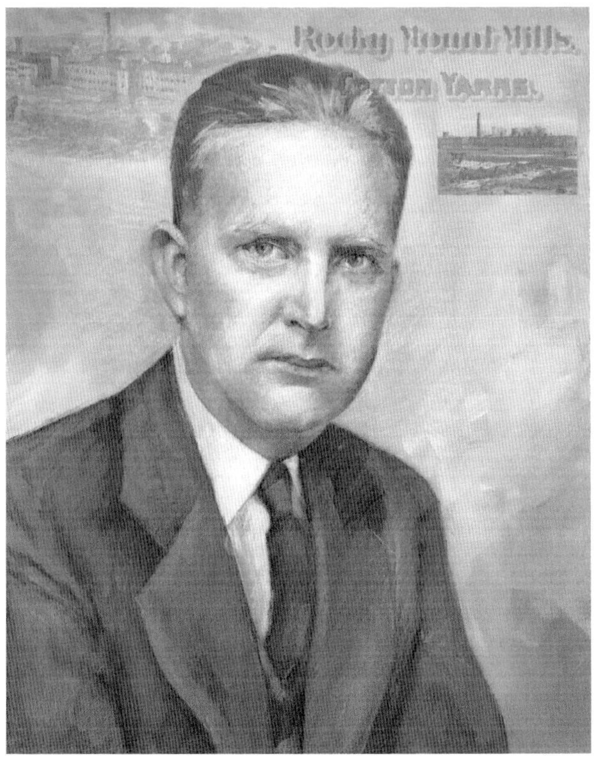

Hyman L. Battle
Rocky Mount native Hyman L. Battle (1896–1972; TCHOF 2007) served in the US Army during World War I. After the war, he returned home to work in the Rocky Mount Mills, eventually becoming president and chairman of the board. A founding member of the Rocky Mount Housing Authority and chairman for 20 years, Battle also served as director of the YMCA in Rocky Mount and was president of the Rocky Mount Chamber of Commerce. (Portrait by Susan Fecho.)

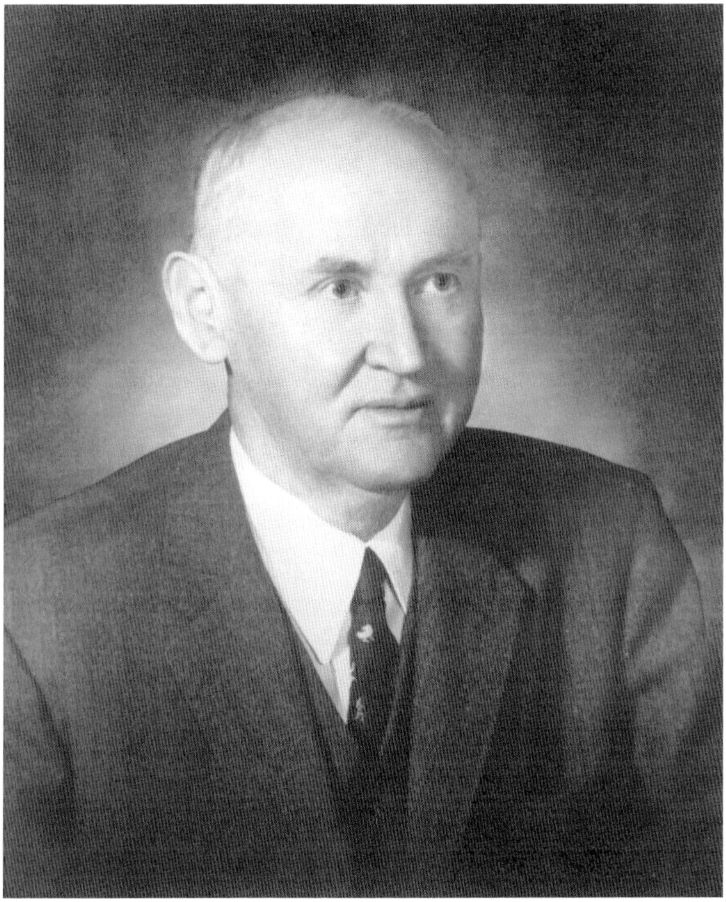

Kemp Davis Battle

After graduating from the University of North Carolina, Kemp Davis Battle (1888–1973; TCHOF 2009) partnered with law school classmate Frances E. Winslow to open a practice that lasted for 62 years, the longest in state history. Battle was also president of the North Carolina Bar Association from 1932 to 1933. He was vice president and chairman of the board of Rocky Mount Mills. A community leader like his father, Thomas, and younger brother Hyman, Kemp worked with many local organizations, including Carolina Telephone, Rocky Mount Public Schools, and Braswell Memorial Library. Concerned about living conditions, he convinced Rocky Mount to pass a housing code to keep people out of dangerous dwellings. A member of the Rocky Mount Kiwanis Club, he also served as the club president. He dedicated many hours to both the North Carolina and National Tuberculosis Associations, the latter of which he served as secretary. He won the Will Ross Medal from the National Tuberculosis Association in 1956. The University of North Carolina gave him an honorary doctor of laws degree in 1960, shortly after his retirement from the board of trustees (there had been a member of the Battle family serving on the board for over 120 years). In the 1960s, Battle spoke out against a Speaker Ban Law passed the by the North Carolina General Assembly and was praised for his eloquent speech by newspapers and supporters from across the state. While Battle received recognition for his many contributions to his hometown of Rocky Mount and to the state, one action earlier in his life had not been widely known. In 1933, at the age of 45, Kemp saved a young boy from rising floodwaters of the Tar River. Battle went into the rushing current and pulled the child toward the riverbank, holding him in a tree just out of the water until a rescue line was formed by mill workers to get them both to safety. This act, in which he risked his own life to save that of a child, may be the finest example of his service to his community. (Courtesy Battle family.)

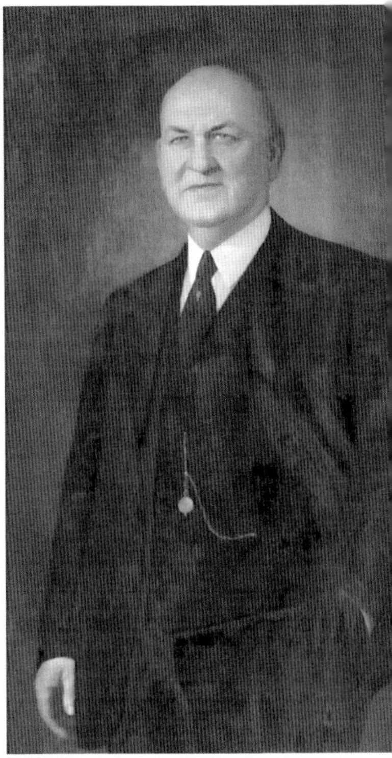

James Craig Braswell

Born in Battleboro, James Craig Braswell graduated from the University of North Carolina in 1890. Less than a decade later, he founded Planters National Bank & Trust Company (pictured below) in Rocky Mount, which became the leading financial institution in the Twin Counties. He served as the chairman of the board from its founding until 1944. He was president of the North Carolina Bankers Association 1911–1912. He also served as president of the board of directors of the Federal Reserve Bank. With his friend Thomas Hall Battle, Braswell pioneered the Rocky Mount School Board. Another community builder, he was a charter member of both the Rocky Mount Chamber of Commerce and the Rocky Mount Kiwanis Club, and he served as chairman of the board of directors of the Methodist Home for Children and the East Carolina Training School in Rocky Mount. When he died in April 1951, all banks, schools, and libraries closed the day of his funeral. His obituary in the *Rocky Mount Telegram* reported, "the city has lost one of its most valuable citizens and the city government one of its more reliable counselors. He gave liberally of his time, energy, wisdom, and financial means for the support of all causes which he felt would make Rocky Mount and this community a better place to live." (Right, courtesy Rusty and Mary Ann Holderness; below, courtesy Simpson Collection, NC State Archives.)

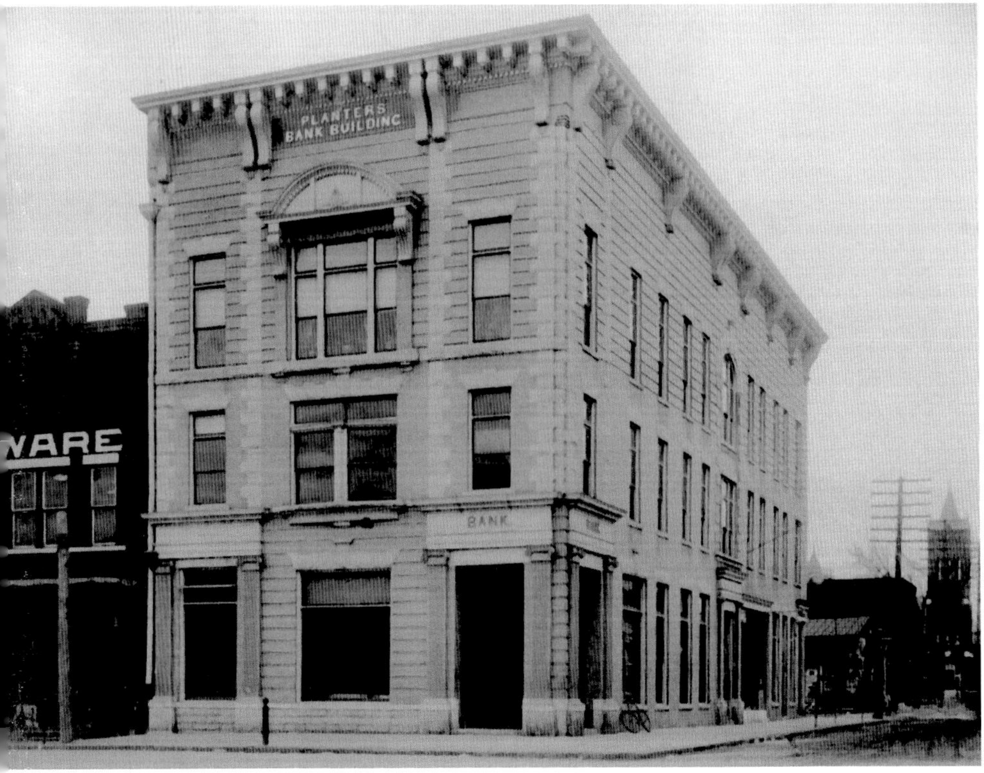

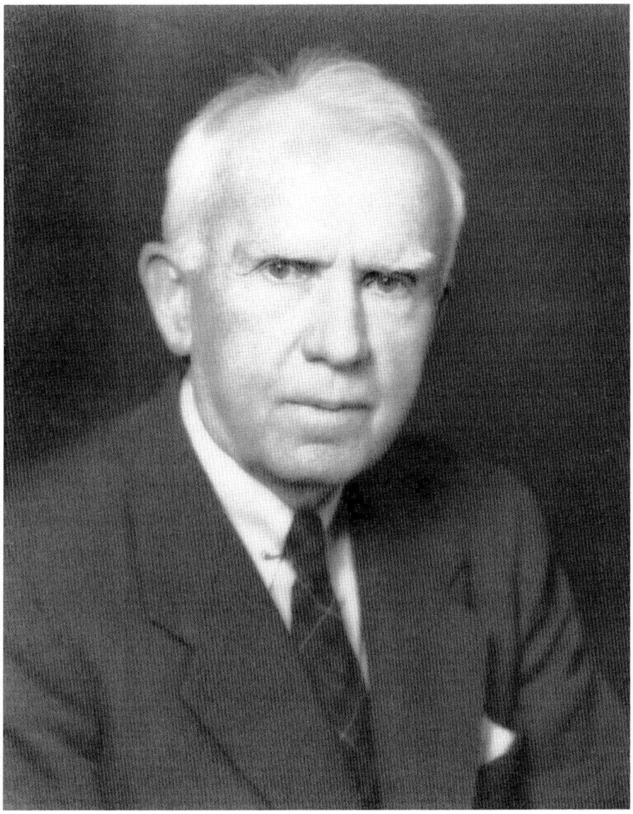

Henry Clark Bridgers and Bridgers Building

Born in 1876, Bridgers is best known for creating the East Carolina Railway, which ran from Tarboro to Greene County, North Carolina. He was also an attorney, having graduated from the UNC Law School. He loved athletics, having played both tennis and golf in college. After returning home to Tarboro, he built a nine-hole golf course (one of the first in the state), which operated from 1899 to 2012. His railroad led to the development of several towns along its route, including Pinetops, Macclesfield, and Fountain. He had the H.C. Bridgers Building constructed in 1907 to house his railroad office. He was president of the First National Bank in Tarboro and established several banks in surrounding small towns. Bridgers died in 1951. (Left, courtesy BBH; below, photograph by the author.)

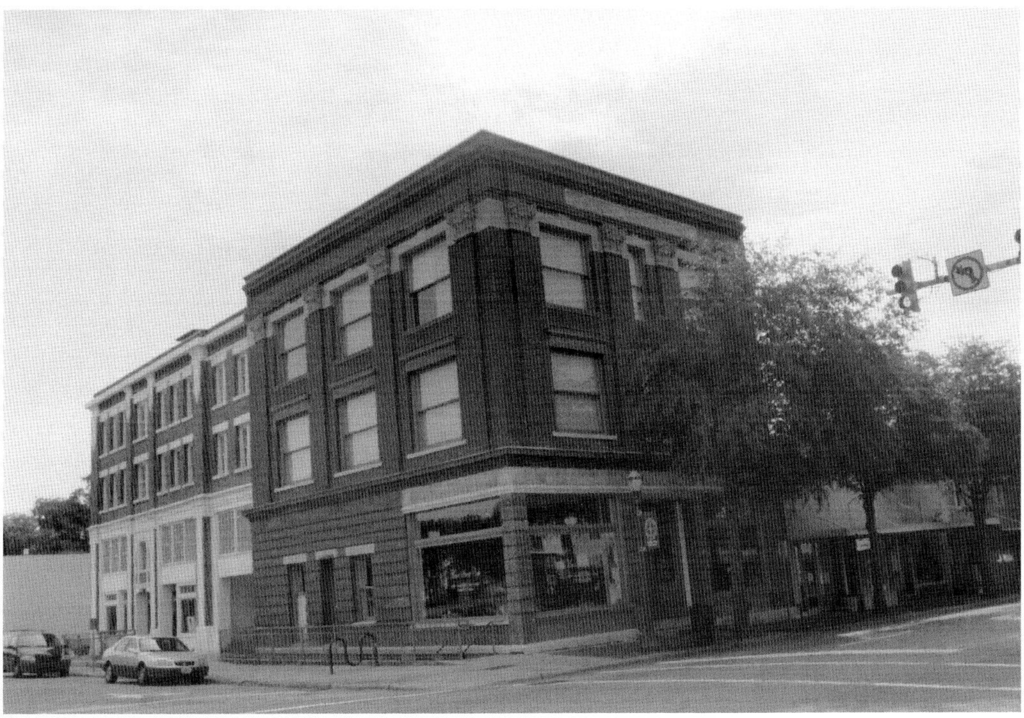

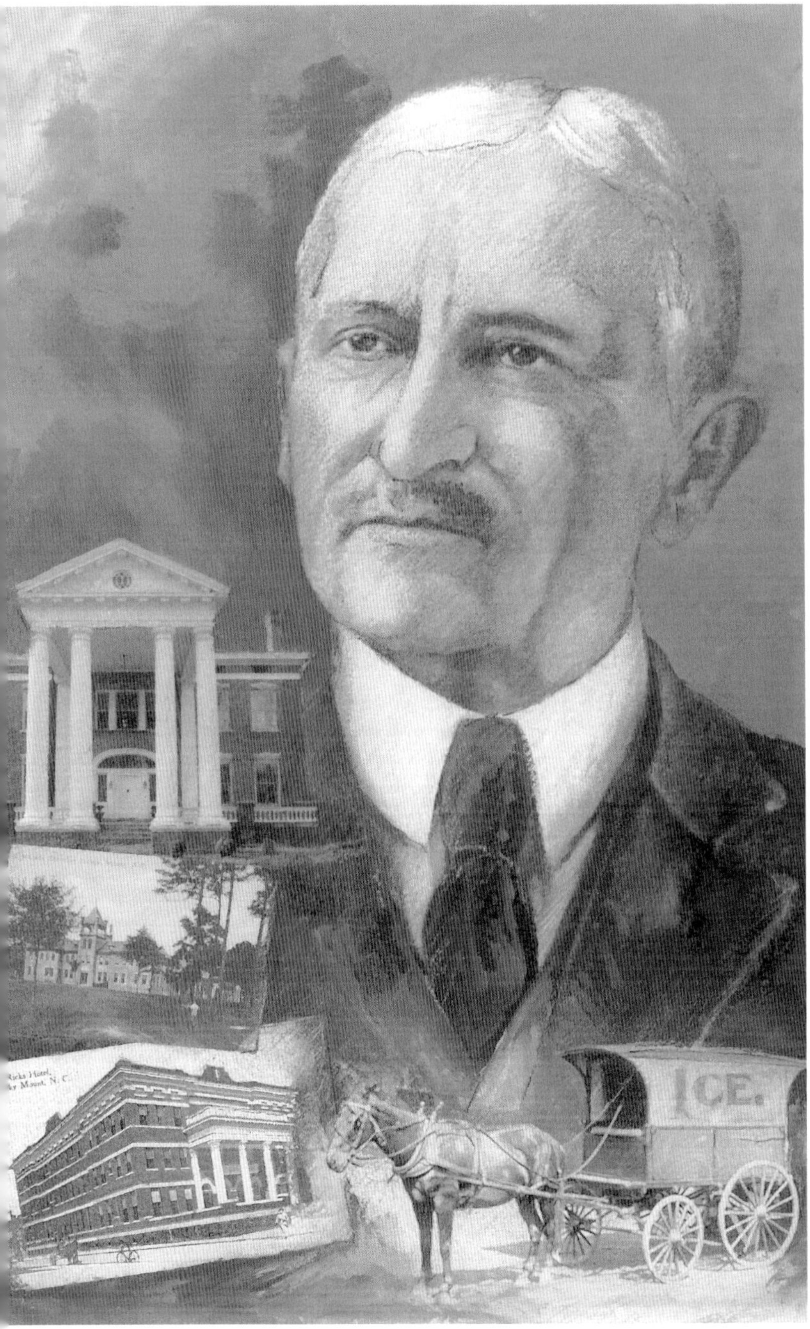

James W. Hines
Known as the "Ice King" in the early 20th century, James W. Hines (TCHOF 2010) was a self-made businessman. When the ACL Railroad set up shop in Rocky Mount, Hines began an ice business, Rocky Mount Fuel & Ice Company, to supply ice for trains carrying fresh produce from Florida to New York. Hines set up contracts with railway companies to provide ice for refrigerated cars. He eventually opened ice shops all across North Carolina. Hines was also involved with the tobacco warehouses in the area. He served on the Rocky Mount Chamber of Commerce, as well as on the boards of trustees of both East Carolina Normal School (now East Carolina University) and Atlantic Christian College (now Barton). He later gave a special endowment at Atlantic Christian College of over $100,000. Hines married Mary Matilda MacEntyre, and they built the stately Neoclassical home on Grace Street. Known as MacHaven, the house is listed in the National Register of Historic Places. Hines died in 1928. (Portrait by Susan Fecho.)

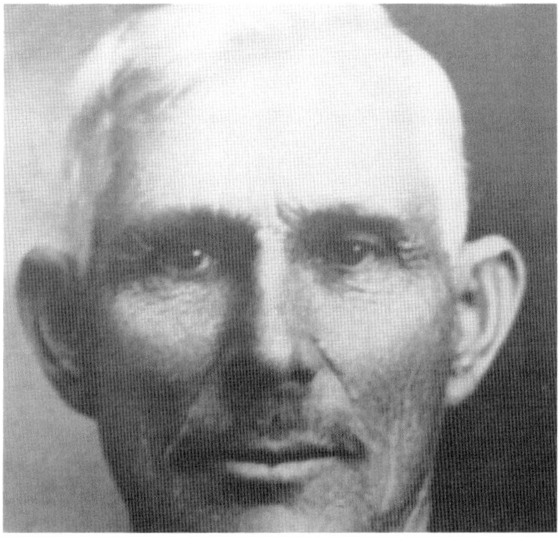

Robert H. Ricks

A confederate veteran, Robert H. Ricks (1839–1920) came home from the war to help develop Rocky Mount. He built the Ricks Hotel and was vice president of the Bank of Rocky Mount, vice president of a textile mill, and was elected as a Nash County commissioner and as a state senator. Ricks earned further recognition for establishing the tobacco market and for funding the construction of the Rocky Mount Civil War monument. (Courtesy Ricks family.)

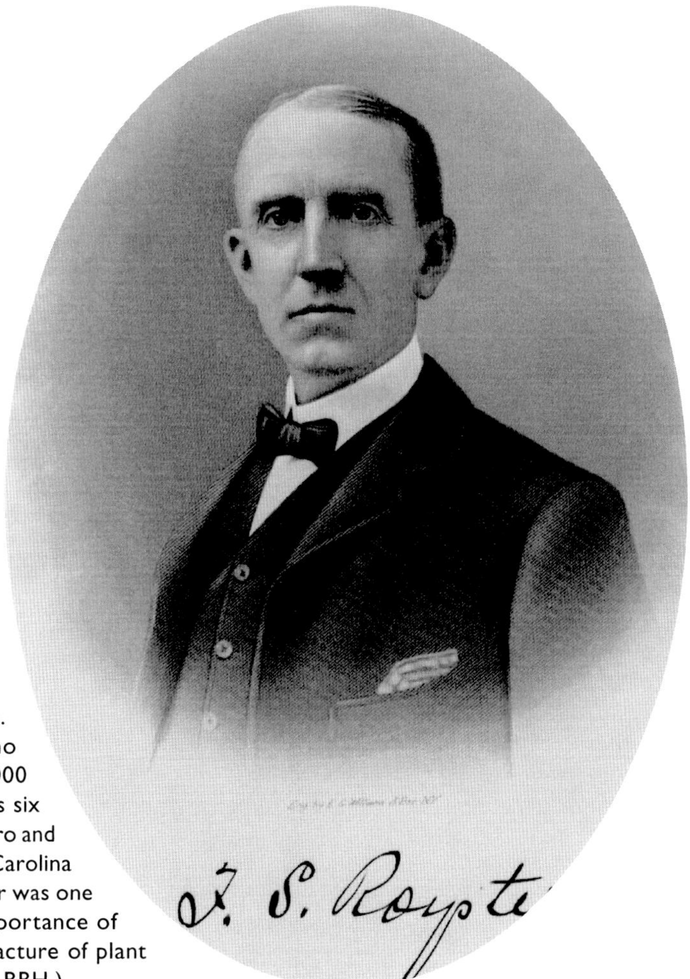

Frank S. Royster

In 1870, Frank S. Royster came to Tarboro to clerk in a mercantile store. Fifteen years later he opened a fertilizer company and soon had a major market across the South. By 1900, the F.S. Royster Guano Company was producing over 75,000 tons of fertilizer annually from its six plants, including the ones in Tarboro and Norfolk, as well as two in South Carolina and two more in Georgia. Royster was one of the first to recognize the importance of scientific methods in the manufacture of plant food. He died in 1928. (Courtesy BBH.)

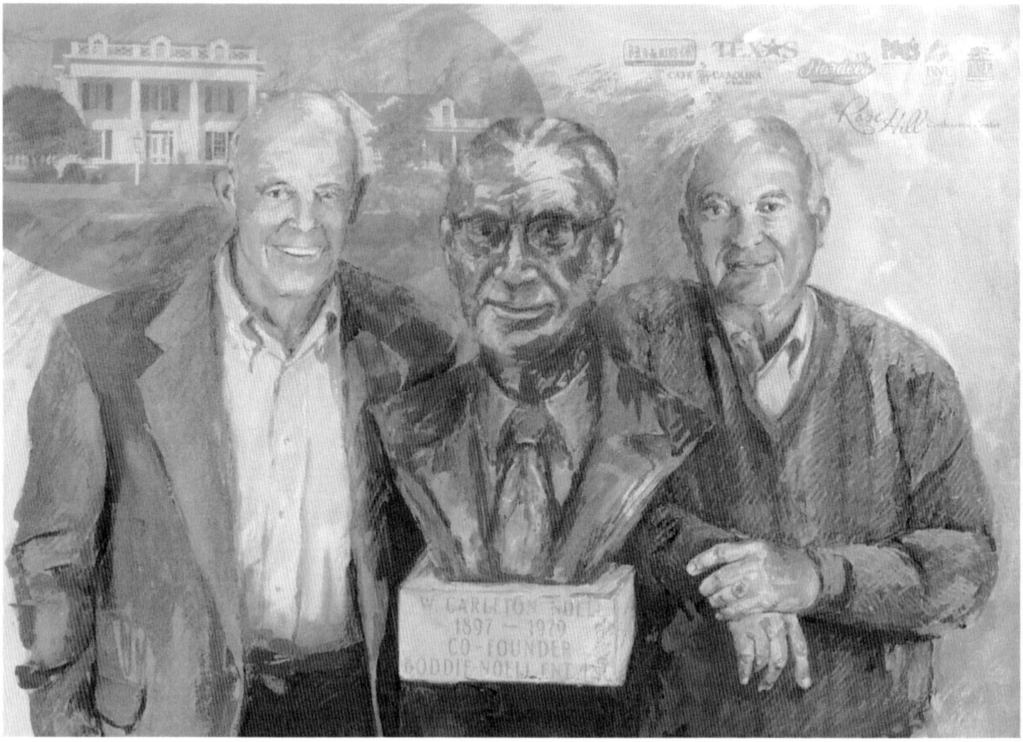

Boddie-Noell

Ben Mayo Boddie Sr., Nicholas Bunn Boddie, and W. Carleton Noell (all three, TCHOF 2006) were the founders of Boddie-Noell Enterprises. Their business accomplishments include the creation of the Carleton House Restaurant & Motel, a Hardee's franchise comprising more than 300 restaurants in four states, and the operation of several other restaurants (such as the Texas Steakhouse and Moe's Southwest Grill). The Boddie brothers were born at Rose Hill Plantation in Nash County. Noell was a native of Danville, Virginia. Each has been active in community groups, including the Boys and Girls Club of Rocky Mount and the Boy Scouts. Noell died in 1979. (Portrait by Susan Fecho.)

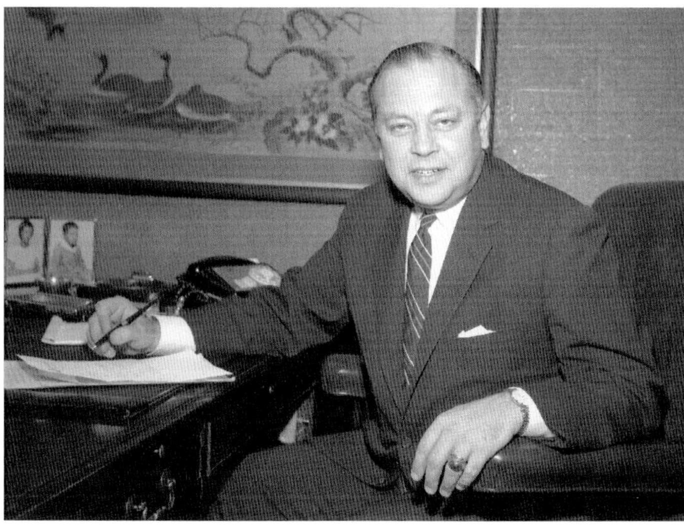

Joseph Leonard Rawls

A Rocky Mount native, Joseph Leonard Rawls Jr. (TCHOF 2012) became chairman and president of a new restaurant operation in Rocky Mount, Hardee's Food Systems, in 1961. When he left the company in 1975, there were more than 900 Hardee's restaurants across the southeast. Rawls was also founder of Canton Station restaurants until his death of a heart attack in 1982 at the age of 51. (Courtesy Braswell, Killbrew Collection.)

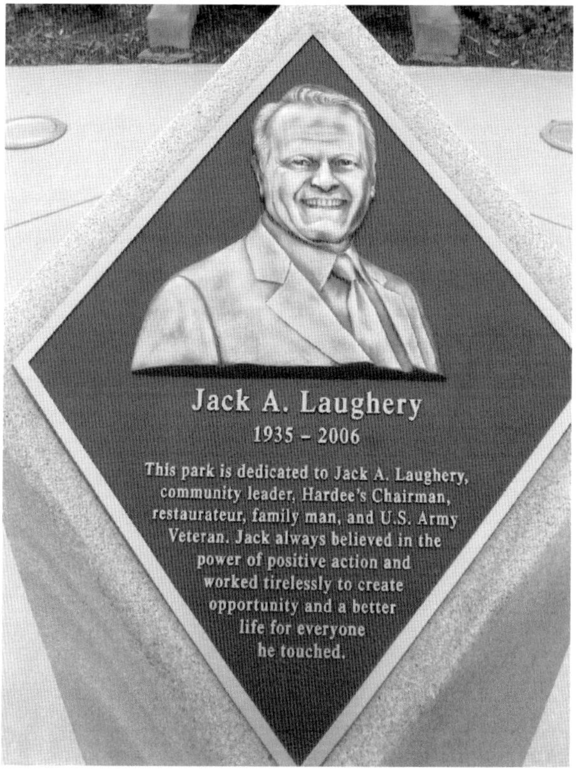

Jack A. Laughery
Iowa native Jack A. Laughery (TCHOF 2006) moved to Rocky Mount in the 1970s and became the president of Hardee's Food Systems. In 1980, he was elected chairman of the board. He was also a partner in Papa John's Pizza and part owner of Rocky Mount Harley-Davidson. Laughery received the North Carolina Restaurateur of the Year Award in 1980. The next year, he won the Gold Plate Award from the International Foodservice Manufacturers' Association, the highest honor in the food service industry. He was then named "Man of the Year" in 1987 in *Nation's Restaurant News*. Laughery was also involved in local business organizations, serving on the Nash County Industrial Development Commission, the North Carolina State Advisory Budget Commission, and the state board of transportation. He died in 2006. (Photograph by the author.)

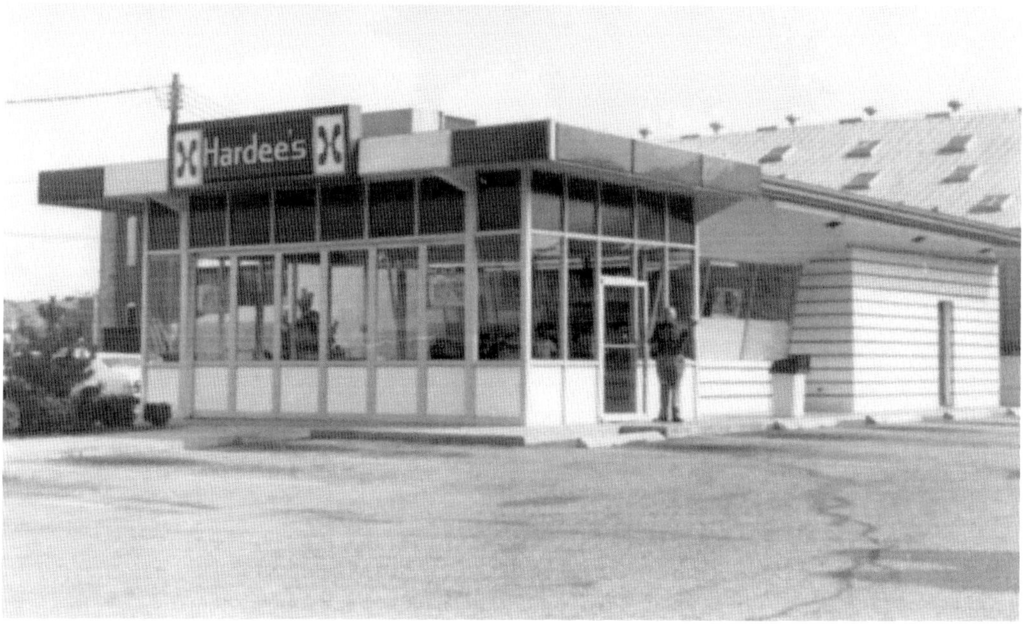

Hardee's
The first Hardee's hamburger restaurant opened on Church Street in Rocky Mount in 1961. It closed in the 1990s and was torn down, and the site became the Jack A. Laughery Park and Veterans Memorial. (Courtesy NCDAH.)

William "Billy" Harrison

Born in Enfield, Billy Harrison (TCHOF 2011) spent most of his life serving the people of Rocky Mount. Harrison graduated in 1935 from UNC with a degree in commerce. He partnered with his son in Harrison & Harrison and developed neighborhoods of Westridge, Farmington, Berkley, Oakside, and Old Farm. A founding member of NC Wesleyan, he served on the first board of trustees. In 2004, the school conferred an honorary doctor of laws degree on him. Rocky Mount recently dedicated the Harrison Family YMCA. Harrison died in 2005. (Courtesy Harrison family.)

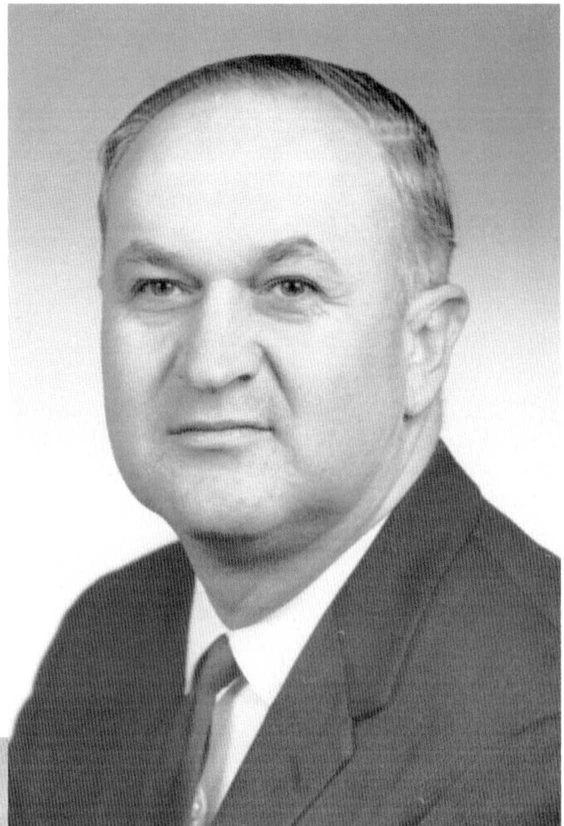

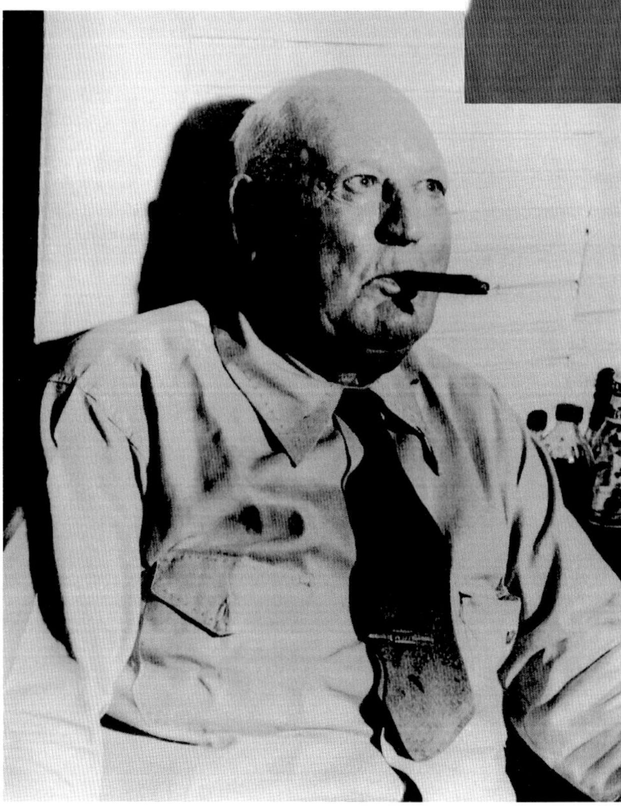

Robert "Bob" Melton

Born in 1872 on a farm near Castalia, Robert "Bob" Melton sought a different occupation. In 1924, he opened the first pit-cooked-barbecue restaurant on the banks of the Tar River in Rocky Mount. All races were welcome inside the restaurant, even though segregation was standard at the time. Melton was known as the Eastern North Carolina Barbecue King, and his restaurant was reviewed in national magazines and international newspapers. Melton died in 1958, but his restaurant continued until it was destroyed by Hurricane Floyd in 1999. (Courtesy Melton family.)

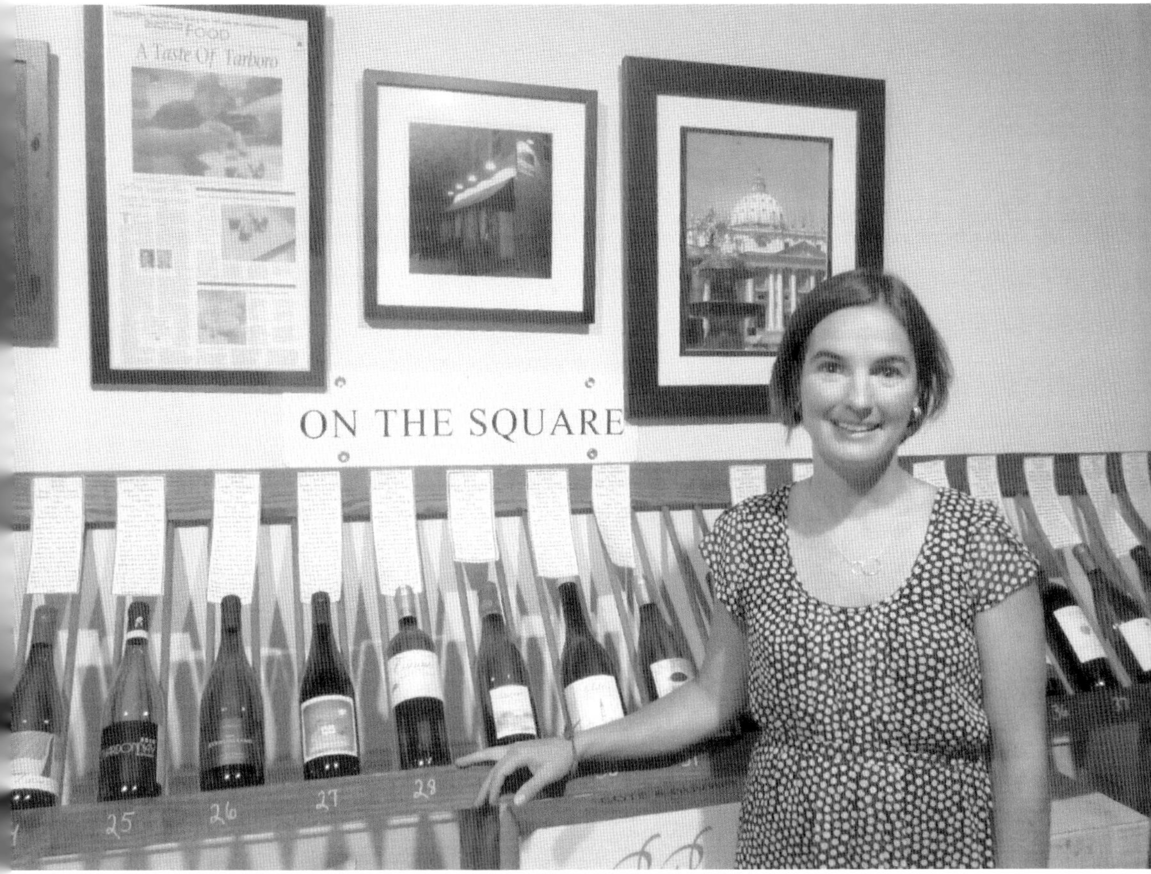

Inez Holderness Ribustello

After graduating from the University of North Carolina, Tarboro native Inez Holderness headed north and attended the New York Institute of Culinary Education. She soon was employed as a beverage director at Windows on the World in the World Trade Center in 2000. While working there she met sommelier Stephen Ribustello, with whom she shared a passion for learning about wine. Stephen was from a cooking family and had worked in several restaurants before coming to Windows on the World. On September 11, 2001, Inez had come home to be in her sister's wedding, and Stephen was not due to work until noon, so both were spared the terror attacks that brought down the World Trade Center. They soon decided New York was no longer the place for them. During a visit to Tarboro in the summer of 2002, a local diner owner approached them to see if they were interested in purchasing her sandwich shop, On the Square. At first, Inez said they had no plans to live in Tarboro. The couple went on a trip to France to learn more about grapes and wine, and when they came back to Tarboro in October, they bought the shop. On the Square became a restaurant of lunches during the week and fine dining on weekends, with a wine shop featuring over 500 labels. Inez and Stephen married in 2003. They have both earned advanced sommelier certification and are the only married couple to have done so. In their 10 years operating On the Square, they have had reviews in *Our State*, on *NC Weekend,* and in the Raleigh *News & Observer. Wine Spectator Magazine* has recognized them with a best of excellence award, a distinction they share with only nine other restaurants in North Carolina (and none east of Raleigh). The fine dining draws customers from the eastern half of the state, and, in 2009, they were selected to provide a dish for the governor's inauguration. Inez and Steve also operate a catering business and recently added a Sushi stand three days a week. They have two children and could not imagine life any differently. (Photograph by the author.)

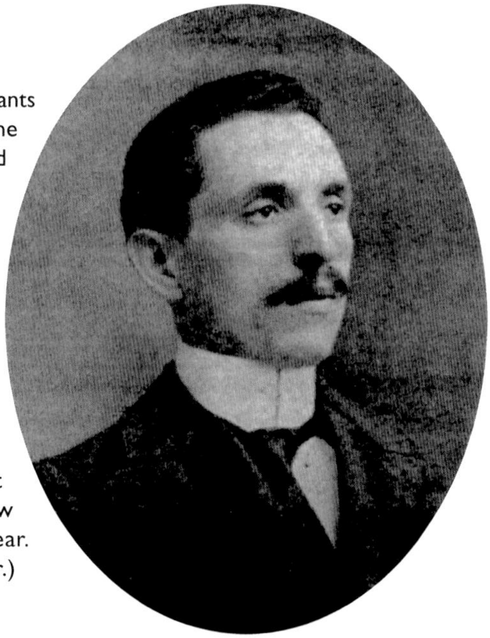

Edward Epstein
One of many Jewish merchants to locate in the region at the turn of the century, Edward Epstein opened his first clothing store in Rocky Mount in 1905. He moved to a prominent location on Main Street in 1912, and the successful gentlemen's clothing operation later expanded into women's wear. The store suffered a major fire in 1988 but reopened under new management the next year. (Photograph by Barringer.)

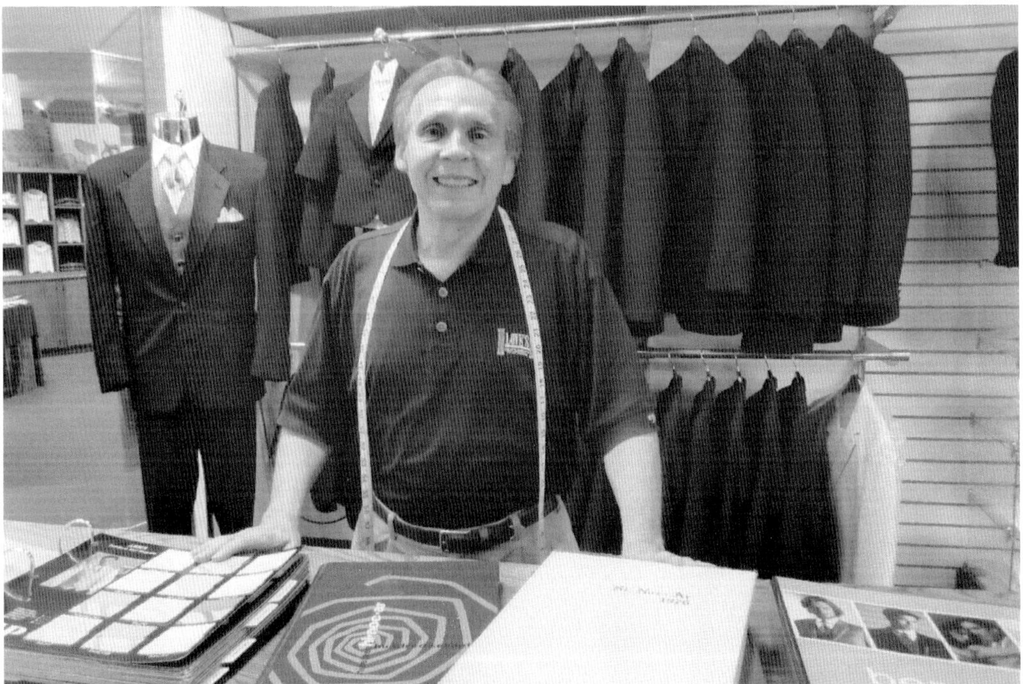

Rudy Love
In the spring of 1992, Rudy Love was brought up from South Carolina to manage Epstein's after it had relocated from downtown to a shopping center in Westridge. The company officially became Love's in 1995 and was recognized by the Rocky Mount Chamber of Commerce as the "Small Business of the Year." Rudy Love was the "2001 Retailer of the Year" in the southeast. (Photograph by the author.)

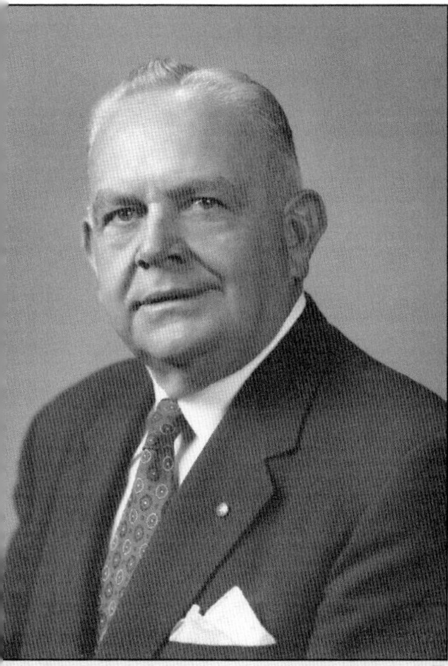

Arthur Tyler

In 1915, nineteen-year-old Arthur Lynwood Tyler (TCHOF 2012) came to Rocky Mount from Richmond to manage Anchor department store. After graduating from Henderson High School, Tyler attended UNC for one year. He left the university to help support his family after his father was seriously injured in a railroad accident. Tyler spent one year in the Army during World War I, after which he returned to Rocky Mount and learned the retail business. In 1931, he joined Henry Belk, and together they opened the Belk-Tyler Store in Rocky Mount; it was the first of a 14-store chain that would eventually employ hundreds and become a leading retailer in the Southeast. Tyler died in 1978. Pictured below is the original Belk-Tyler store, opened on Main Street in Rocky Mount in 1931. (Left, courtesy Tyler family; below, photograph by Barringer.)

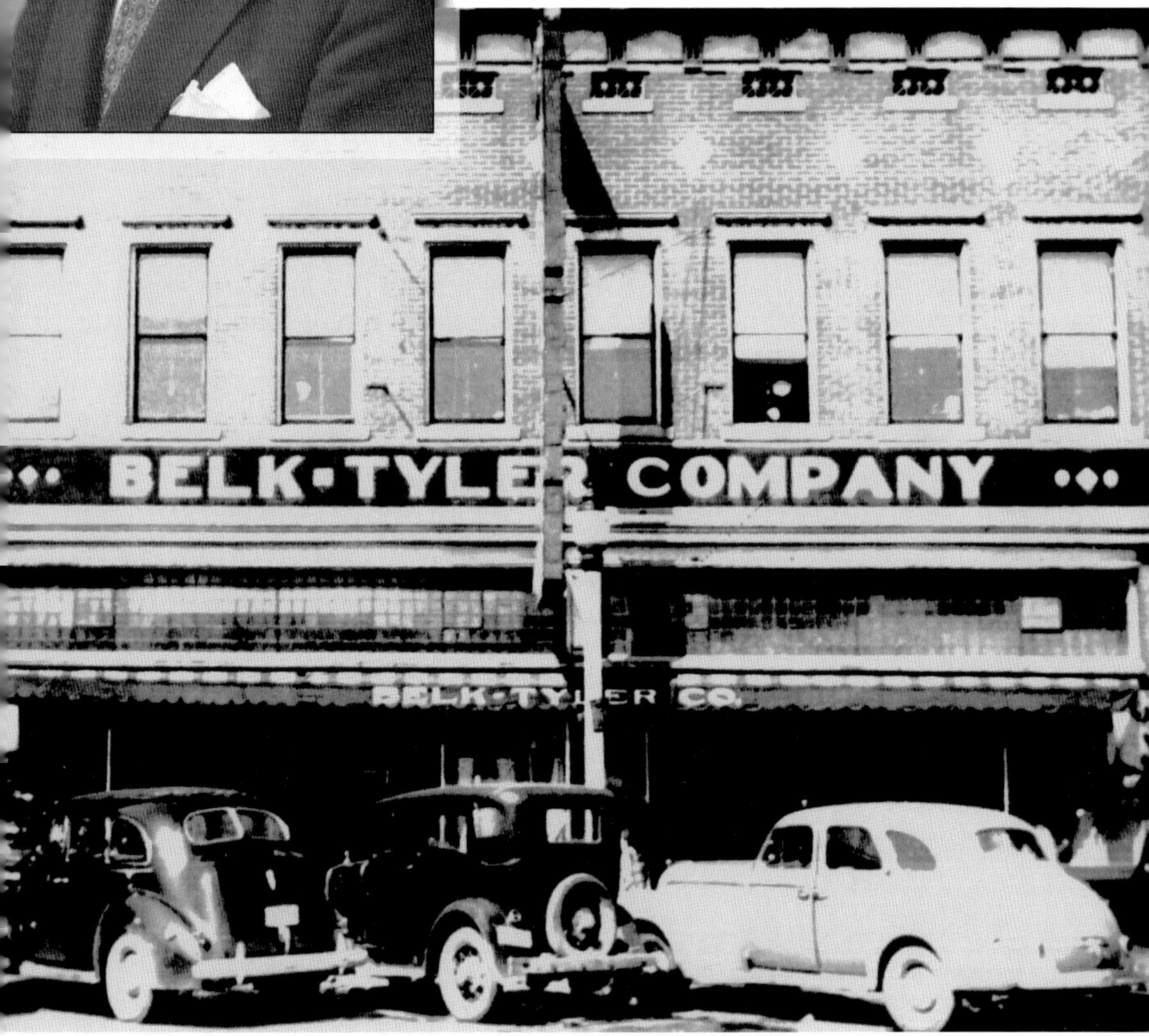

Marrow Pitt Hardware—Joseph W. Pitt and William Mears Pitt

In 1913, William C. Pitt Sr. and Thomas F. Marrow opened Marrow Pitt Hardware store on the west side of Main Street in Tarboro. Four years later they moved across the street to the location they would occupy for the next 56 years. William C. Pitt Jr. returned home after earning a business degree and took over part of the business, working with Ching Marrow. William Pitt Jr. also served as a county commissioner, and both men were active in community programs. The firm expanded, adding a radio and record store to the hardware business. After Marrow retired, Joseph "Joe" Whitehead Pitt (right) became the third generation of the Pitt family to take over the business, in 1969. The Pitts bought out the Marrows' interest in the business but kept the name that had been in place for over half a century. On December 26, 1973, the main hardware store was destroyed by fire; the Pitts, determined to continue, relocated to the former Belk-Tyler building (the department store had moved to Parkhill Mall). Like his father, Joe Pitt was active in community programs, serving the chamber of commerce and acting as a chair for the Tarboro Community Outreach. He was also a leader in the Tarboro Redevelopment Corporation, which sought to revitalize downtown. In 1995, the firm moved to its fourth location on north Main Street and became an affiliate of Ace Home Centers. Joe has received recognition as "Small Business of the Year" in 1988 and 1997, for Excellence in Hardware Retailing in 1999, and twice has won the Ace High Performance Retail Award. In 2000, he received the Best Customer Service Award. Marrow-Pitt Hardware supported Little League teams, area Boy Scout troops, 4-H youth programs, and Distributive Education Clubs of America (DECA) students. Several of the Pitts' loyal employees have remained with the store upwards of 40 of 50 years. In 2002, William Mears Pitt (left) became the fourth generation to serve as president of Marrow-Pitt, Ace Hardware. Four times in the past decade, the store has received the Ace Vision Achievement Award. In 2005, it was recognized as the Best Hardware Store in the Twin Counties by the *Rocky Mount Telegram*. Joe and his wife, local State Farm agent Bernice Pitt, were honored for their contributions to the area as the 2005 "Tarboro Citizens of the Year." (Courtesy Mears Pitt, Marrow-Pitt Ace Home Center.)

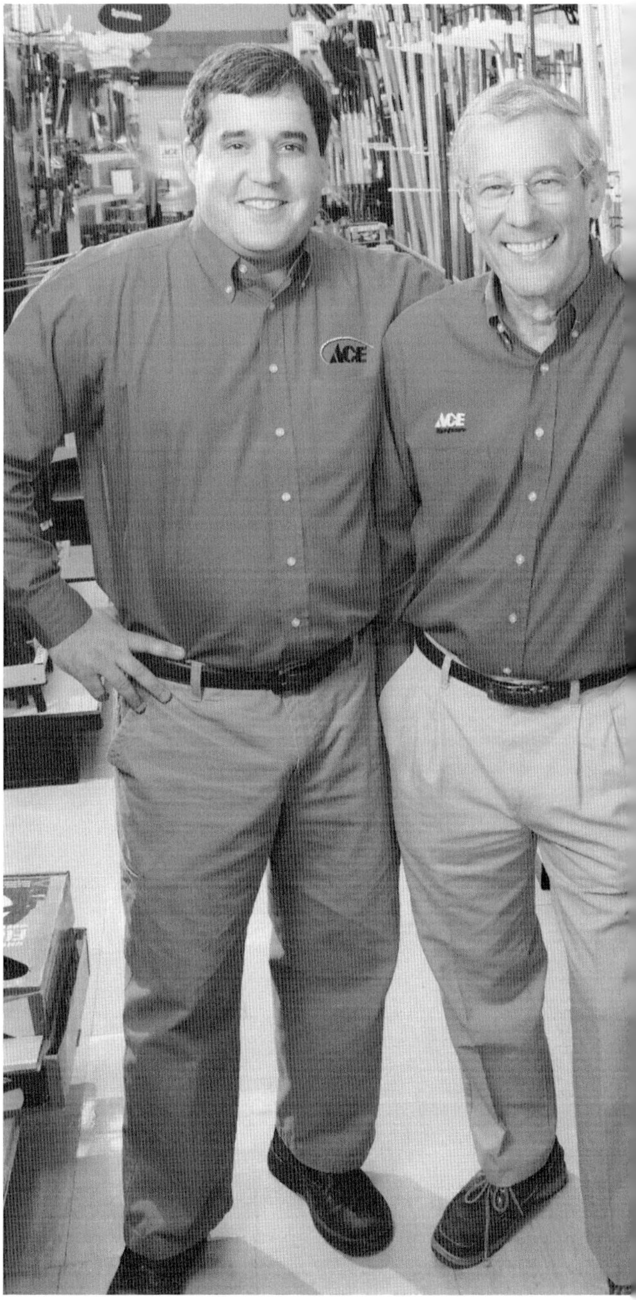

CHAPTER TWO

Community

The Twin Counties began as farmland, with a few small towns developing in the first century of settlement. County seats Tarboro and Nashville were the most populated areas, but the area remained primarily rural. Some towns, like Old Sparta, grew along the river, while others, such as Battleboro, Whitakers, and Sharpsburg (and later, Pinetops and Macclesfield) formed along the railroad. The village of Rocky Mount incorporated as a town in 1867 and encouraged new businesses in the area. With the increase of people moving to these counties came a variety of contributions, which greatly enhanced the region's communities. In the first part of the 20th century, two home extension agents brought change and improvement to the rural area. Other residents became the voice and eyes of the region, preserving the Twin Counties' history through newspapers and photography. George Howard Sr. brought the first newspaper, the *Tarboro Press,* to Tarboro in 1826. Today, the *Tarboro Southerner* is the second-oldest continuous newspaper in the state, and the *Rocky Mount Telegram* (begun in 1910) has been reporting events in the Twin Counties for over a century. Still others formed historical societies and museums to preserve the historical and architectural richness that had developed over the past two and half centuries. This endeavor is exemplified by the community museum in Spring Hope, the arts center in Nashville, the arts council in Edgecombe County, and the Centennial House in Pinetops. There is even a special museum just for children in Rocky Mount, which was reorganized in the Imperial Center after the flooding caused by Hurricane Floyd in 1999. Some individuals worked to make their communities better for future generations by giving of their time, experience, and dedication to community groups like Scout troops, churches, and community centers. The hard work of the many citizens was reflected in the naming of Rocky Mount and Tarboro as All-America Cities, in 1970 and 1977, respectively.

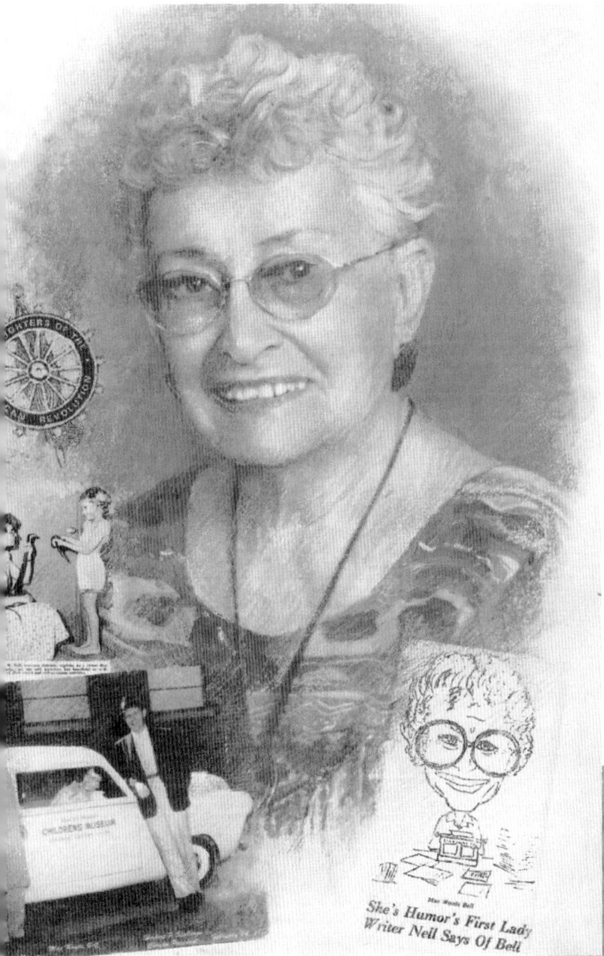

Mae Woods Bell

A native of England, Mae Woods Bell (TCHOF 2010) has spent the past 60 years in Rocky Mount. In 1951, she began the Children's Museum, which grew from a few exhibits to a major community program. Lifetime dedication and 30 years as director earned her the Southeastern Museums Distinguished Service Award in 1978. Bell has been active with the East Carolina Council of the Boy Scouts of America, serving as vice president of the Cub Scout program, and has earned the Compass Award, the highest honor given to non-Scouters. (Portrait by Susan Fecho.)

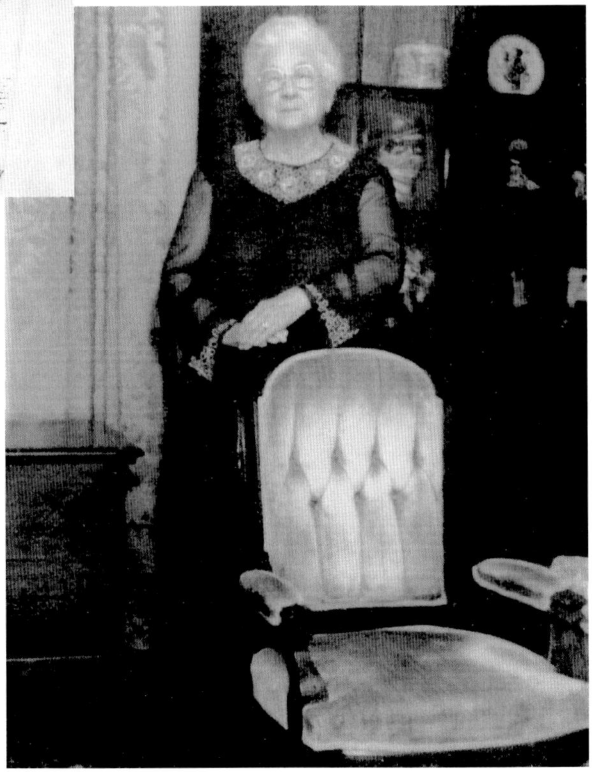

Hazel Valentine

Schoolteacher and Nashville postmaster Hazel Valentine's (1895–1997; TCHOF 2007) legacy is in her volunteer work. She began the Coastal Plain Craft Show and helped establish the Nash Arts Center. She was a member of the Nashville Chamber of Commerce, a lifelong member of the North Carolina Art Society, and a member of several garden clubs. At the age of 91, she carried the Olympic Torch when it traveled through Nash County for the 1988 Olympics. (Courtesy Valentine family.)

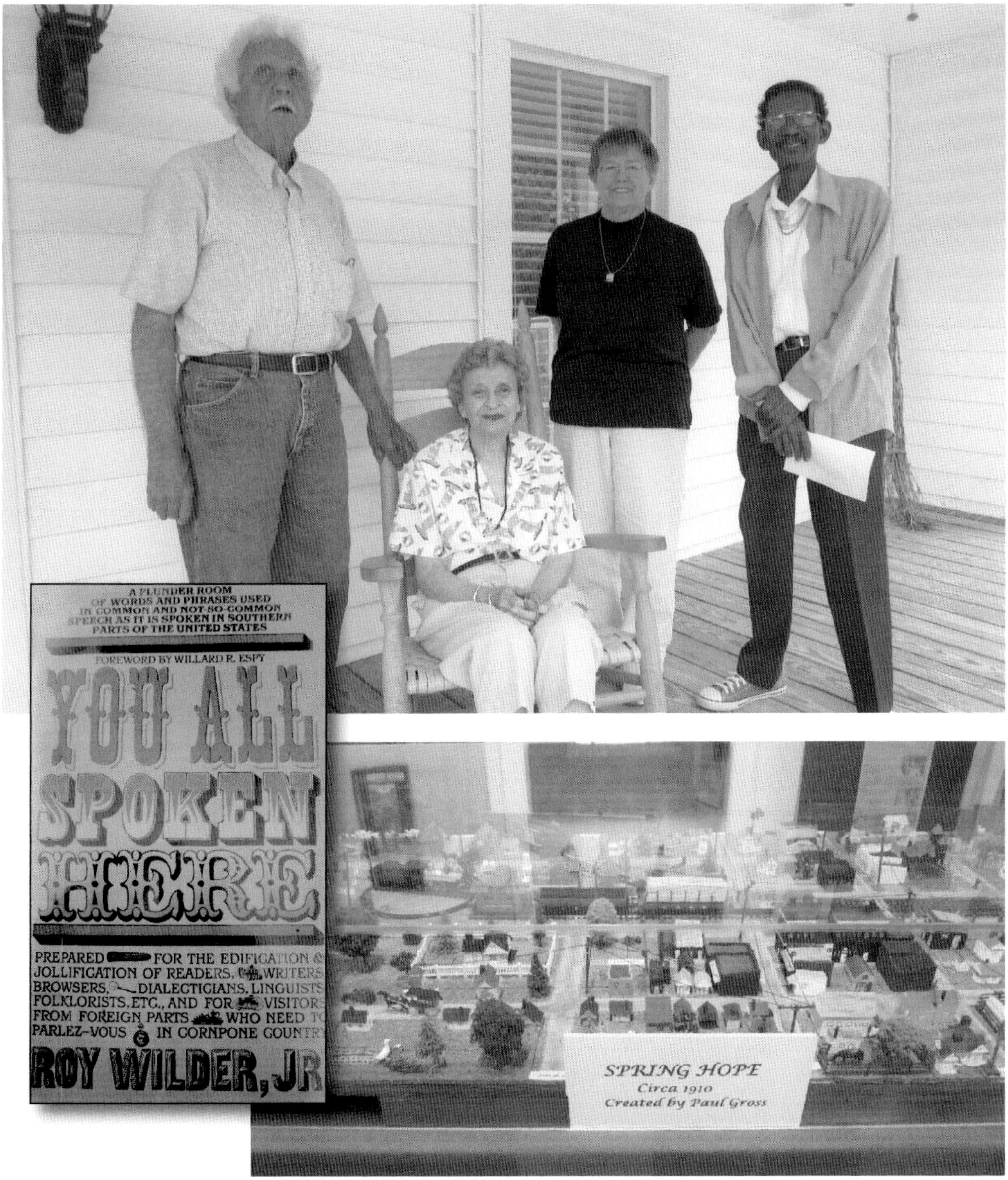

Spring Hope Historical Association

In 1983, Anna Pearl Brantly, Hazel Mae Little, Lena Morgan, and Pauline Boone formed the Spring Hope Historical Association. Pauline (seated), the only surviving founding member, is still active in the organization. Their original goal was to have a permanent home to preserve the area's history. A shotgun-style house given to the organization was moved to its current location and opened in February 1989, in time to celebrate the town's centennial. Others soon joined the organization, and the Spring Hope Museum now hosts rotating exhibits of the community's history. Pictured from left to right, officers Warren Boone Pauline Boone, Gay Sturgeon, and Bill Newkirk also bring in guest speakers. Resident Paul Gross made a diorama representing a view of the town around its 1910-era peak. Agricultural artifacts belonging to local author Roy Wilder Jr., whose book *You All Spoken Here* is a classic in Southern dialects, are a part of the museum's permanent collection. (Photograph by the author.)

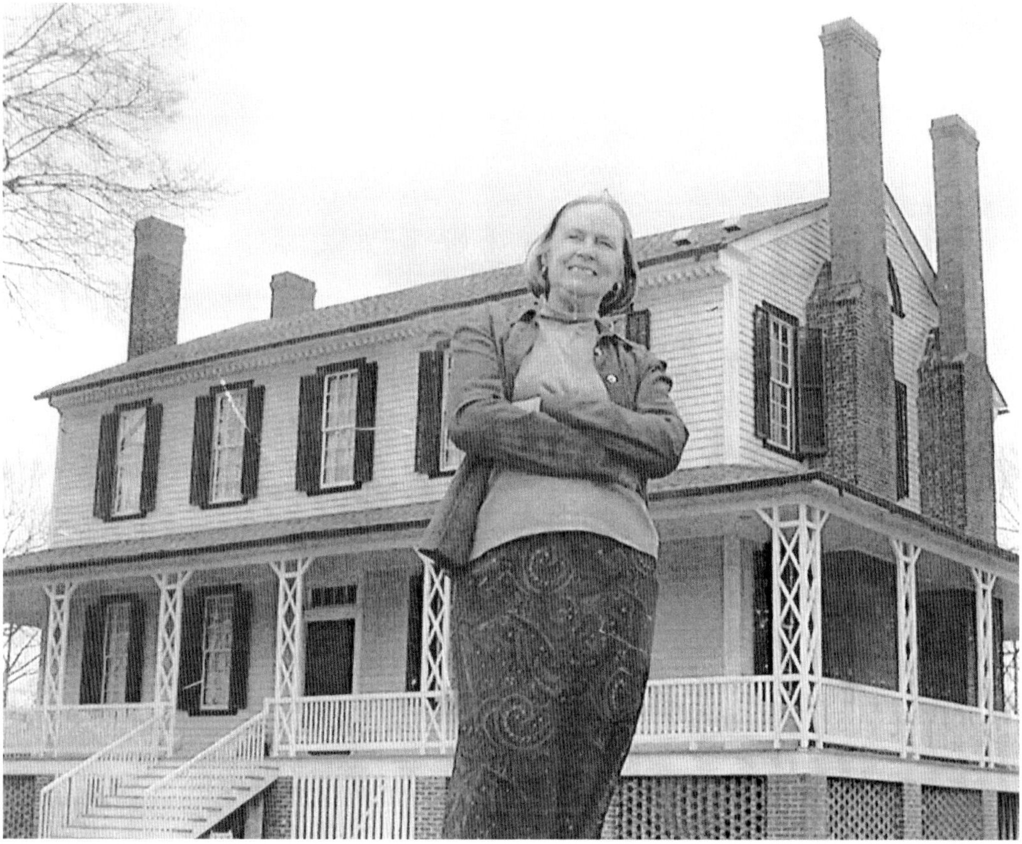

Meade Bridgers Horne

Meade Bridgers Horne's family history goes back for several generations in Edgecombe County, where her relatives were active in community service, in the military, and in business. Meade continued the family tradition. Although she was born in Durham, she visited family in Tarboro often on holidays. A graduate of Vassar College, she earned her master of arts degree from Johns Hopkins University. She married and raised a family, but her roots eventually brought her home. In 1982, the Blount-Bridgers House, which had been her ancestors' residence in the 1850s and had served as a community house in Tarboro since the Depression, was dedicated as a house museum and art gallery, with Horne as the first director. Her job involved managing the house and its furnishings, giving tours, directing the Edgecombe Arts Council, supervising her small staff, and providing cultural activities for the community. Meade managed to juggle all these hats equally well for over 23 years until she retired in 2005. She organized the Happening on the Common, a multicultural arts event of music, food, fun, and family entertainment that was held each spring on the Tarboro Common. She arranged art shows in the Hobson Pittman Gallery (on the second floor of the house) featuring local and regional artists' works in all media, from painting and photography to pottery and sculpture. She wrote a book, *The Poet's Palette*, about local artist Hobson Pittman. For at least a dozen years, Horne and the arts council sponsored the Great Tarboro Art Bazaar each November, which showcased the work of dozens of local artists just in time for holiday gifts. She brought in authors and historians for lectures, readings, and book signings. The Blount-Bridgers House also maintains records about many families and residents of the area, as well as about historical homes. Meade and her staff often fielded questions from around the country about former Edgecombe citizens. Working with the Town of Tarboro, Meade helped produce a walking-tour brochure of the historic district. In addition to her work at the museum and the art council, she was active with the Calvary Episcopal Church choir for three decades. (Courtesy BBH.)

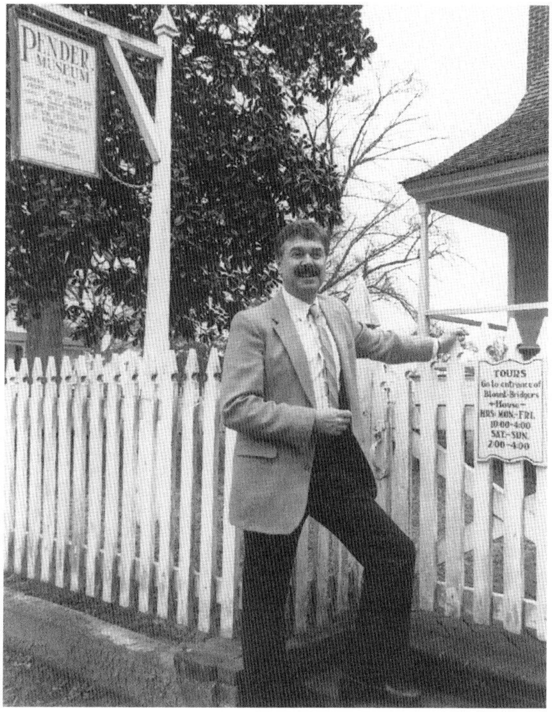

Earl Roberson
Edgecombe County native Earl Lynn Roberson dedicated his life to making his community a better place to live through education and preservation. In 1972, he joined Edgecombe Community College as head of the literacy programs, a position he held for 17 years. He was very active in the Edgecombe County Historical Society; in the preservation movement, restoring his 19th-century home; and in the Conetoe Methodist Church. (Courtesy ECC.)

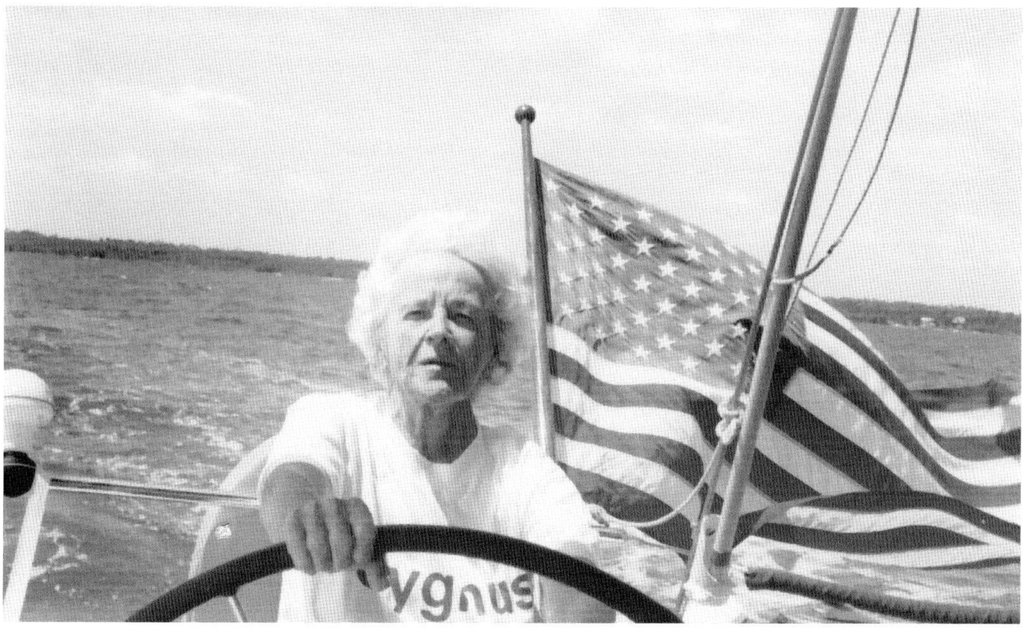

Jaquelin Drane Nash
A native of Charlotte, Nash moved to Tarboro upon her marriage to Pembroke Nash and became one of the community's active supporters. She wrote *A Goodly Heritage*, the history of Calvary Episcopal Church. She published articles in the *Dictionary of North Carolina Biography* and was founding director of the Edgecombe County Historical Society. Nash won the Carraway Award of Merit from Preservation North Carolina. (Courtesy Sylvia Nash.)

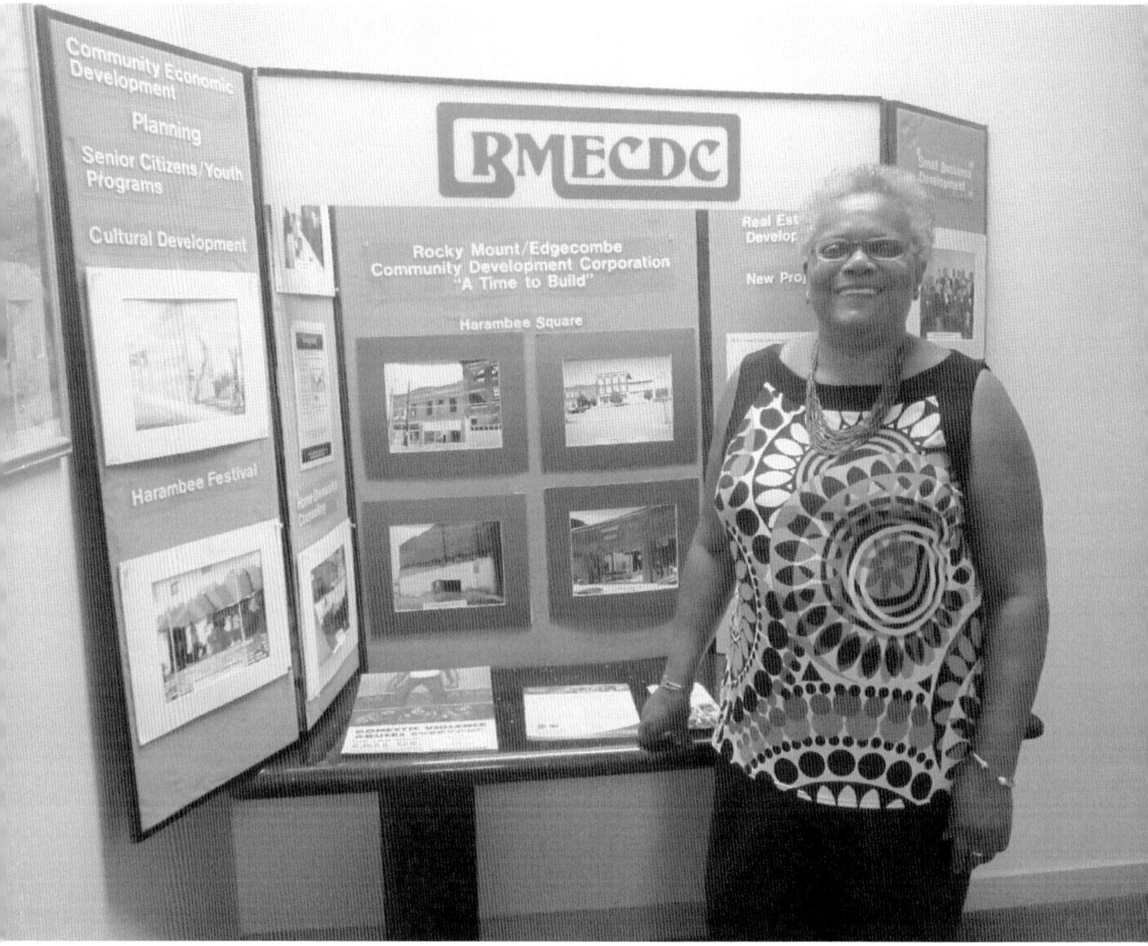

Joyce Dickens

In 1988, the Rocky Mount/Edgecombe Community Development Corporation (RMECDC) was chartered. Founder Joyce Dickens, a Pinetops native, has been the director of the nonprofit organization since the beginning. One of the organization's goals was the preservation of the African American heritage of the area. This was carried out with the redevelopment of Washington Street and the creation of Harambee Square, home of the annual Harambee Festival.

The free annual event has over 100 vendors featuring food and art displays that showcase the area, with the highlight being the Thelonious Monk Jazz Concert, which features performances by gospel, blues, and jazz artists. Monk was born in a neighborhood that has been redeveloped into single-family housing; working with the City of Rocky Mount and the Phoenix Society, RMECDC dedicated a park in 2002 near his birthplace. Other focuses of RMECDC are housing for the elderly and a program in public arts. Over the years, Dickens and the RMECDC have helped thousands of area residents through housing projects, assistance with business startups, and aid during the recovery from Hurricane Floyd. Recently, working along with City of Rocky Mount employees Steve Raper, Charles Penny, and Pete Varney, Dickens saw the realization of a long-held dream: the complete revitalization of Douglas Block, an essential part of Rocky Mount's African American community. Old, abandoned buildings were restored; the Booker T. Theater now serves as a conference area, and several other buildings house new businesses. The latest project of Dickens and the RMECDC is the 64 Crossing, a location for new businesses at the junction of old Highway 64 and the 64 Bypass. (Photograph by the author.)

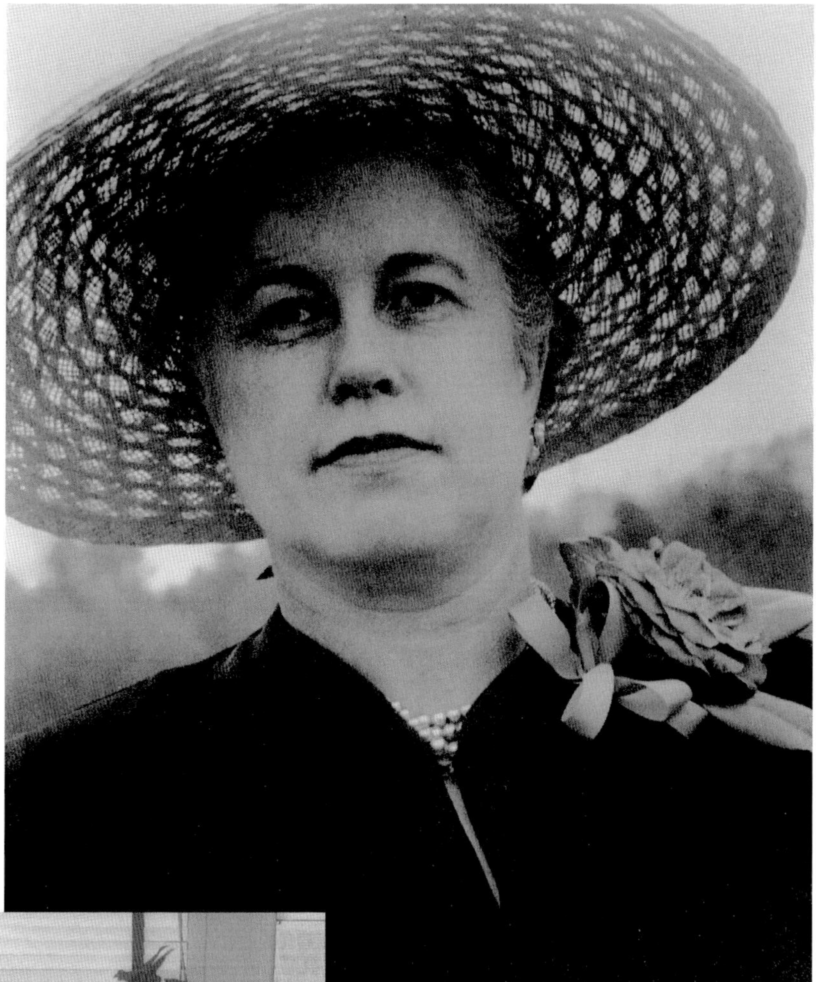

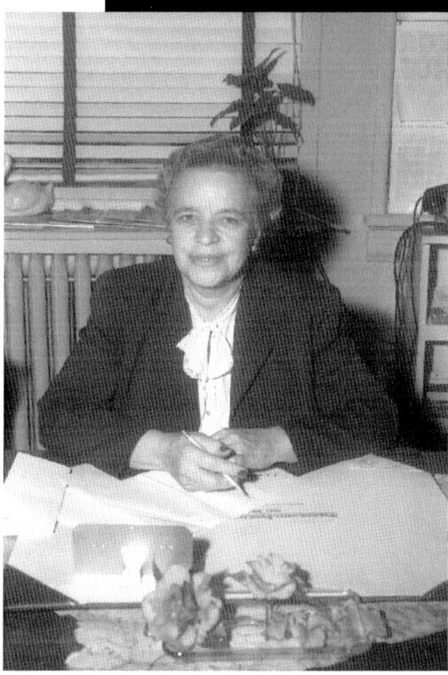

Effie Vines Gordon and Eugenia Van Landingham
These two outstanding women left their mark on the Twin Counties through their service as home extension agents. Effie Vines Gordon (left), an Edgecombe County native, served as the first home demonstration agent in 1915, then spent two years doing emergency work during World War I. In May 1922, she went to Nash County as the home extension agent, a position she held for 28 years. During her tenure, she helped start the curb market in Rocky Mount and expanded membership in local farm clubs. In 1948, *Progressive Farmer* recognized her as "Woman of the Year." Eugenia Van Landingham (above), known as "Mrs. Van," spent over 33 years as an Edgecombe extension agent until she retired in 1971. She developed a highly recognized homemaker program in the state. (Left, courtesy Braswell, Killibrew Collection; above, courtesy ECML, Brown collection.)

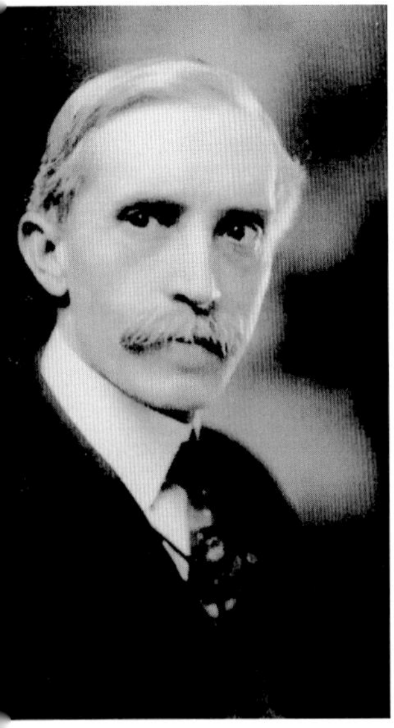

Sidney Rufus Alley and Osmond Long "Bugs" Barringer

The Twin Counties have been home to several outstanding photographers. Sidney Rufus Alley (left) operated a studio in Tarboro from the 1880s to 1920. Alley took portraits of most of the citizens, as well as school photographs for yearbooks and pictures of many of the historic houses. He took the area's first news photographs in 1897 when he captured images of the burning of the Bryan House Hotel on Main Street. Bugs Barringer (right), originally from Charlotte, came to Rocky Mount in 1939 to work for the *Telegram*; by 1942 he had opened a photography studio on the side. Bugs won "Best Picture of the Year" in 1942 from the North Carolina Press Association. He contributed photographs and stories to the Raleigh *News and Observer*, including a weekly gardening column, which ran for over a decade. (Left, courtesy ECML; right, courtesy Barringer.)

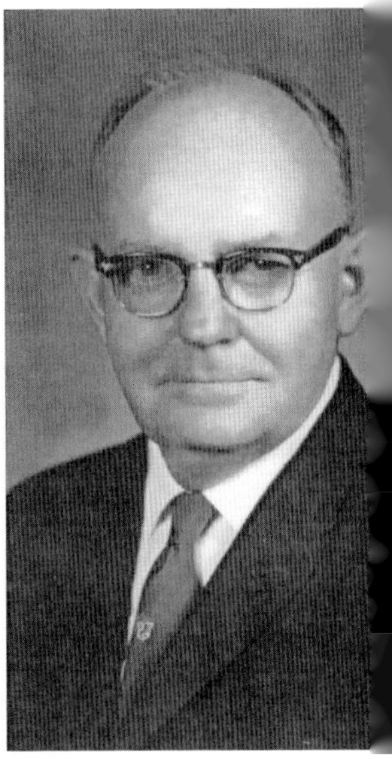

Milton Steele "Coca Cola" Brown (OPPOSITE PAGE)

Almost 100 years ago, Milton Steele Brown came to Tarboro to open a Coca-Cola plant. Had that been all he did, he would have been a footnote in Tarboro history for beginning a business that operated for over 50 years and employed many people. But M.S. Brown, better known in his day as "Coca Cola" Brown, did so much more. Active in local government, business, and community organizations, he helped establish the Tarboro Merchants Association and Chamber of Commerce and was eventually elected president of the organization. He served on the town council for a number of years and, along with Dr. Spencer Bass, led a drive to have a milk plant. He also was on the town commission when the Community House (today the Blount-Bridgers House) was set up in the 1930s. Brown was recognized as the "Father of Progress" for our community for giving "unselfishly of his mental and physical energy and his material and spiritual resources to the end that Tarboro now is a clear, healthier, richer, bigger, better, finer and more wholesome place in which to live." But M.S. Brown is best remembered today for his hobby, which has left a rich legacy for local citizens. Brown loved taking pictures, and he and his camera frequented many community events between 1912 and the 1950s. Through his camera, Brown witnessed and recorded life in the community. He loved sports, especially swimming and baseball, and worked tirelessly to keep the local minor-league team, the Tarboro Tars, a part of the Coastal Plain League. Brown sponsored the athletic teams and the marching band. Brown's love for the band was recognized in the fall of 1951 in an article in the Raleigh *News & Observer*, in which it was reported that the "local civic leader [was] perhaps the only man in Eastern Carolina [to have] a band march named in his honor." The article explained that Brown had two mobile bandstands constructed for concerts and celebrations and had raised funds for a trip to Atlantic City for a performance at the Lions International event. A record crowd of more than 1,000 citizens showed up at the Municipal Stadium (the ball park across from Martin Middle School) to hear the band perform a new song dedicated to Brown. It was called the "M.S.B. March." (Courtesy ECML, Brown Collection.)

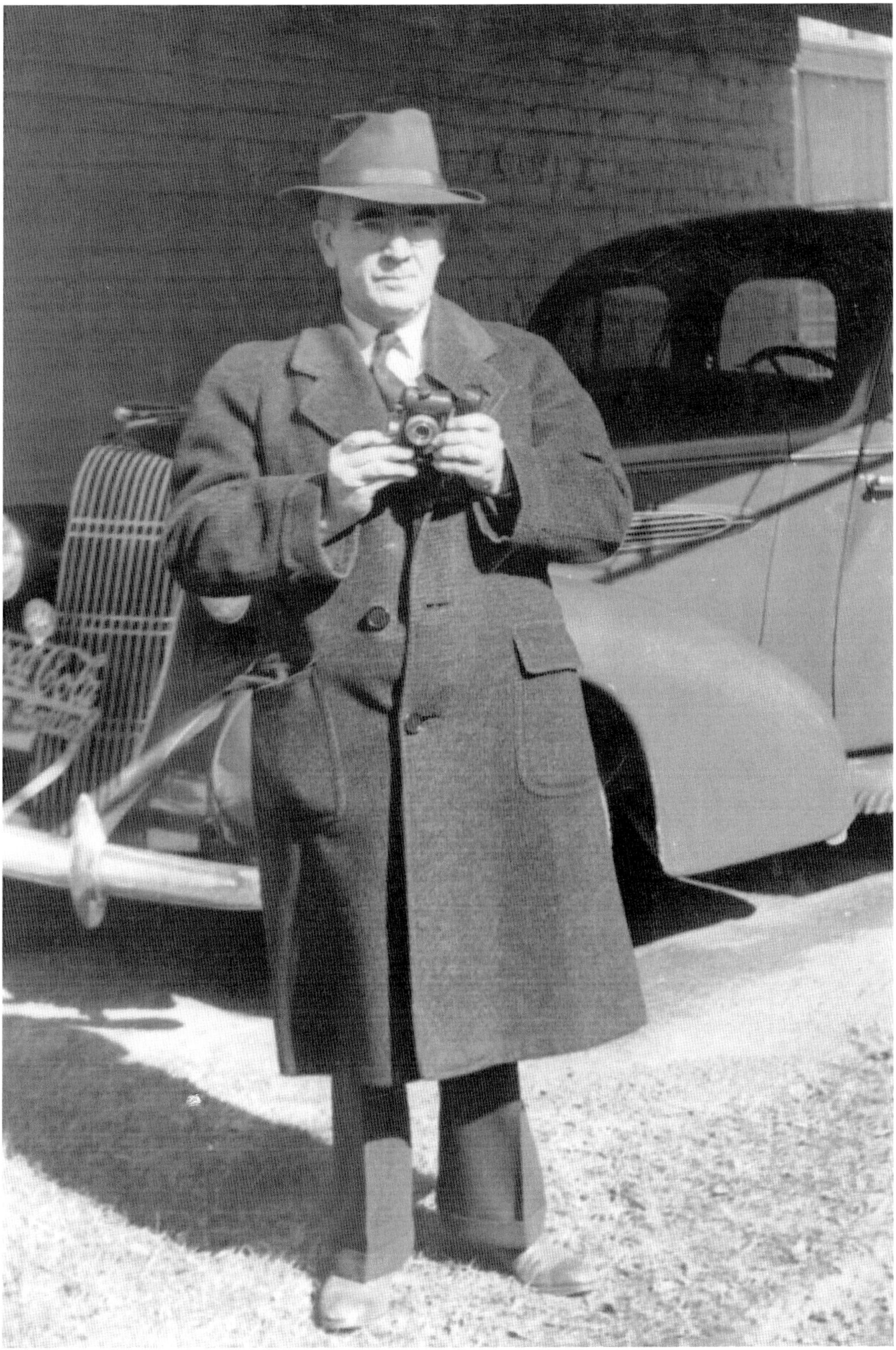

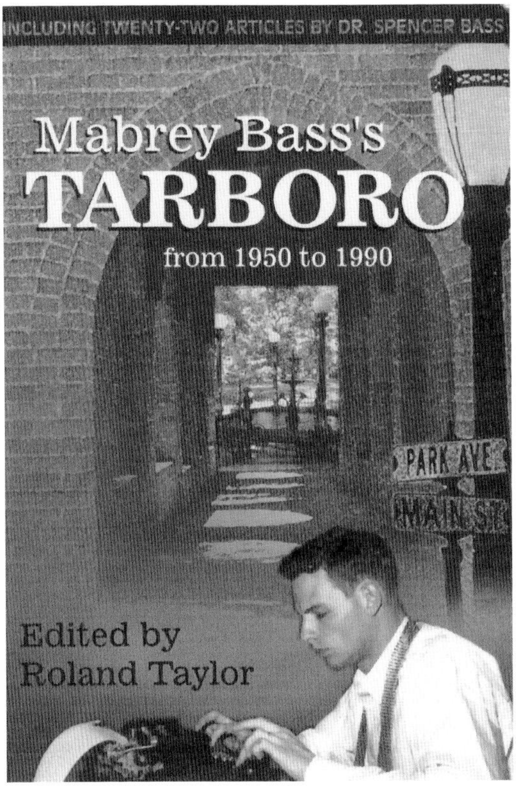

Baker "Mabrey" Bass Jr.
For 40 years, Mabrey Bass worked at the *Daily Southerner* in Tarboro, spending 35 of those years as editor. Bass grew up in Tarboro in a family with roots dating back several generations. After serving in the Army in World War II, he went to work at the paper. His weekly column, "Ramblin'" described observations of the community. After his death, Mabrey's brother Bill Bass published selections from the more than 2,000 columns. (Photograph by the author.)

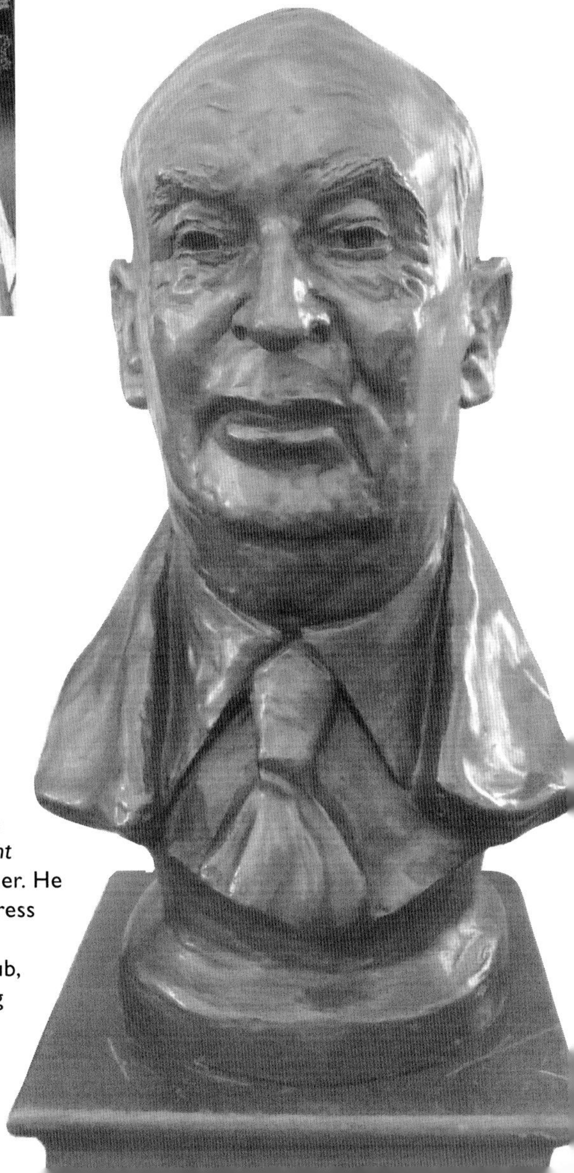

Joshua Lawrence Horne
Nash County native Josh Horne began a 60-year newspaper career with the *Rocky Mount Record* in 1910. Two years later, he founded the *Rocky Mount Telegram* and served as editor, publisher, and owner. He also served as president of the North Carolina Press Association and founded two area radio stations. He was a charter member of the RM Kiwanis Club, and served on the YMCA board. A bust honoring his service can be found at the Braswell Library. (Photograph by the author.)

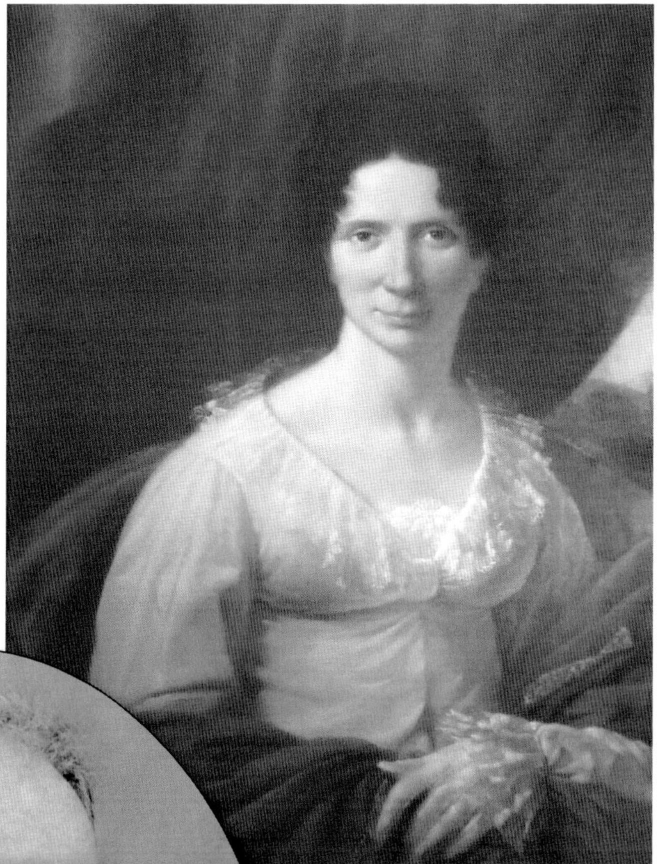

Mary "Jackie" Blount
The wife of congressman Thomas Blount, Mary "Jackie" Blount lived in what was described as the grandest house in the county in 1810. She had no children, but left a remarkable legacy in her will, which, in 1822, freed slaves, set up a fund for widows and orphans, and helped establish Christ Episcopal Church in Raleigh. (Copy of portrait courtesy BBH; original at Mordecai House in Raleigh.)

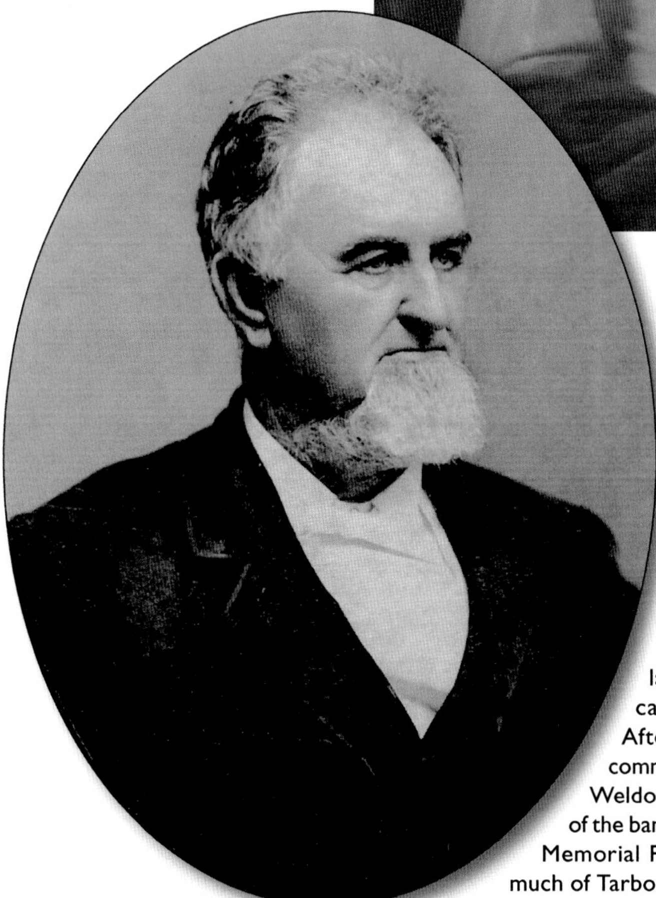

George Howard Jr.
The son of the founder of the first area newspaper, George Howard Jr. first worked on the paper as editor. After going to UNC, he became a lawyer and judge. In 1855, he led the campaign to create Wilson County. After the Civil War, Howard was a town commissioner, director of the Wilmington & Weldon Railroad, trustee of UNC, president of the bank, elder of what is now called Howard Memorial Presbyterian Church, and owner of much of Tarboro. (Courtesy BBH.)

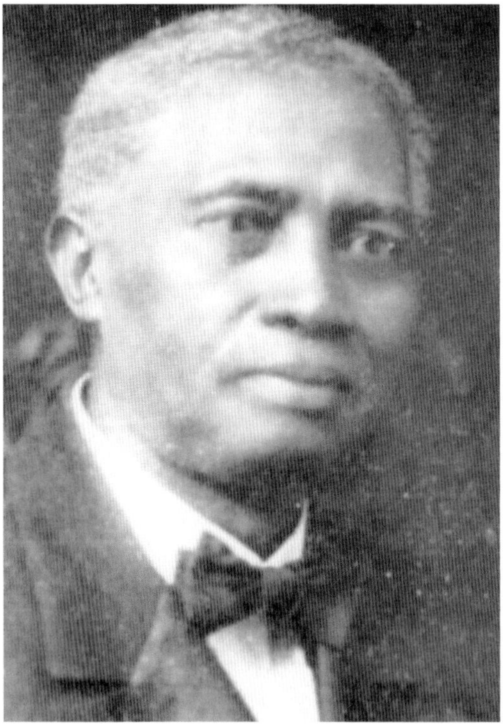

John C. Dancy

The son of a former slave, John C. Dancy was born free in 1857. He attended a local school before going to Howard University in Washington, DC. A state historic marker recognizes Dancy's work as editor of the African Methodist Episcopal Zion Church papers and as a customs collector in Wilmington. He was active in Reconstruction politics and was appointed to the US Treasury Department; he was later the recorder of deeds in Washington, DC. (Courtesy NCDAH.)

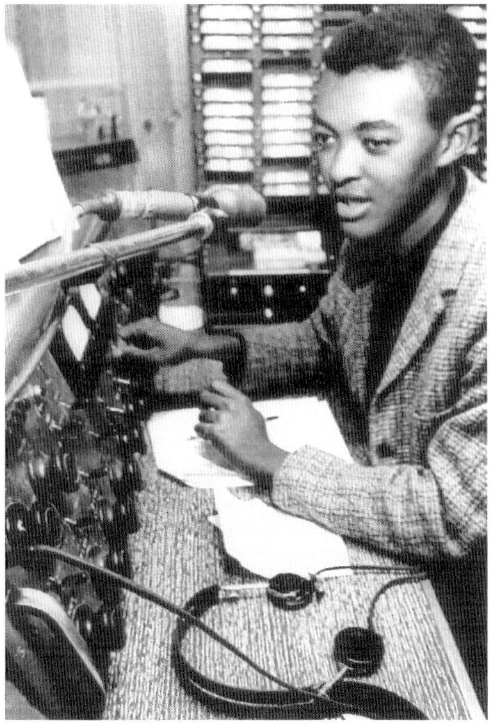

Charles Johnson

Charles Johnson (TCHOF 2009) grew up in Enfield and became a manager, then owner, of the local radio stations WRSV-FM and WEED-AM. He started out hosting radio programs, bringing gospel and rhythm-and-blues music to local audiences back in the 1960s. He spent more than 40 years in the broadcasting business serving the African American community. (Johnson family photograph.)

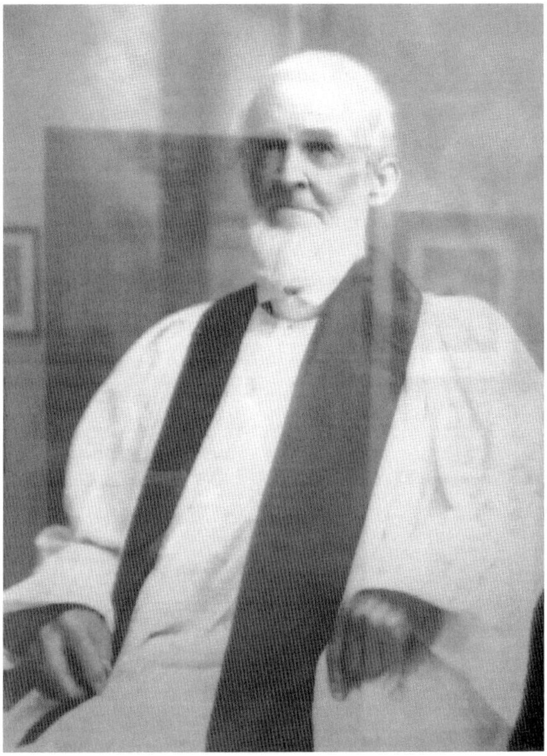

Rev. Joseph Blount Cheshire
Rector of Calvary Episcopal Church for nearly 50 years, Joseph Blount Cheshire landscaped the churchyard with a variety of plants that are not native to the area. Tradition indicates that he asked visitors to send him plants or seeds from other areas. With his interest in botany, he created a beautiful arboretum. He also led the campaign to build the current church in 1859; it was completed in 1867. (Courtesy Calvary Episcopal Church.)

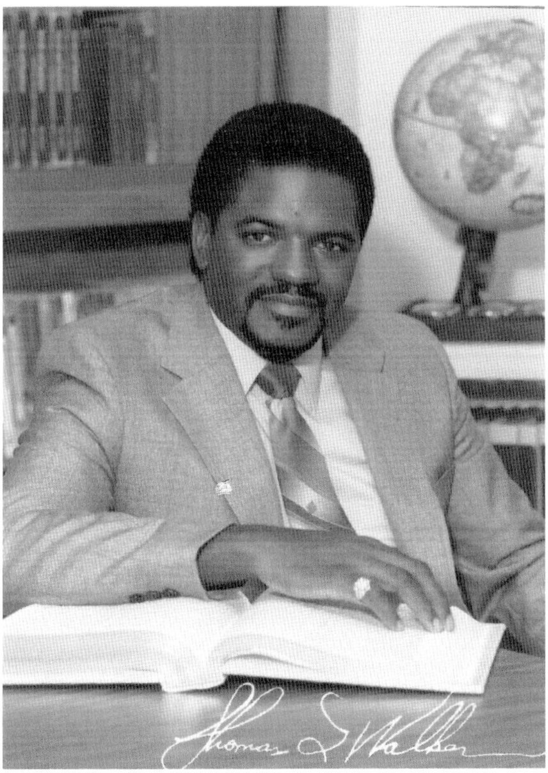

Rev. Thomas Lorenzo Walker
Edgecombe native Thomas Lorenzo Walker (TCHOF 2010) has been pastor of Ebenezer Baptist Church in Rocky Mount for 40 years. Active in his community, Walker founded EBC-Atom, a nonprofit organization that focuses on housing, health, and community outreach. After recovering from prostate cancer, the Reverend Dr. Walker authored *Brother to Brother—You Don't Have to Die of Prostate Cancer.* (Courtesy Reverend Walker.)

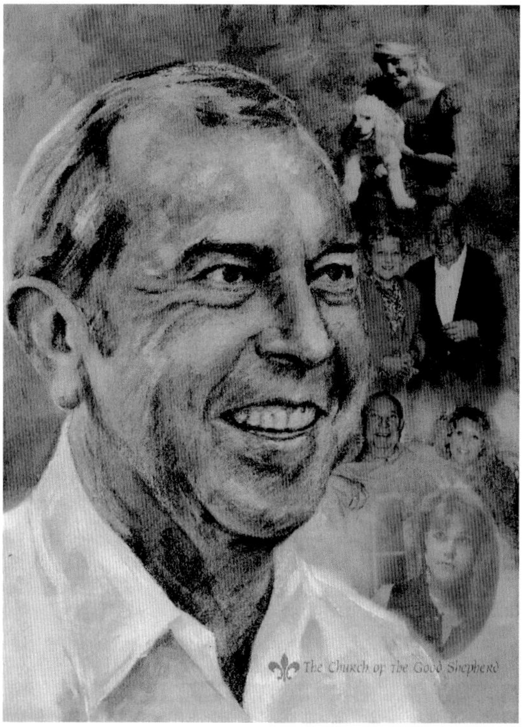

Jesse Claude Mayo
In addition to his longtime business interest in the area, Duke University graduate Jesse Claude Mayo (TCHOF 2009) has served as a Nash County Commissioner, as well as on the board of trustees of NC Wesleyan. He has served on numerous boards in his church, as well as on health care agencies and on the East Carolina Council of the Boy Scouts of America. (Portrait by Susan Fecho.)

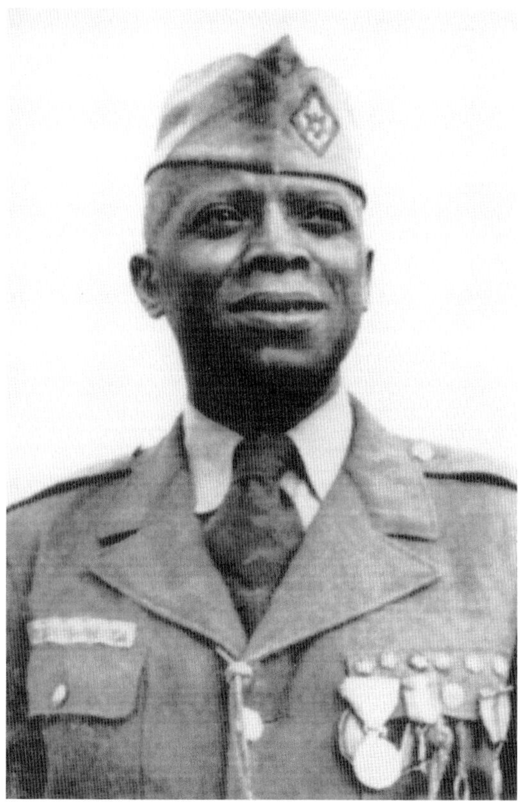

Thomas Stith
After serving in World War I, Thomas Stith Sr. (TCHOF 2005) worked for Rocky Mount schools for 20 years and spent 18 years with the US Post Office. He is most recognized, though, for his dedication to area youth in his role as founder of Boy Scout Troop 161. He was active in developing the baseball park for the Negro League. He also founded the Southeastern Business College in Durham and taught Sunday school at the St. James Baptist church for 15 years. (Courtesy Stith family.)

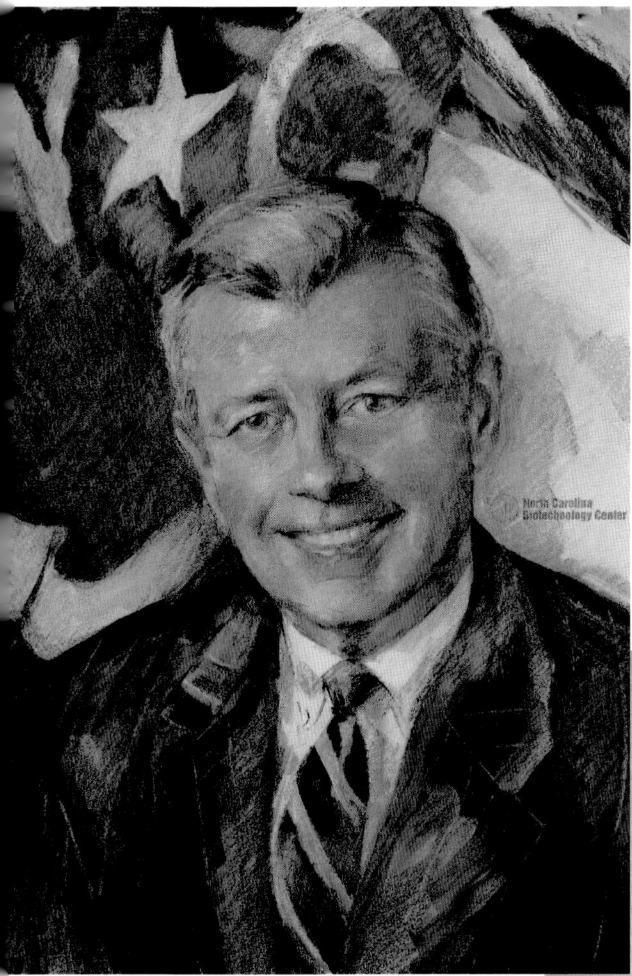

Norris Tolson
Tolson (TCHOF 2008) grew up on a farm but, after graduating from NC State, went to work in industry. Tolson ran the marketing division of agrichemicals at Dupont for 28 years, traveling all over the world. He returned to North Carolina and tackled many problems for the state. He was a state legislator, then secretary of commerce, secretary of transportation, and secretary of revenue. He was also director of the North Carolina Hurricane Floyd Relief Fund. (Portrait by Susan Fecho.)

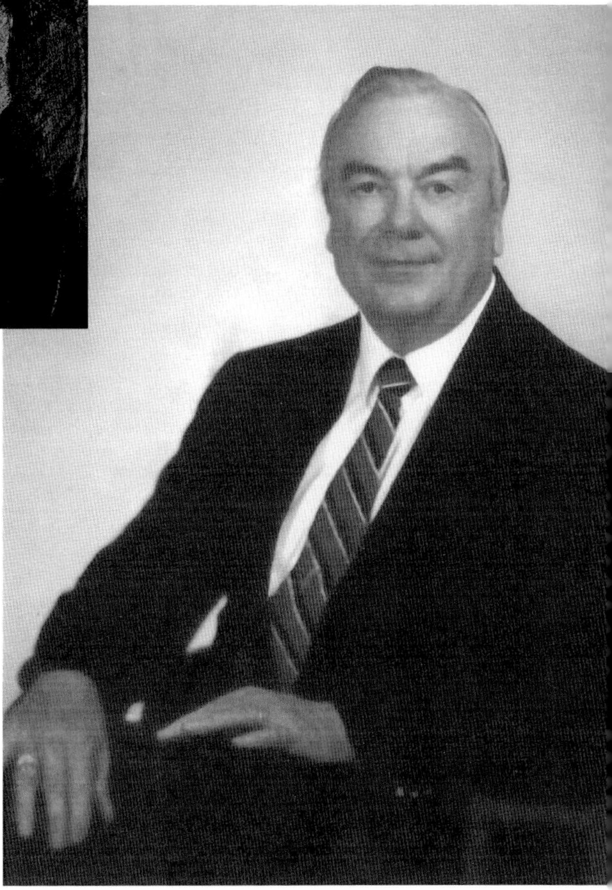

Norfleet "Fleet" Sugg
Born in Pinetops, Fleet Sugg (TCHOF 2011) earned a bachelor of science degree in agronomy from North Carolina State University (NC State). In World War II, he served in the Navy in the Pacific theater. Sugg is a leader in the field of agriculture, serving as chairman of the Agriculture Council of America, executive vice president of the North Carolina Agribusiness Council, and chief executive officer of the North Carolina Peanut Growers Association. Sugg is also a member of both the American Legion and the Pinetops Lions Club, in addition to being a Scoutmaster. (Courtesy Norfleet "Fleet" Sugg.)

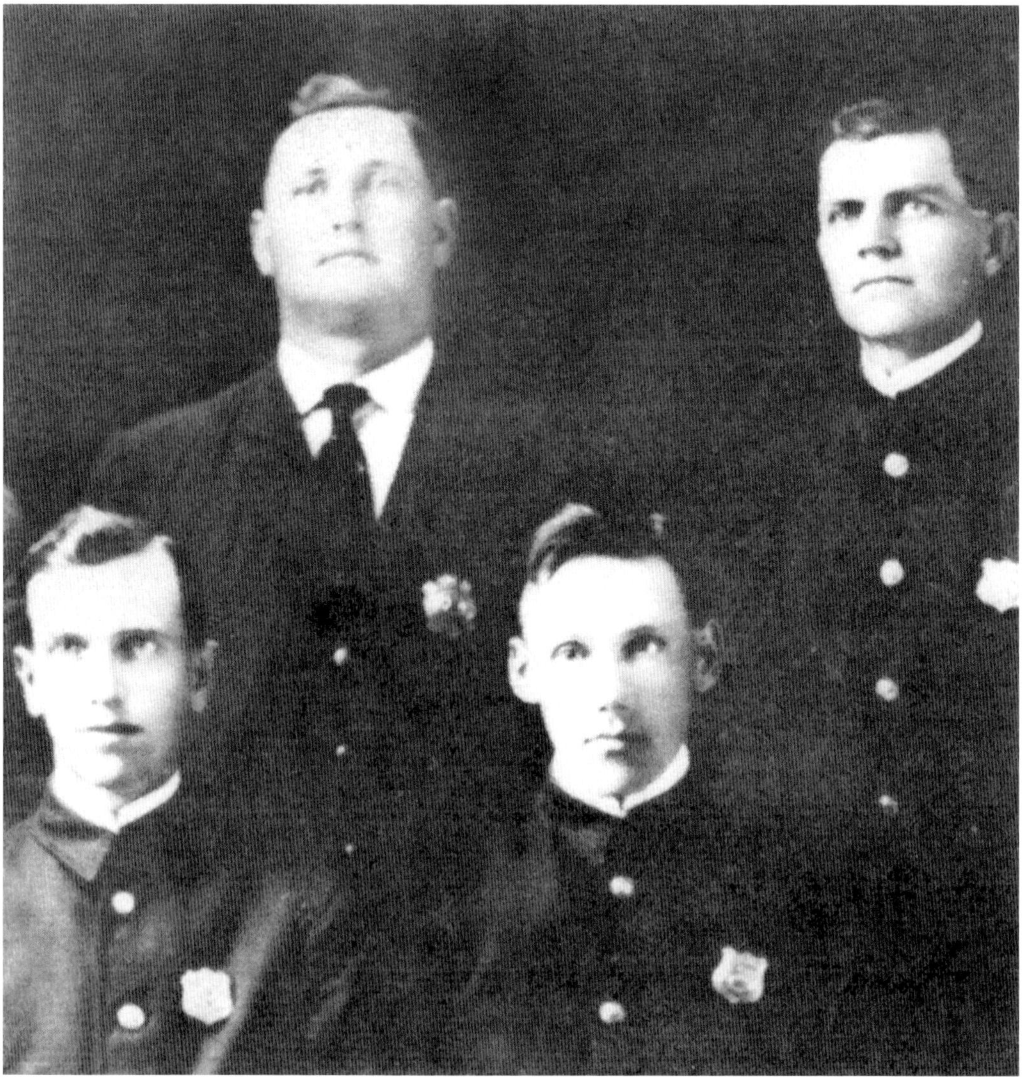

Tarboro Officers Killed
On March 3, 1917, two Tarboro police officers were shot and killed during a raid on a residence suspected of selling illegal alcohol; the mayor was also wounded in the incident. Matt Ransom Gwatney (top right) and Plummer Ray Riggen (bottom left) were the first Edgecombe County officers to die in the line of duty. They were buried under a joint tombstone with a single word, "duty," appearing after their names. (Courtesy BBH.)

Patrick Jackson (OPPOSITE PAGE)
Patrick Jackson, a fire engineer with the Rocky Mount Fire Department, has invented a smart-phone and tablet application that allows for quicker and more informed responses to fires. It shows locations of hydrants near the fire and also sends out alerts. Jackson is continuing to develop this application to assist firefighters. (Photograph by the author.)

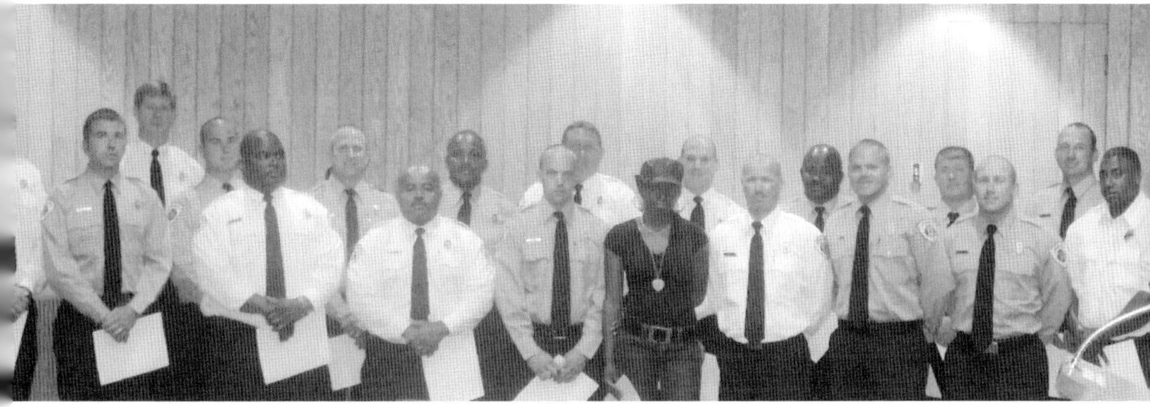

Rocky Mount Fire Department

On January 5, 2012, fourteen-year-old Taniya Wiggins of Rocky Mount saved four of her siblings (ages 12 years, 6 years, 3 years, and 11 months) by safely getting them out of their house when it caught on fire. When Rocky Mount firefighters arrived, Taniya realized her five-year-old sister Taylor was still in the house. The firefighters rescued the child, and, after spending two months at the North Carolina Jaycee Burn Center at UNC Hospitals in Chapel Hill, she returned home. In June, the Rocky Mount City Council honored Taniya along with members of the battalion that rescued the child and put out the fire. Pictured are, from left to right, (first row) Jamey Vaughan (battalion chief), Mark Williams (fire engineer), Corey Mercer (captain), Tracey Drewery (captain), Billy Baker (captain), Tyler Hinton (firefighter), Taniya Wiggins, Tyler Whitely (firefighter), Mark Guy (senior firefighter), Maurice Woodley (senior firefighter), and Danny Walker (Edgecombe County paramedic); (second row) Trey Mayo (fire chief), Bradford Price (fire engineer who found the child), Stephen Wolf (senior firefighter), Lamont Morgan (fire engineer), Ronnie Raper (battalion chief), Joe Vindigni (captain), Earl Williams (fire engineer), John Miller (firefighter), and Jett Webb (firefighter). Just two months earlier, in November 2011, three Rocky Mount city employees became hometown heroes. Brian Marshall, Terry Johnson, and Brad Short were working on a gas line when they noticed a residence on fire. They cut the power and gas to the home, called the fire department, and helped the residents evacuate. The three were later recognized for their efforts in saving Rocky Mount citizens. (Courtesy RMFD.)

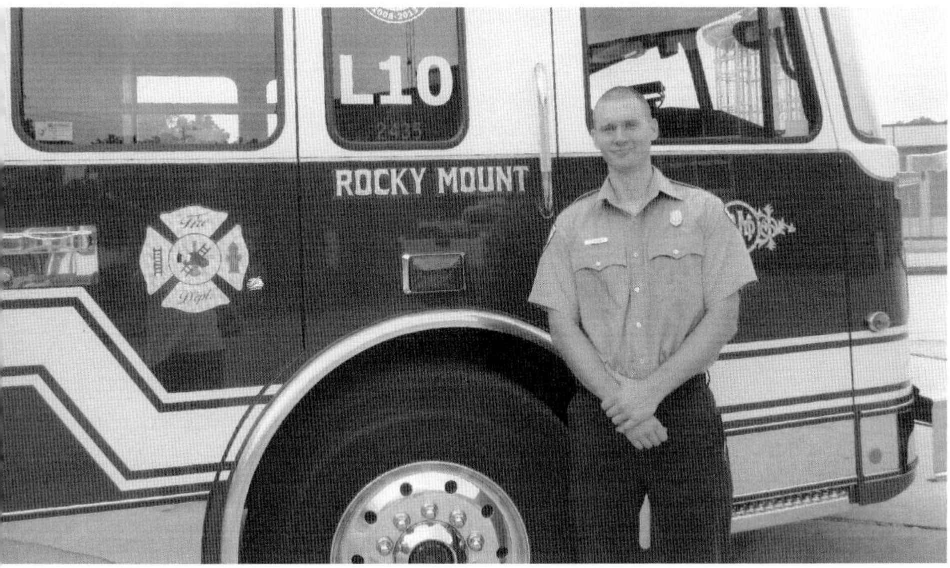

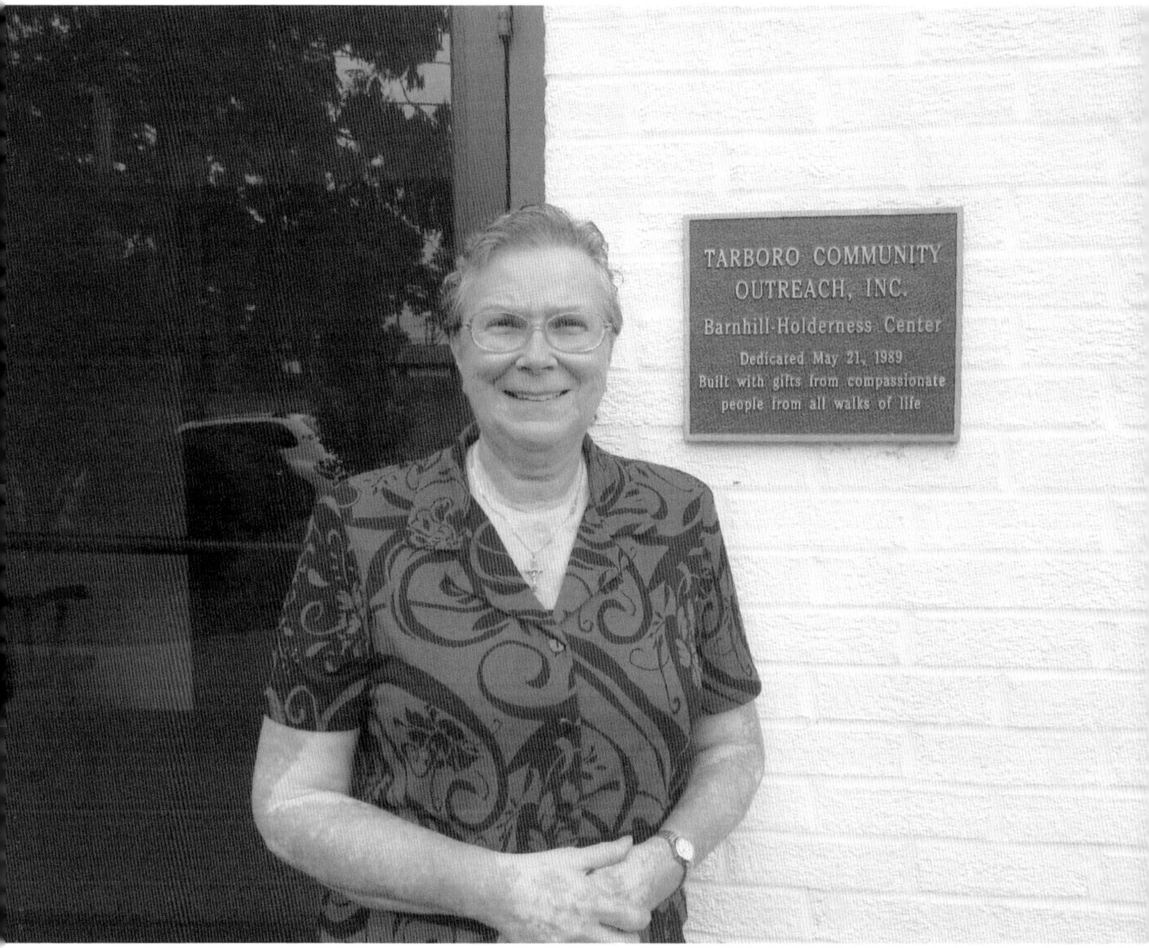

Sister Mary Ann Czaza and Tarboro Community Outreach
In 1981, a Catholic nun from Wisconsin reported to the Diocese of Raleigh to work for the good of the poor. Sister Mary Ann located in Tarboro, where Nancy Braswell Holderness and Robert Barnhill were developing a community organization to help the area poor. The next year, the organization, Tarboro Community Outreach (TCO), opened a food pantry at Calvary Episcopal Church, and rector Doug Reimer requested Sister Mary Ann to operate it. Four years later, the food pantry expanded into a soup kitchen at the farmers market. The soup kitchen was a multidenominational program, receiving support from several churches. Soon, more needs became apparent and the goal for community improvement led to the building of permanent a location on Cedar Lane, which opened in 1989. The facility provides temporary shelter for up to 26 men and also includes accommodations for homeless families. The program is open to any resident of Edgecombe County, not just those in Tarboro. TCO still operates the soup kitchen and the food pantry, and also now offers recycled clothing and furniture. Today, the organization serves more than 6,000 meals a month in the soup kitchen and assists over 1,000 households each month with food, clothing, furniture, and transportation needs. Sister Mary Ann still supervises all the programs and activities at TCO, operating in a position she has held for more than 30 years. (Photograph by author.)

CHAPTER THREE

Culture

Talent and creative inspiration has been plentiful in the Twin Counties for at least the past century. Arts were surely appreciated during the late 19th century, as records show that an opera house existed in Tarboro in the 1880s and a performance stage was built in the Tarboro Town Hall in 1890. Newspaper advertisements indicate that traveling acting troupes visited the area. Tarboro opened its first motion picture theater in 1919, and Rocky Mount soon followed suit. The Rocky Mount Masonic Lodge, built in the 1920s, included a stage and auditorium on the second floor. Not only did locals enjoy going to the theater, many also became talented artists, musicians, and writers. Several have won awards in their respective fields, and others, like Kay Kyser, Kaye Gibbons, and Allan Gurganus, have earned national attention or seen their work featured in motion pictures or special television movies. Some nonfiction authors have provided insights into Southern life, such as Roy Wilder Jr. with his dialect study, *You All Spoken Here*, and Smithsonian historian Pete Daniel with both *Standing at the Crossroads: Southern Life in the Twentieth Century* and *Lost Revolutions: The South in the 1950s*. Both Edgecombe and Nash Counties have arts councils that actively display local works in a variety of media. The Imperial Center in Rocky Mount is a renovated tobacco warehouse complex that is now home to a children's museum and an art gallery. Another gallery can be found at the Dunn Center on NC Wesleyan's campus. Tarboro has exhibits at the Blount-Bridgers House, while the Nashville Arts Center hosts exhibits in Nash County. There are also annual festivals that encourage new artists to display their art or perform their music. The Happening on the Common, a spring festival, has been held in early May for over 30 years. Spring Hope has a National Pumpkin Festival each fall, which features both art and musical talent. There are also community theaters that showcase the talents of actors and playwrights. The Playhouse and Tank Theater was active for many years in Rocky Mount, until being destroyed in Hurricane Floyd. The Tar River Players in Tarboro perform at Edgecombe Community College.

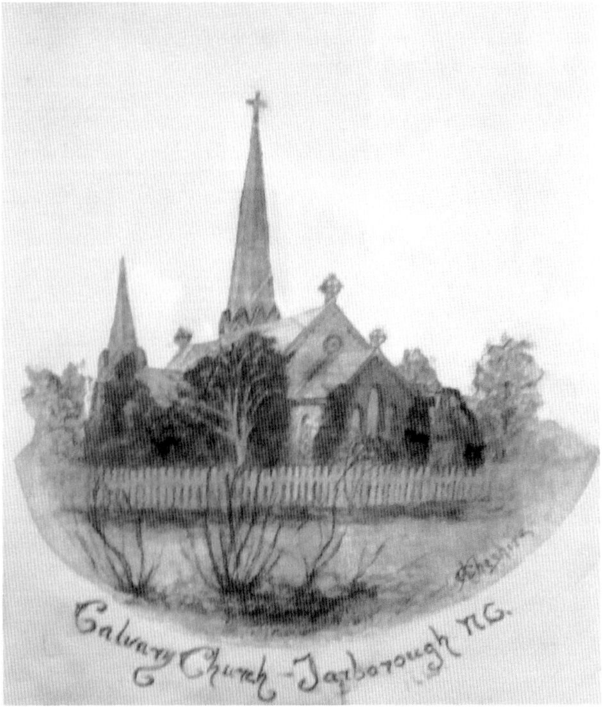

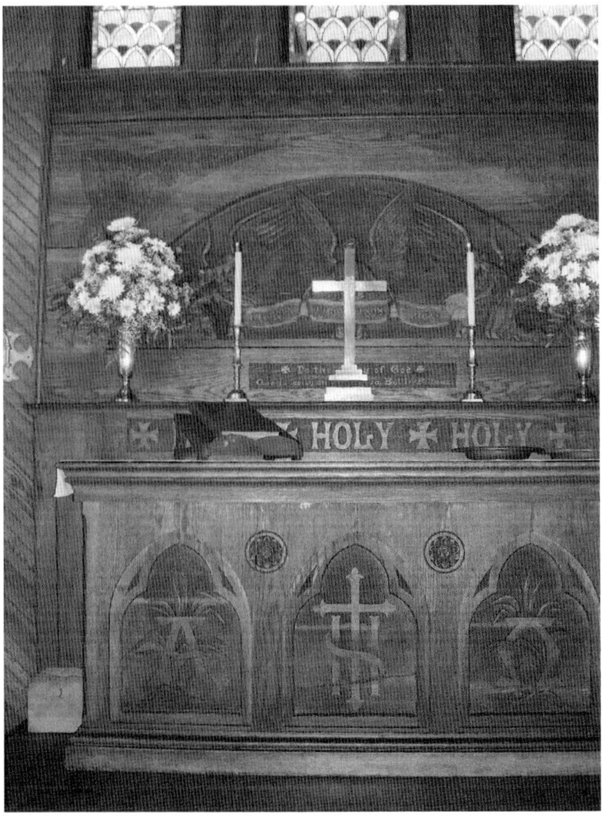

Katherine "Kate" Draughn Cheshire
The daughter of an Episcopal rector, Kate Cheshire grew up influenced by the church but with a natural artistic talent and perspective on nature. She painted in oils and watercolors and did some work in charcoal. A series of views of Calvary Episcopal Church and the churchyard, completed in the 1920s, are on display in the church. She also made pottery and ceramic tiles. Her best work, though, was her wood carving, and she created a beautiful baptismal font cover with carved ivy, doves, and fleur-de-lis that is still used in the church today. Her carving is also exemplified in the mantles of a few Tarboro homes, as well as in a series of fireplace tiles in the Cheshire-Nash House. At 30, Kate carved the front panel of a desk that became the centerpiece of the North Carolina Exhibit at the 1893 Columbian Exhibition in Chicago. The desk featured panels of carved holly and included Sir Walter Raleigh's coat of arms and an image of a doe, reflecting the legend of Virginia Dare. Her largest work is the altar at Grace Episcopal Church, completed in 1895. (Photographs by the author.)

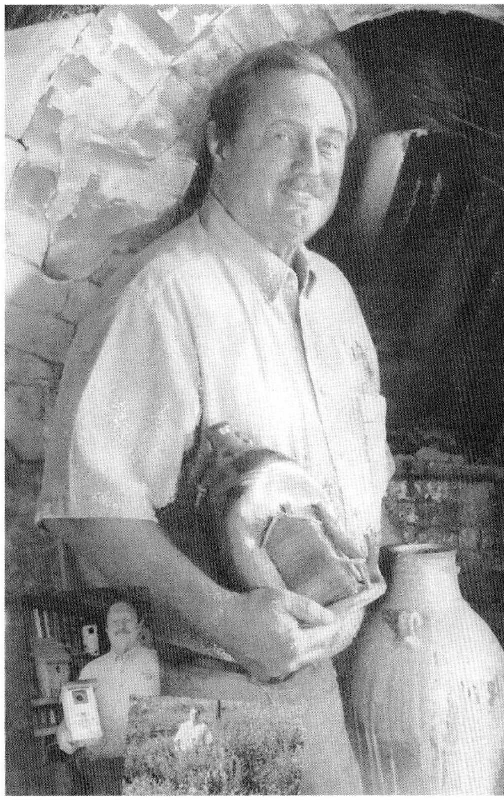

Daniel R. Finch
Born in Wilson County, Daniel R. Finch (TCHOF 2010) has spent his life in Bailey, where he has a pottery studio. His artistic talent and his dedication to teaching others the craft have made his name well known in the art world. For over 25 years, he taught at various area schools, engaging others in learning about art and pottery. His work has been featured in exhibits all over the southeast. (Portrait by Susan Fecho.)

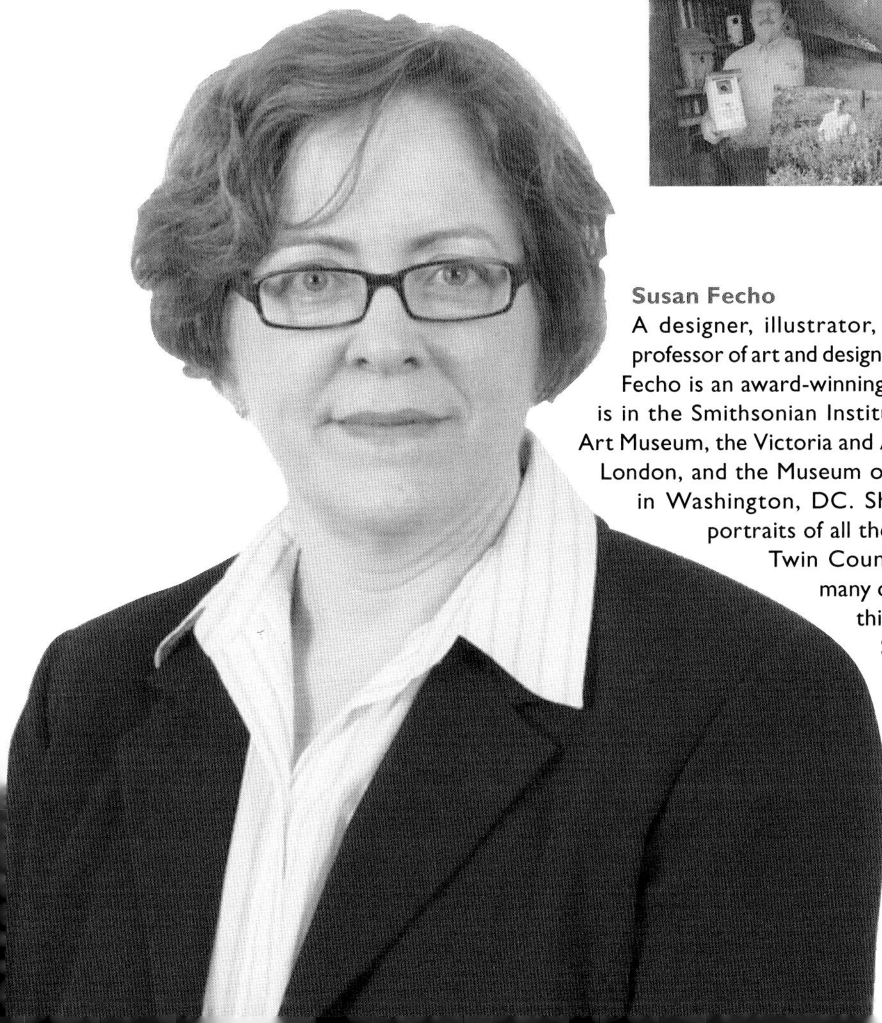

Susan Fecho
A designer, illustrator, printmaker, and professor of art and design at Barton College, Fecho is an award-winning artist. Her work is in the Smithsonian Institution's American Art Museum, the Victoria and Albert Museum in London, and the Museum of Women Artists in Washington, DC. She has produced portraits of all the members of the Twin County Hall of Fame, many of which appear in this book. (Courtesy Susan Fecho.)

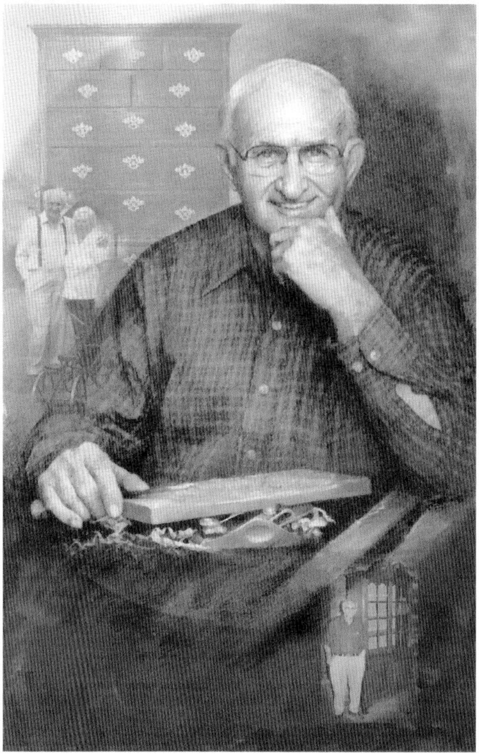

Preston Augustus "Pug" Moore

Delivering furniture for his father's business Pug Moore (TCHOF 2011) developed an appreciation for crafting fine furniture. In 1940, he opened Moore's Antique Shop and began making furniture in addition to repairing and selling antique pieces. After visiting Colonial Williamsburg, Pug discovered a passion for 18th-century furniture and became a master craftsman of fine reproductions of 18th-century styles. His work is in the governor's mansion and various historic homes. (Portrait by Susan Fecho.)

Hobson Pittman

Hobson Pittman began painting when he was 10, and his landscapes attracted a lot of attention. After high school, he attended the Pennsylvania Academy of Fine Art in Philadelphia. He completed a European study tour, after which he returned to the academy and taught art for almost 50 years. Pittman worked in oils, watercolor, copper etchings, and printmaking. He produced covers and art for major magazines like *Life* and *Holiday*. He also produced still lifes and Southern Gothic landscapes. (Courtesy BBH.)

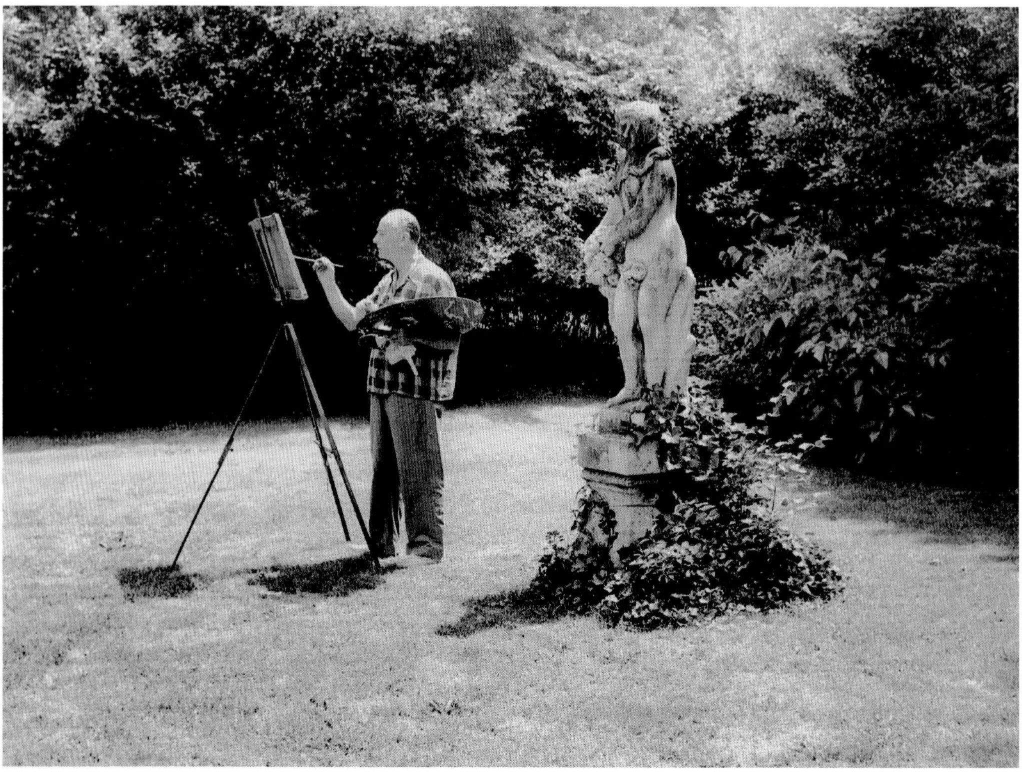

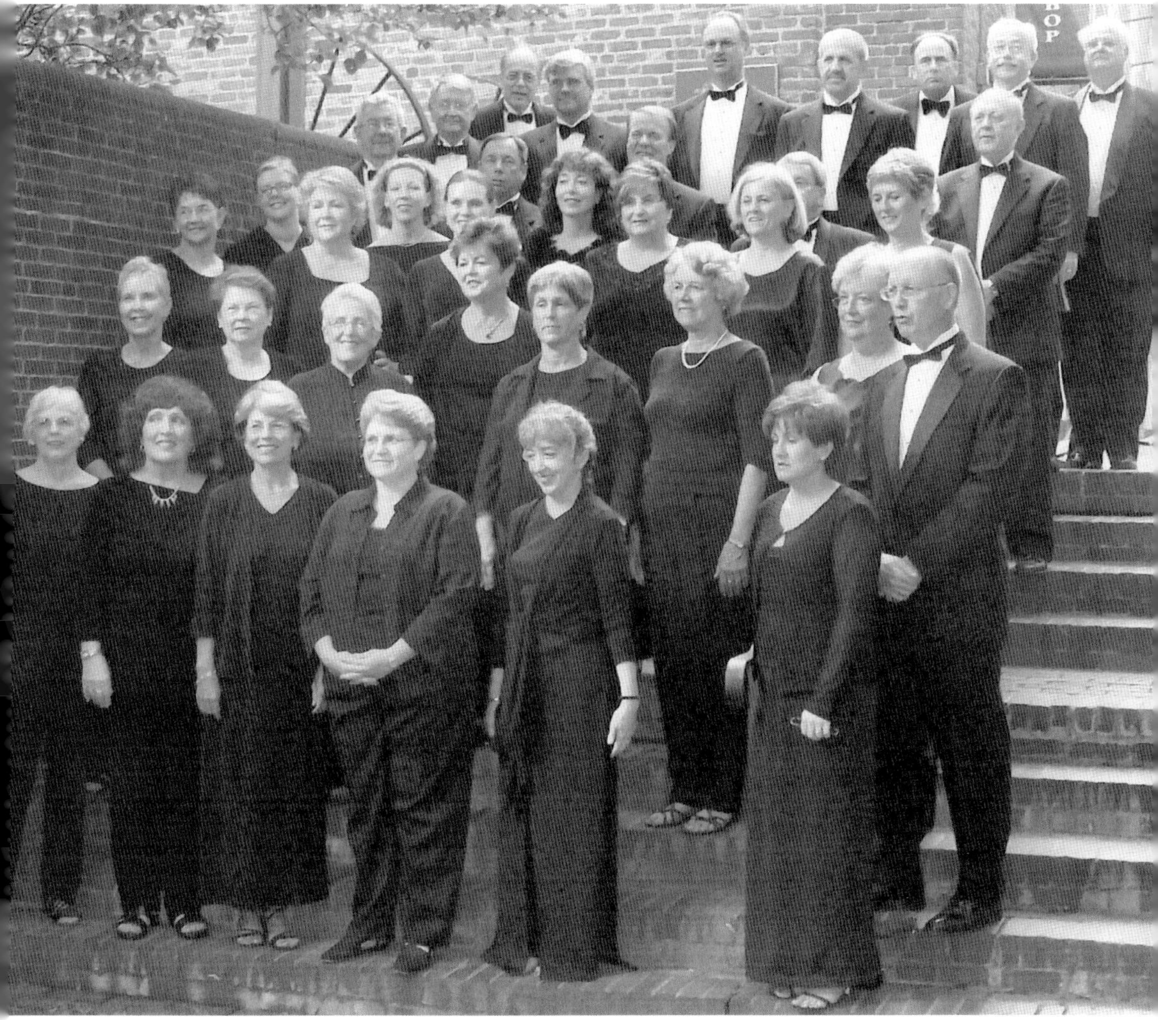

Sounds of Gold Community Chorus

Jesse Shearin, a music lover and choir director, formed a group of talented singers in 1995 known as the Sounds of Gold. Based in Rocky Mount, the group includes 35 individuals from all over the Twin Counties. They perform a cappella sacred and secular music at community venues. They have performed in Williamsburg, Virginia, and in New York City, as well as at Canterbury Cathedral in England and Christ Church in Dublin. Shearin also directed the Tar River Coral and Orchestral Society. (Courtesy Carol Banks.)

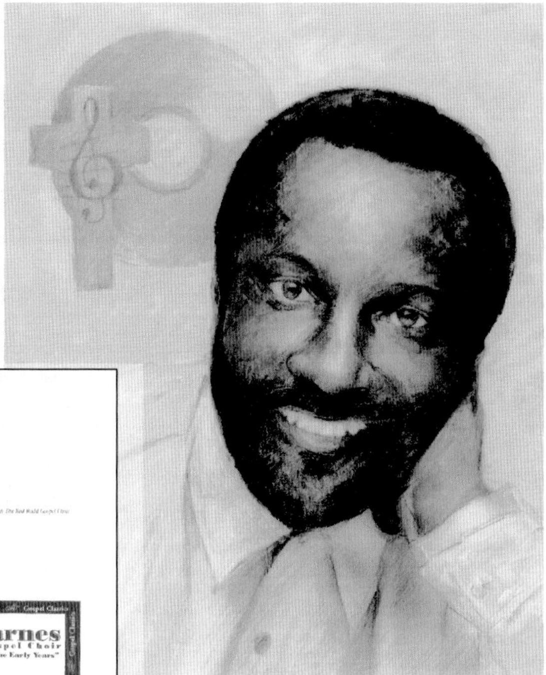

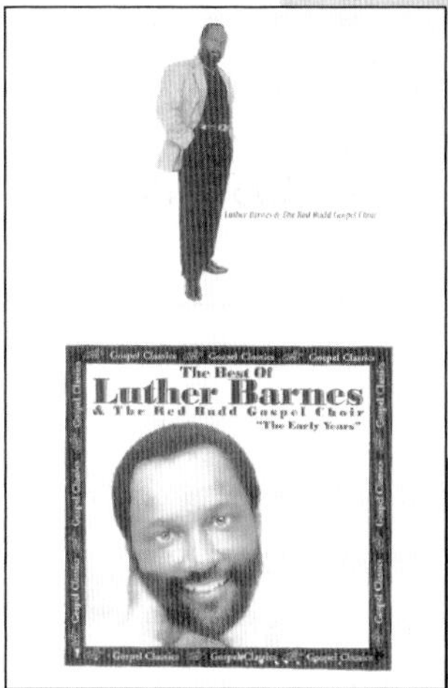

Luther Lee Barnes
Barnes (TCHOF 2006), International Gospel Hall of Fame 2005 Inductee, is a songwriter, producer, composer, arranger, performer. A Nash County native, he earned his bachelor of arts degree in music education from St. Augustine's College in 1977. He has recorded more than 19 albums of gospel music since 1989, either individually, with the Sunset Jubilaires, or with the Red Budd Gospel Choir. Barnes performs gospel music concerts across the nation. (Portrait by Susan Fecho.)

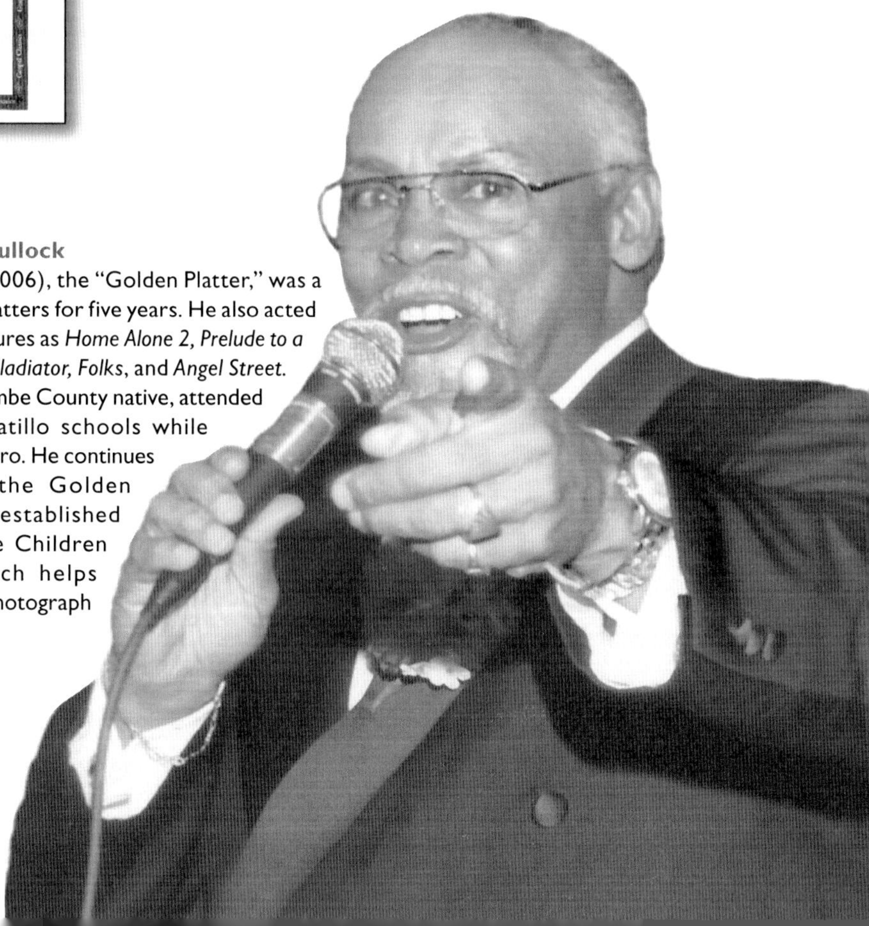

Milton Russell Bullock
Bullock (TCHOF 2006), the "Golden Platter," was a vocalist with the Platters for five years. He also acted in such motion pictures as *Home Alone 2, Prelude to a Kiss, Straight Talk, Gladiator, Folks*, and *Angel Street*. Bullock, an Edgecombe County native, attended Princeville and Patillo schools while growing up in Tarboro. He continues to perform as the Golden Platter, and has established the Do it for the Children Foundation, which helps children in need. (Photograph courtesy TCHOF.)

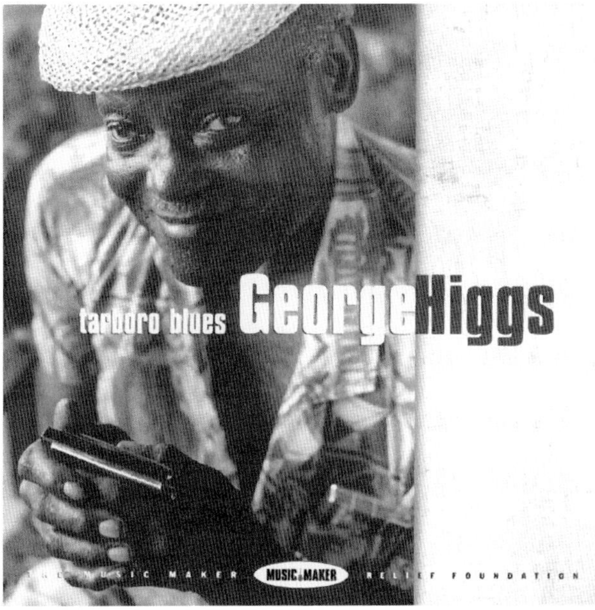

George Higgs

Trained as a carpenter, George Higgs (TCHOF 2010) is better known for his music, playing harmonica and guitar in a style recognized as Piedmont blues. Born near Speed in 1930, Higgs learned to play the harmonica from his father, who taught him gospel and folk tunes. Higgs has been honored with the North Carolina Folklore Brown Hudson Award and the North Carolina Folk Heritage Award. In his 80 years, he has performed all over, touring throughout the United States, Switzerland, and Australia. (Courtesy George Higgs.)

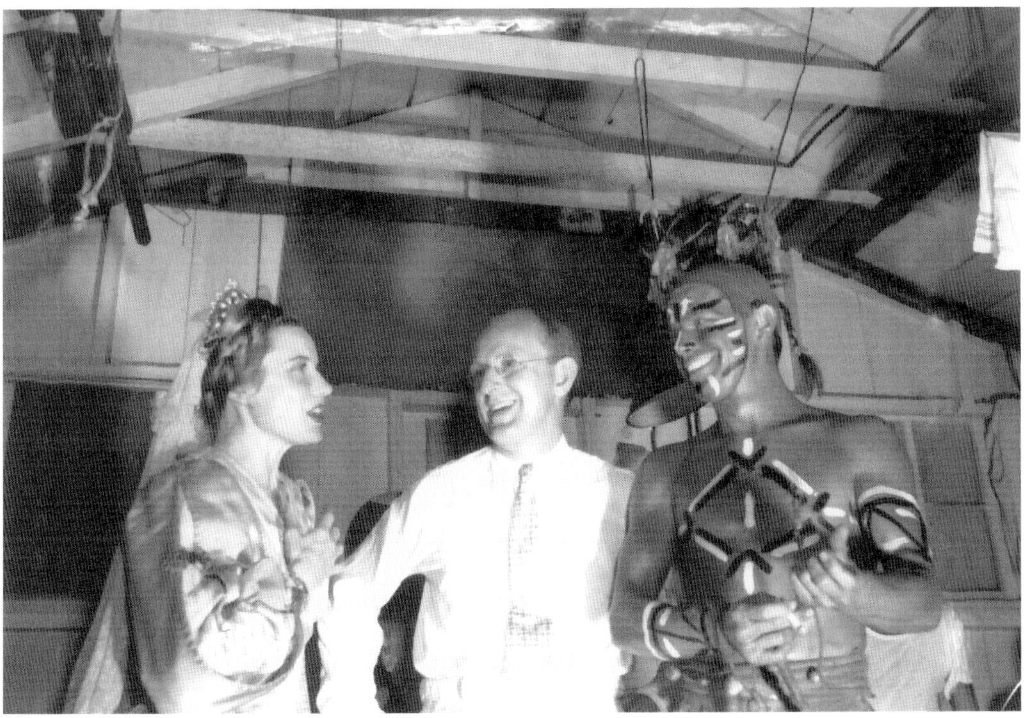

James Kern "Kay" Kyser

Big-band leader Kay Kyser (TCHOF 2004) was born in Rocky Mount and created the Kollege of Musical Knowledge on NBC radio and television, which ran from 1938 to 1950. He starred in movies of the 1930s and 1940s, alongside Lucille Ball. During World War II, Kyser (center) performed over 600 shows for the troops. He retired at the height of his popularity and devoted his life to public service and working to bring public television (UNC-TV) to North Carolina. (Courtesy NCDAH.)

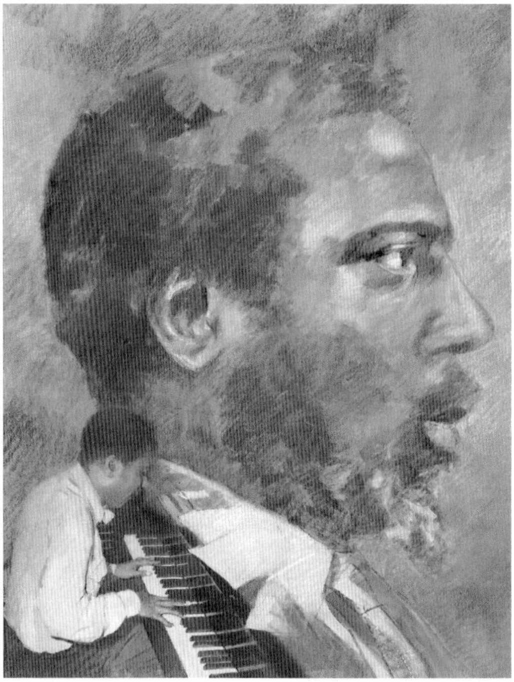

Thelonius Monk
Born in 1917 in Rocky Mount, Monk (TCHOF 2008) relocated with his family to New York when he was a child. Considered an imaginative solo pianist, he made immense contributions to the development of jazz. He wrote over 70 compositions, among them "Round Midnight" and "Blue Monk." He is one of the world's greatest jazz musicians, and his work is the most recorded of any jazz composer. (Portrait by Susan Fecho.)

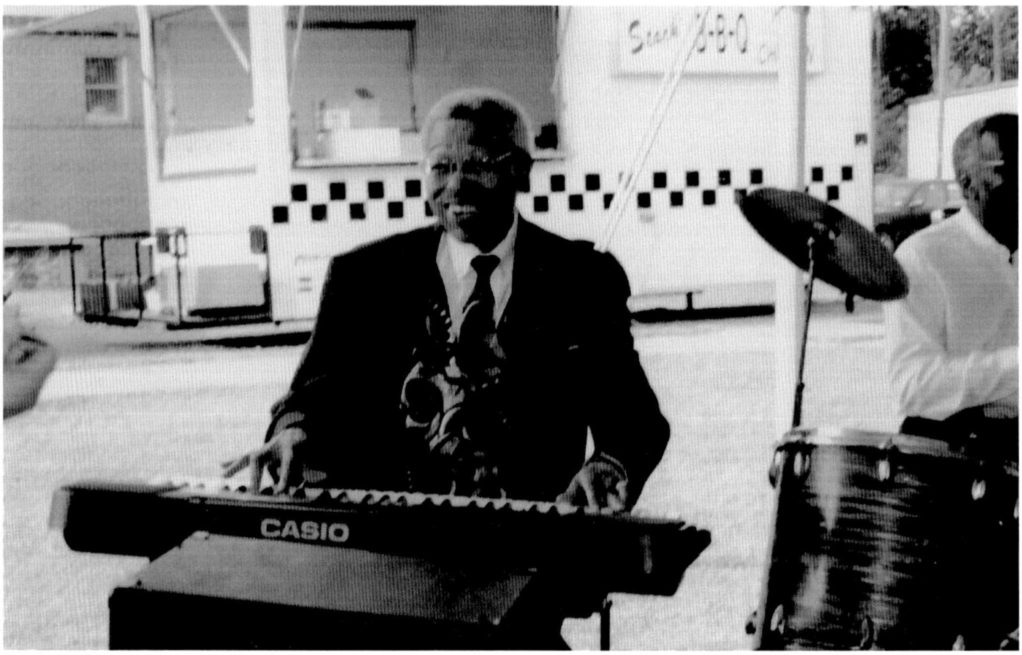

Walter Plemmer Jr.
Born in 1921, Plemmer (TCHOF 2011) taught music and English at county schools for 36 years and was selected "Teacher of the Year" in 1971 for the county and the district. He was band director, choral director, music director, drama director, and director of cultural arts. This Edgecombe County "Father of Music" played guitar, banjo, clarinet, saxophone, trumpet, piano, and organ. He taught piano for over five decades and developed several choral groups. (Photograph by the author.)

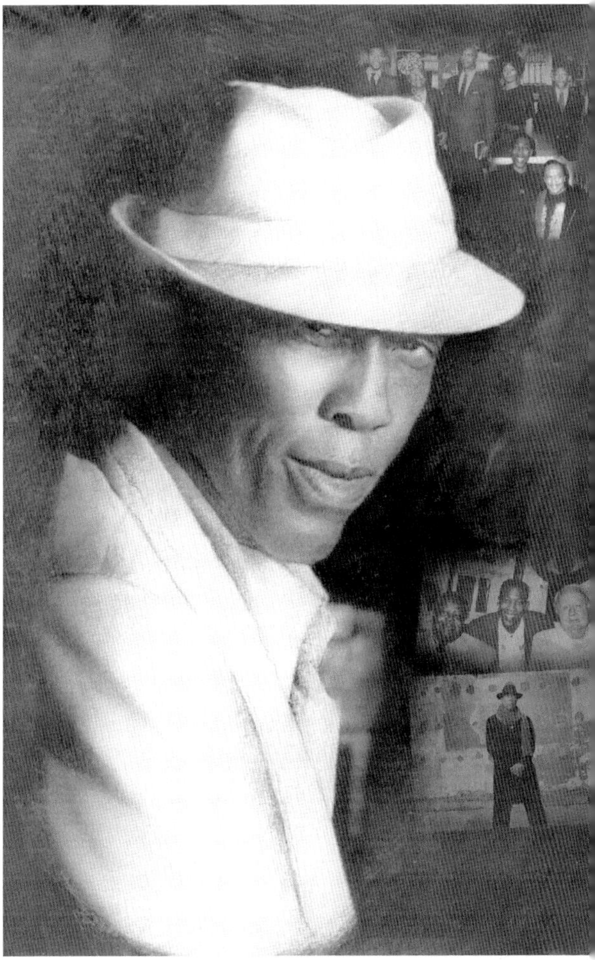

Warren Slim "Pony" Williams
Pony Williams (TCHOF 2011) spent his formative years in Rocky Mount. After graduating from high school, he pursued his love of music, winning the televised talent contest *Star Search* in 1986. He soon found work with The Spinners, The Drifters, and The Temptations. During his solo career, he performed with the Neville Brothers, Joe Cocker, Oscar Peterson, and Smokey Robinson. In 1996, Williams was the musical director for the Atlanta Olympic Games. (Portrait by Susan Fecho.)

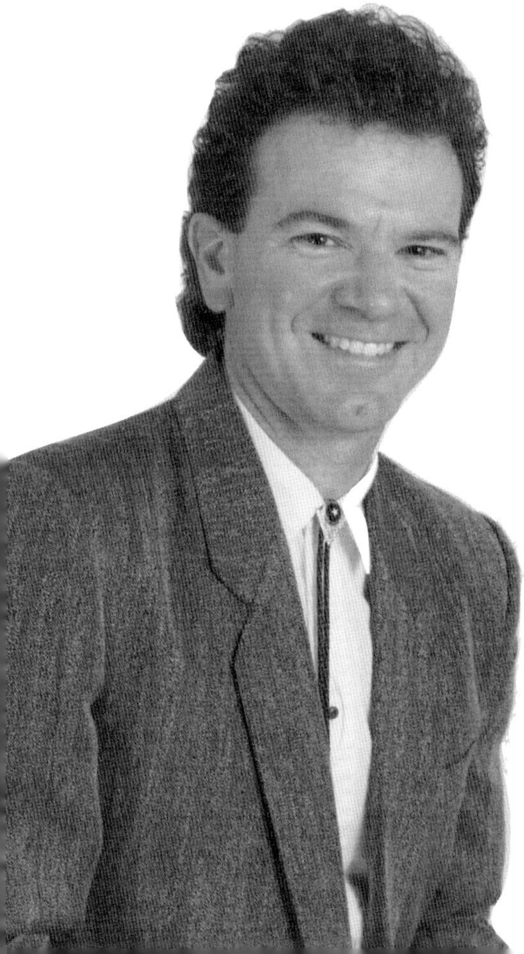

Donnie Weaver
Rocky Mount native Weaver (TCHOF 2009) and his band the O'Kaysions had a hit song in the summer of 1968 with "Girl Watcher," composed by Donnie and guitarist Wayne Pittman. Other Weaver songs include "Too Many Broken Hearts" and "Starvin' for Love." (Courtesy Donnie Weaver.)

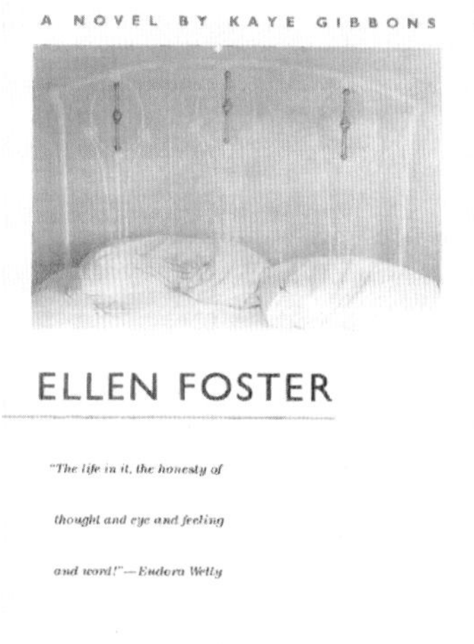

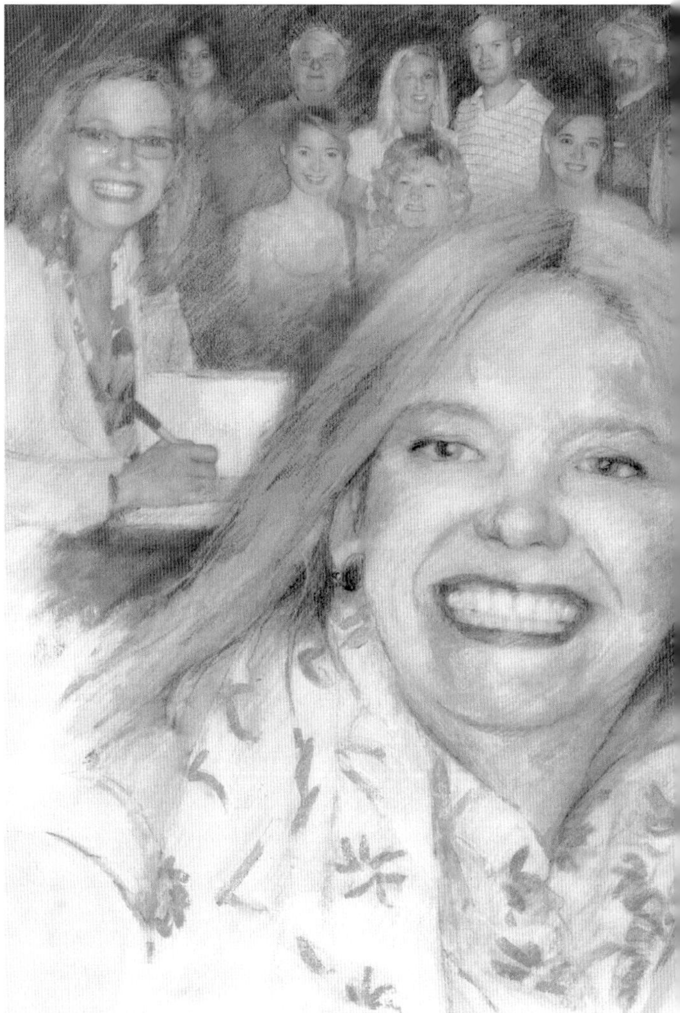

Kaye Gibbons

Born Bertha Kaye Batts in Nash County, Kaye (TCHOF 2009) survived a difficult childhood, losing both parents before she was in her teens. She lived with various relatives and foster families before going to college. Kaye married Michael Gibbons in 1984, and the couple had three children before they divorced. At UNC she was encouraged by English professor Louis Rubin to write fiction. Her first novel, *Ellen Foster*, was published in 1987. The work, which is somewhat autobiographical, was told in such a style that it won numerous awards and was eventually made into a *Hallmark Hall of Fame* television movie in 1997. In the decade between the novel and the film, Kaye continued to write. *A Virtuous Woman* appeared in 1989, *A Cure for Dreams* in 1991, and *Charms of an Easy Life* in 1993. The latter was also was made into a TV movie, this time produced by Showtime. In her fifth novel, *Sights Unseen*, Gibbons revealed her own tragic childhood and her experience with mental illness. She changed genres for her sixth work, a historical novel set in the antebellum South. Called *On the Occasion of My Last Afternoon*, it was published in 1998. By that time, Kaye Gibbons was almost a household name, having appeared on *The Oprah Winfrey Show* and had her first two novels selected for Oprah's book club. Gibbons has received the Sue Kaufman Prize for First Fiction, the Sir Walter Raleigh Award for Fiction, the PEN Revson Award, and the North Carolina Award for Literature. NC State awarded her an honorary degree of doctor of humane letters. (Portrait by Susan Fecho.)

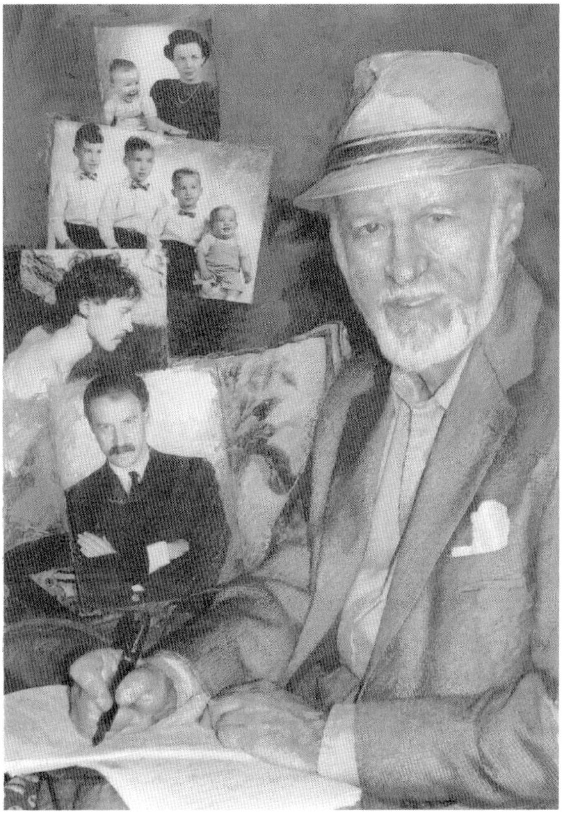

Allan Gurganus
Rocky Mount native Allan Gurganus (TCHOF 2010) studied at the Pennsylvania Academy of Fine Arts as a painter before serving in the US Navy during the Vietnam War. It was during his time in the service that he began writing. Gurganus published his first novel, *The Oldest Living Confederate Widow Tells All,* in 1989, and it made the *New York Times* best-seller list and won the Sue Kaufman Prize from the American Academy of Arts and Letters. Selected by the Book of the Month Club, the novel sold more than four million copies. The story was adapted into a television special movie and a one-woman Broadway play. (Portrait by Susan Fecho.)

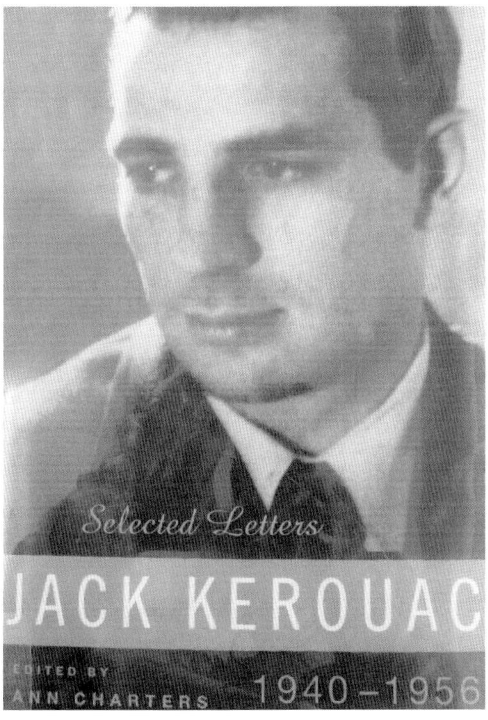

Jack Kerouac
Although he came from Massachusetts, Kerouac (TCHOF 2012) spent some of the most productive years of his life split between New York and Rocky Mount. During the 1950s, he lived with his sister and brother-in-law in the Easonburg Woods area. It is there that Kerouac composed his most famous work, *On the Road.* Kerouac is considered to be the father of the Beat Generation, a new style of writing that appeared in the 1950s. Kerouac died in 1969. (Book jacket courtesy Braswell.)

John Spencer Bassett
Born in Tarboro, Bassett was educated at the local academy. A state historic marker denotes his birthplace and acknowledges his work as a professor at Trinity College. He founded the *South Atlantic Quarterly* history journal and was one of the founders, as well as the secretary, of the American Historical Association. He wrote texts about US history and monographs about African American history. (Courtesy NCDAH.)

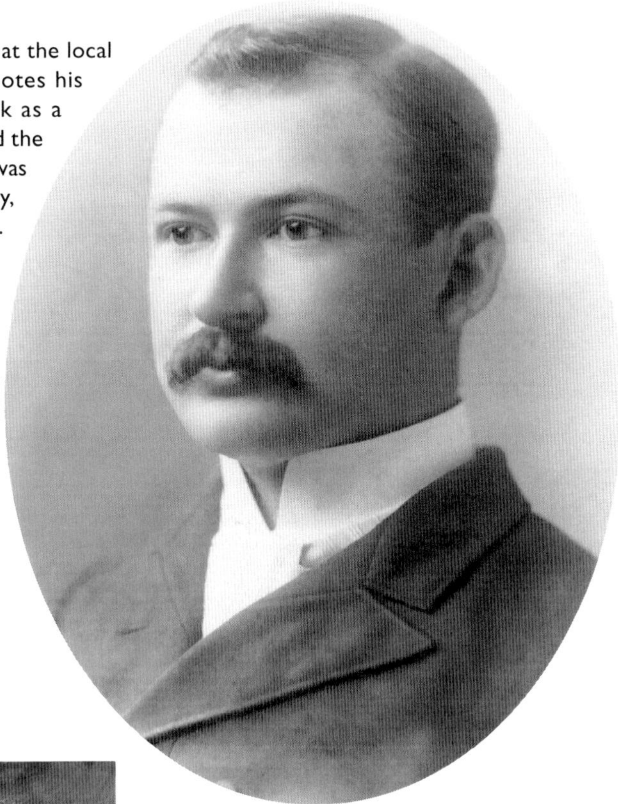

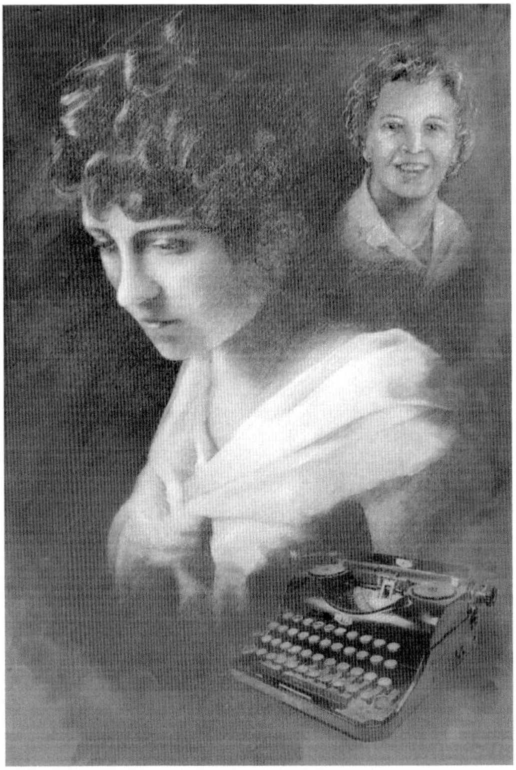

Julia Cherry Spruill
A 1916 graduate of Rocky Mount High School, where she was one of only a few suffragists, Julia (TCHOF 2011) earned an English degree from the North Carolina College for Women. She taught for two years at her alma mater before marrying and moving to UNC, where she was the only woman in the graduate history program. Her research won the William Jennings Bryan Prize for Excellence. Her work was first published as articles, but in 1938, UNC Press published *Women's Life and Work in the Southern Colonies*, one of the first historical works about Southern women. (Portrait by Susan Fecho.)

CHAPTER FOUR

Education

The first schools in the Twin Counties were private academies, existing in Tarboro and on surrounding plantations in both counties by the 1820s. Although the revised North Carolina Constitution of 1835 recommended public schools be established in each county, it was not law until after the Civil War. A few public schools did exist in the 1850s, but they were for white children only and were basically one-room schools covering grades one through eight. According to the 1860 census, there were 34 public schools in Edgecombe County, each with only one teacher serving a total of 1,020 students. There were 13 private academies serving 300 students. After the Civil War, public schools were mandatory in each county. They were also segregated, and the education often ended at the eighth grade. The American Missionary Association helped establish a school for the upper grades for African American students, which eventually became a junior college. In the last part of the 19th century, there were 75 public schools in Edgecombe County, with over 40 of them serving African American students. The number began to decrease in the early 20th century. In a report on the school system, published in 1913, each elementary teacher had 35 students. By 1913, public education was required through the 11th grade. It was during the first quarter of the 20th century that some schools were consolidated, especially after school buses and paved roads made it easier to transport students. Some of the educators included in this chapter helped establish many of these early schools. By mid-century, there were multiple school districts, with each town having at least one school and several schools serving the rural areas in a county district. Integration in the late 1960s closed some schools and consolidated others. Then, in the 1990s, city and county districts merged so that there are now just two districts: Edgecombe County Public Schools has 15 schools and Rocky Mount Nash Schools has 27. There are also two community colleges (one in each county) and one private four-year college. Each of the colleges has been serving the community for more than 45 years.

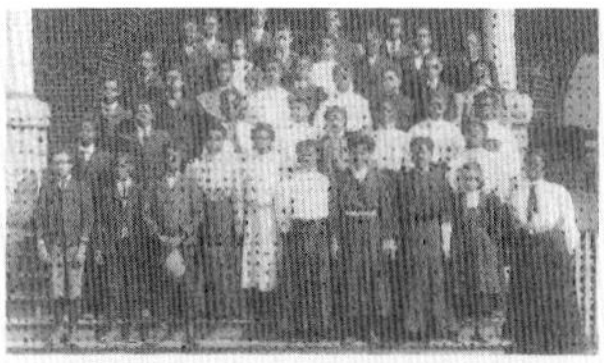

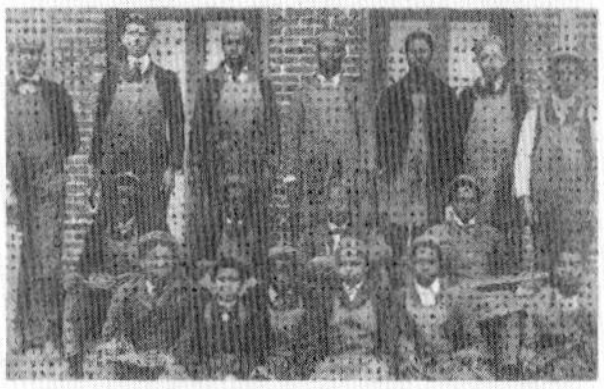

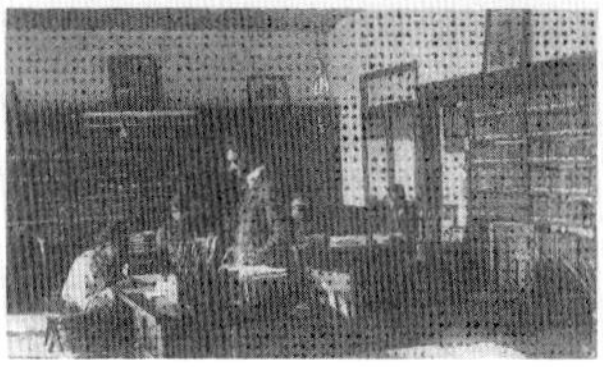

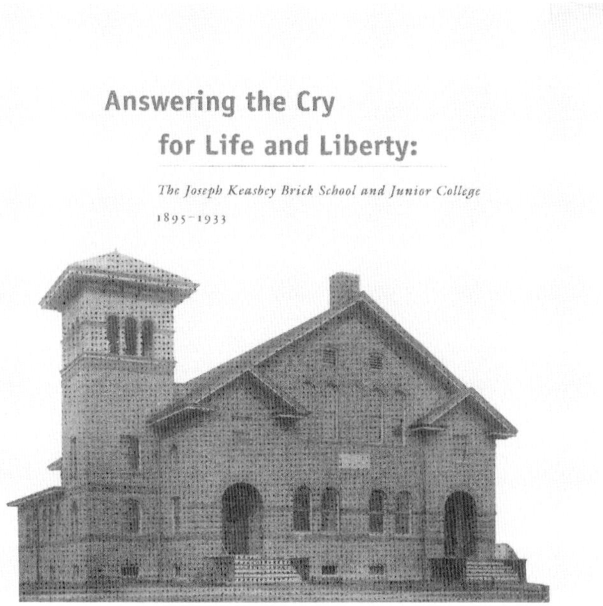

Brick School and Thomas S. Inborden

During the Jim Crow era of segregation at the end of the 19th century, the American Missionary Association worked to offer quality education to African Americans in the South. In North Carolina, public schools had been provided since 1870, but in most places that education stopped at the eighth grade. The state did authorize the development of several public and private colleges, mainly for the purpose of producing teachers, but the nearest of these colleges were hours away from this area. In 1895, Brick School opened in the northern part of Edgecombe County near Whitakers, on the former Estes plantation. Named in honor of the husband of benefactor Julia Elma Brewster Brick of New York, the school operated for over 30 years, finally closing during the Depression. The first principal was Thomas Sewell Inborden, a graduate of Fisk University. Brick provided education in the liberal arts, agriculture, domestic science, and manual arts. Students from across the state and, eventually, the nation, arrived by train (which ran on the edge of the campus). Originally a secondary school, in 1925, Brick became the first junior college in the Twin Counties, offering teaching, arts and sciences, and premedical curriculums. Today, the campus is operated by a nonprofit agency, The Franklinton Center, as a community center. (Courtesy Brickites, the Brick Alumni Association.)

Kanawha ZeBlon Chavis

K.Z. Chavis (TCHOF 2004) was nationally recognized as an innovative educator, published author, human rights activist, and North Carolina Educational Hall of Fame inductee. The principal of Bailey School and the first principal of South Nash Elementary, Dr. Chavis's innovations in education included preschool instruction and readiness programs, curriculum modification, team teaching, and the use of teacher aides. He initiated the use of standardized tests in all grades. (Courtesy Chavis family.)

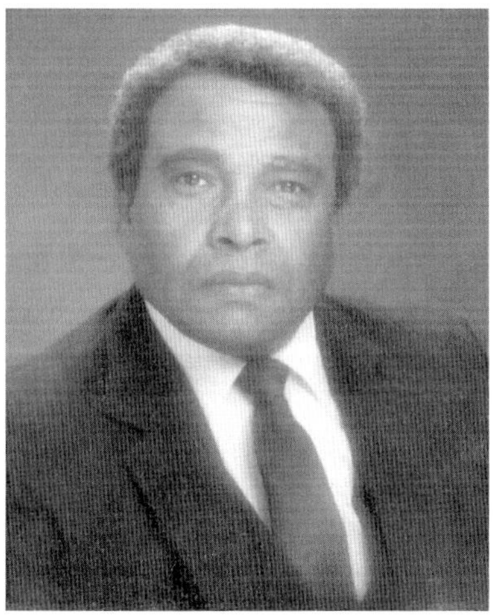

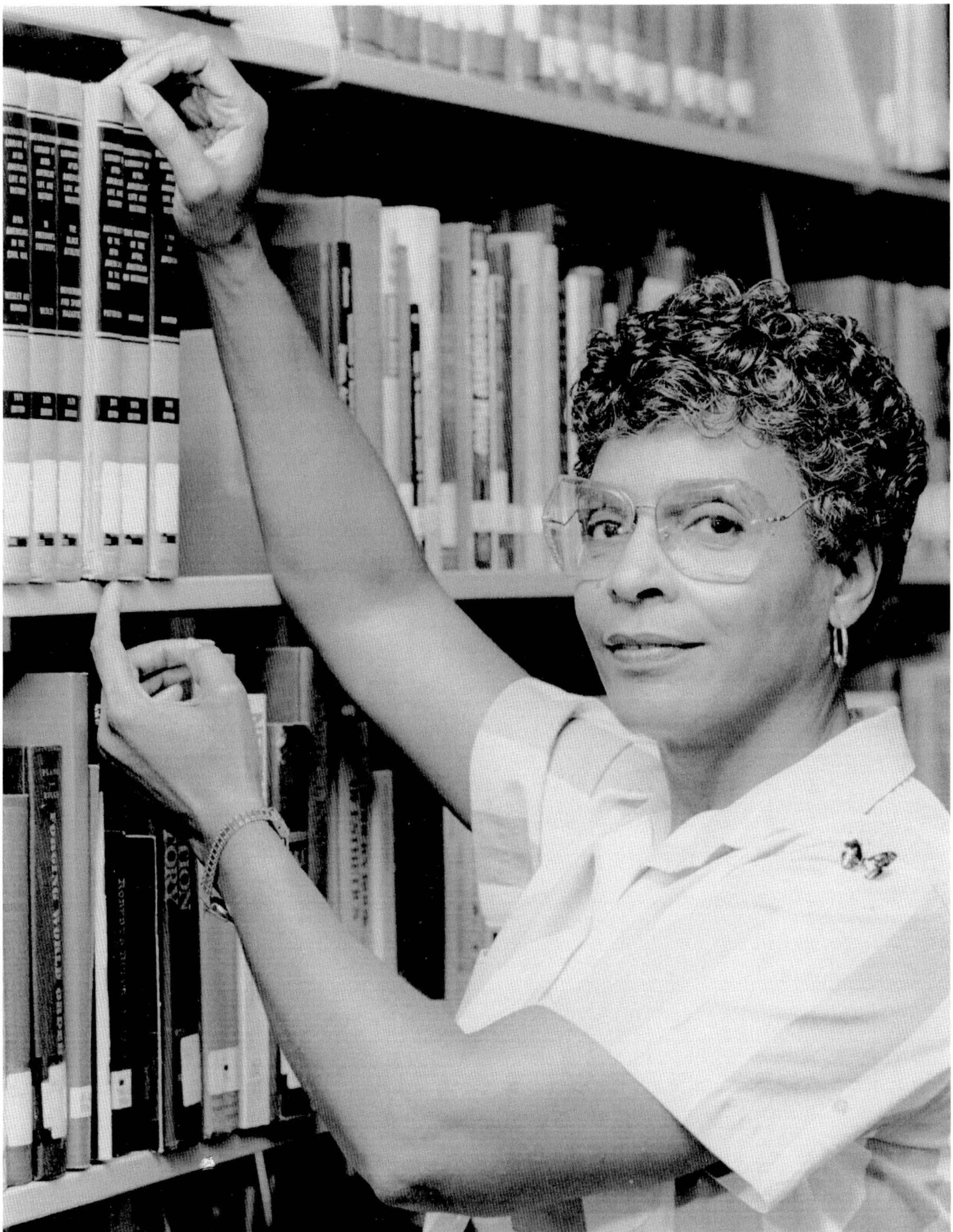

Rosa Andrew Broadie

With degrees from St. Augustine's College in Raleigh and Howard University, Broadie began teaching in 1957 at Nash County Schools. She then spent 24 years at Nash Community College, where she earned an excellence in teaching award. She served eight years on the Rocky Mount City Board of Education and was a charter member of Opportunities Industrialization Center (OIC). In 1989, the City of Rocky Mount awarded her the J.B. Harren Award for her community service. (Courtesy Rosa Broadie.)

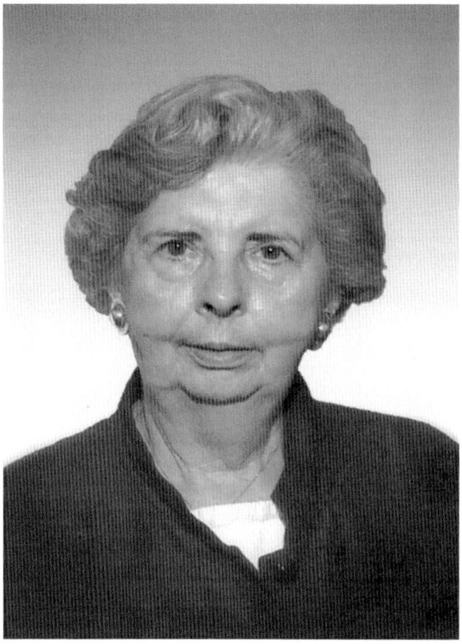

Ann Pitts Cobb

Aside from being choir director for more than 30 years at her church, Cobb also taught music, Spanish, and English as a second language in Wilson and Edgecombe Counties for 35 years and served a cultural arts director. Cobb offered private voice lessons to over 100 local students. She served on the state board of the North Carolina Music Educators Association and was twice president of the Edgecombe chapter of the North Carolina Symphony Society Board. (Courtesy of the Cobb family.)

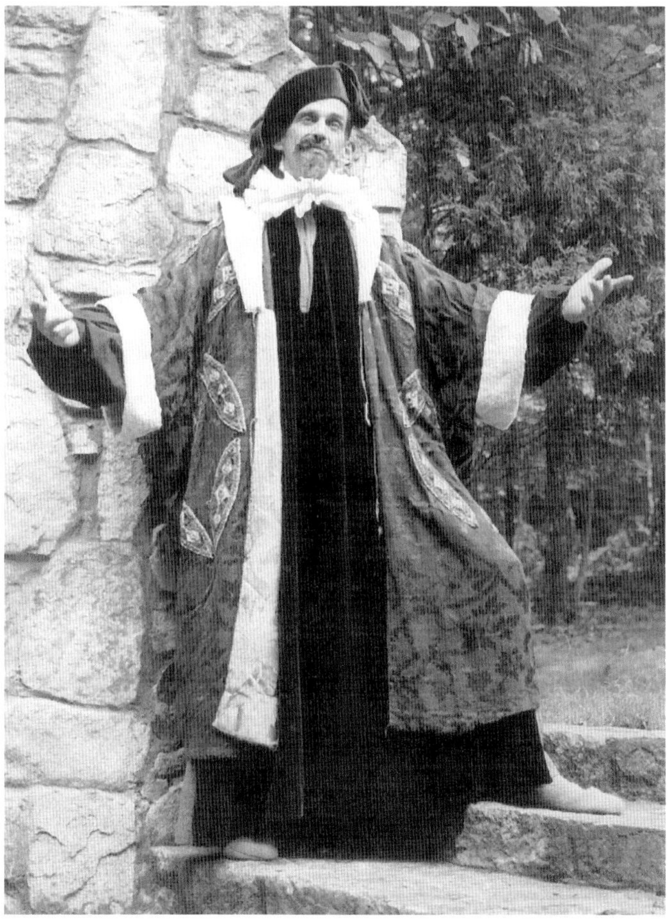

Cyrus "Cy" Melvin Edson

Cy Edson spent 43 years educating students, beginning in 1933 at West Edgecombe. After service in World War II, he returned to Rocky Mount as head of the dramatics department. Edson and his students won 10 first-place and three second-place awards in statewide dramatic competitions. He soon became principal of Rocky Mount High School and retired as associate superintendent of the city school system. (Photograph by Roberta King, courtesy Jon Wiggs.)

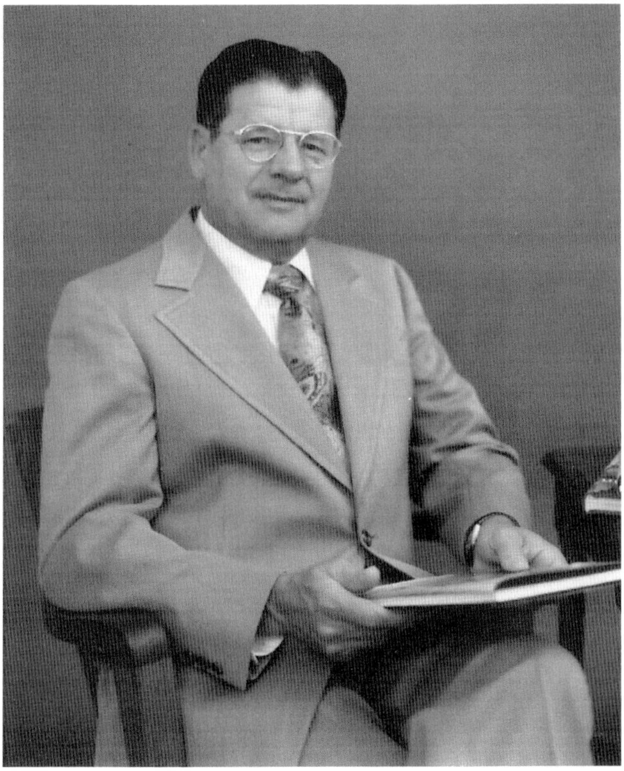

Channing Hilliard Fries Jr.
Fries (TCHOF 2012) worked as a teacher, soldier, and principal in Nash County before and after World War II. He became assistant superintendent for Nash County Schools and eventually progressed to the position of superintendent, which he held for 16 years before retiring in 1977. He led the system through both integration and the consolidation of the Nash County School System, which led to the creation of two new high schools. (Courtesy Fries family.)

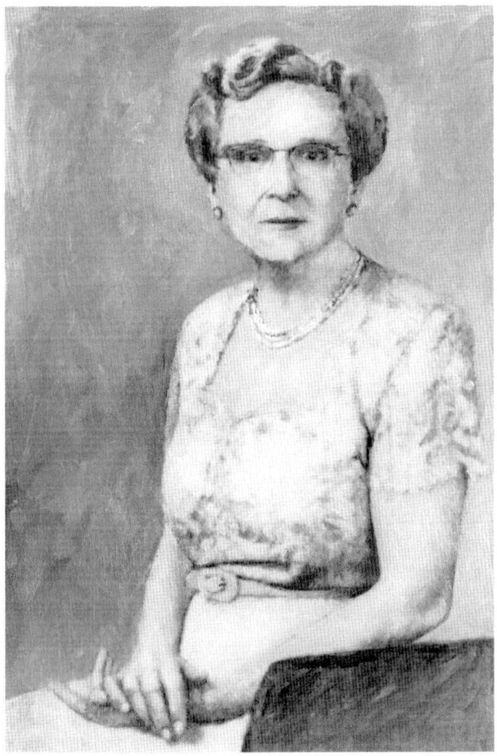

Frances "Fannie" Gorham
"Miss Fannie" Gorham (TCHOF 2005), a Rocky Mount native, graduated from college in 1904. She is recognized for her more than 50 years of unparalleled service in education as a teacher and principal in the Edgecombe County, Nash County, and Rocky Mount City schools. She was also principal of East School and Edgemont School, later renamed the Fannie W. Gorham School in her honor. (Portrait by Susan Fecho.)

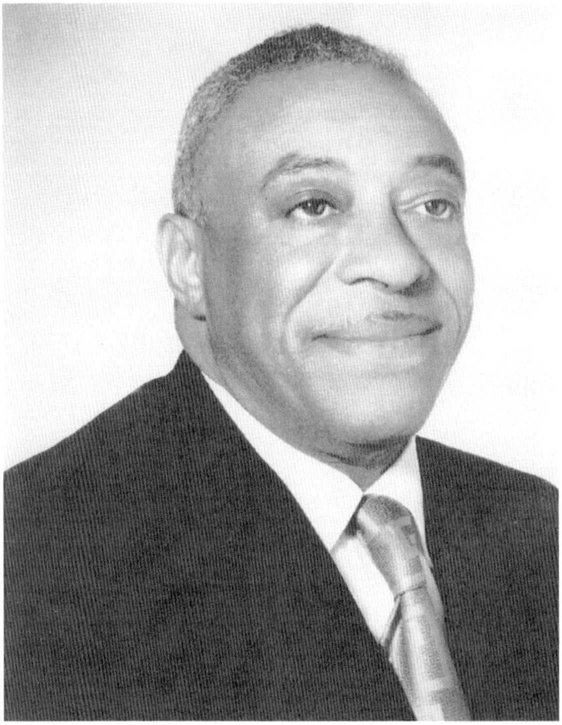

Samuel Guilliam
A graduate of Shaw University and North Carolina Central University, Guilliam (TCHOF 2009) served in education for 40 years in Edgecombe County. He established G.W. Carver High School in 1941 and was its first principal. He was also active in the Red Cross, the Edgecombe County Planning Board, and the Nash/Edgecombe Mental Health Board. (Courtesy Guilliam family.)

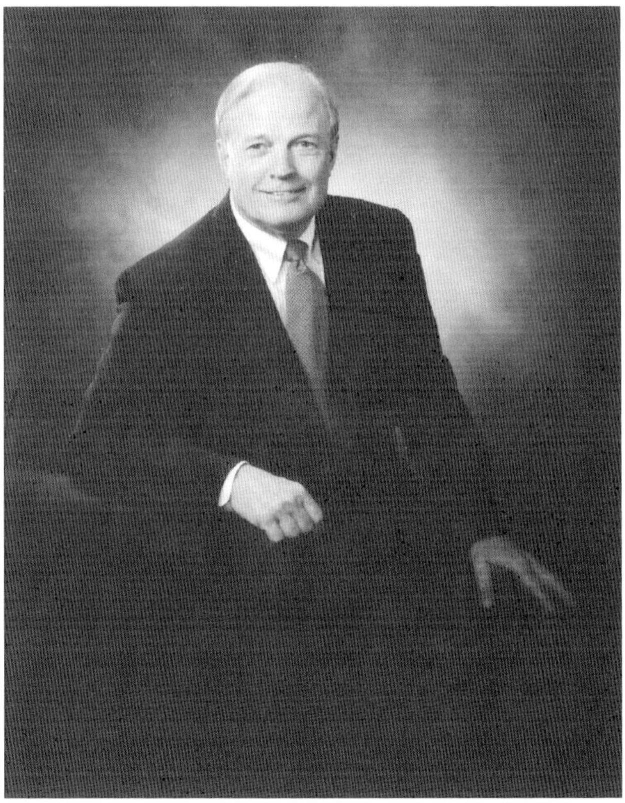

Lee Rawlings Hall
In 1968, Hall (TCHOF 2012) came to Edgecombe County as the superintendent of the Edgecombe County Schools, a position he held for 25 years. During his tenure as superintendent, he consolidated several county schools to establish the integrated high schools of North Edgecombe and SouthWest Edgecombe. The athletic complex at North Edgecombe was named the Lee R. Hall Complex in 1993, upon Hall's retirement. (Courtesy Lee Rawlings Hall.)

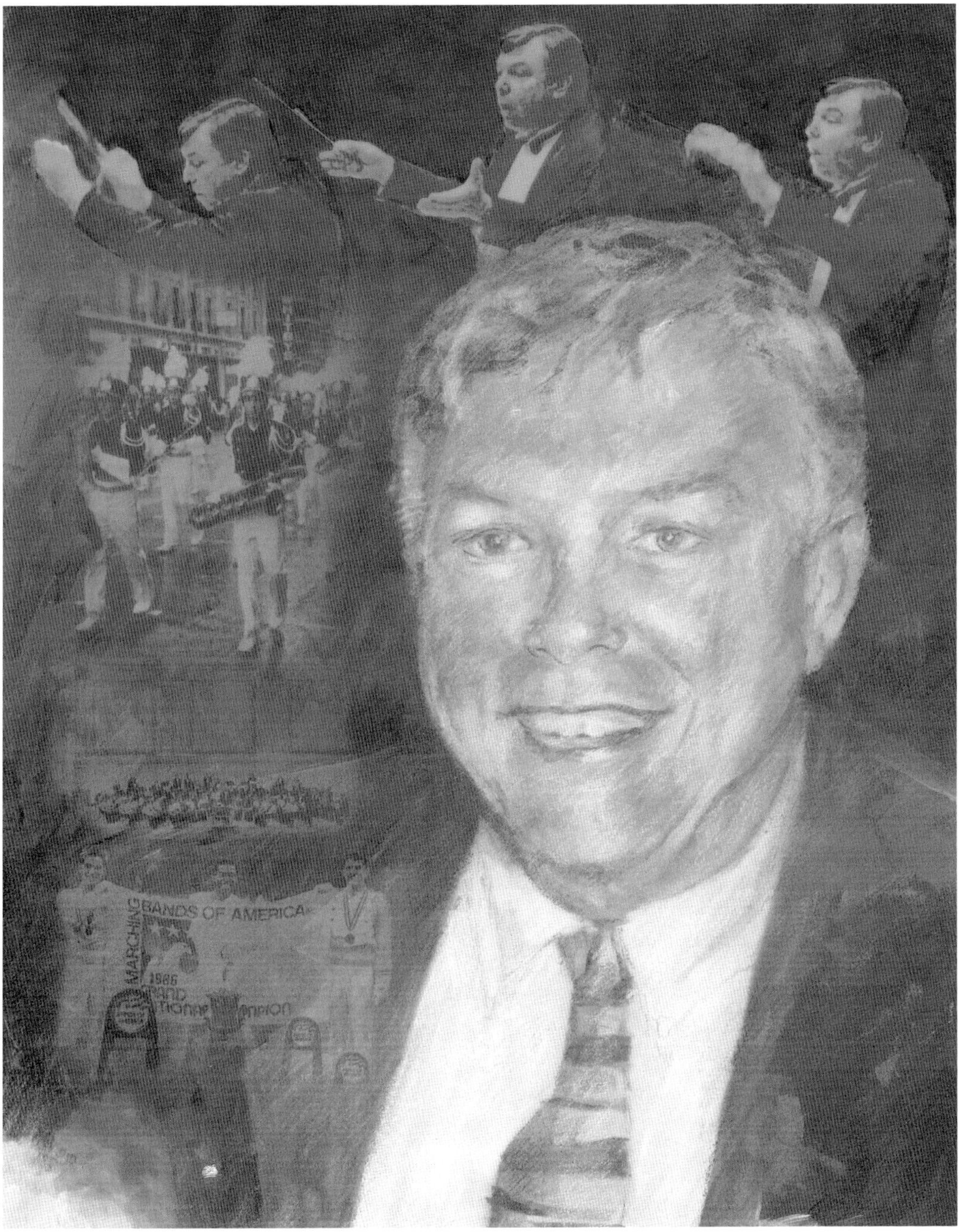

John Sykes

John Sykes (TCHOF 2009) spent 30 years directing junior high and high school bands in Rocky Mount after getting his music degree from East Carolina University. His bands competed in state and national events, earning "superior" ratings 22 times. The excellent bands performed for the president of the United States, for two Orange Bowls, and for the Tournament of Roses; they also won three Grand National Championships. Sykes also performed in and directed the Tar River Swing Band and the Tar River Orchestra. (Portrait by Susan Fecho.)

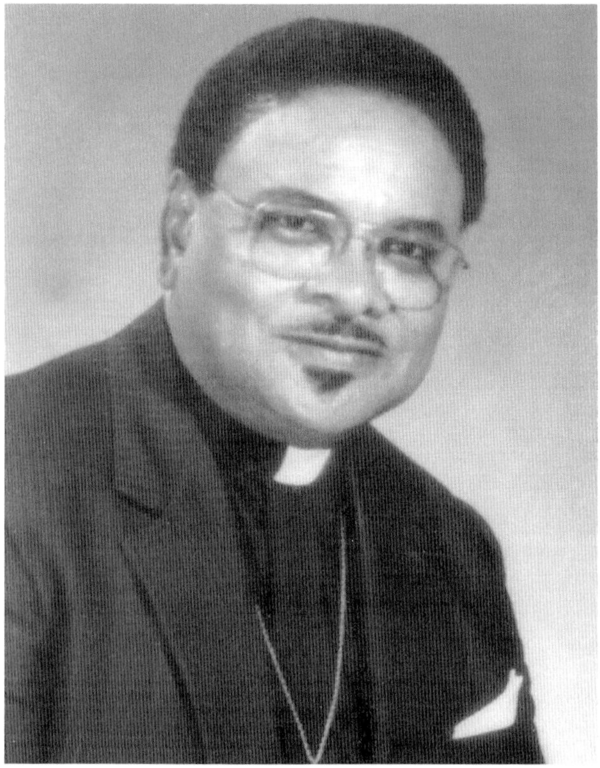

Frank Byrd Weaver
After graduating from Fayetteville State College, Edgecombe native Weaver (TCHOF 2012) returned to the area as the principal of Providence Rosenwald School. He organized and served as principal of Roberson School and then of Willow Grove. His outstanding work with elementary education led to a role as the state supervisor of elementary education for the North Carolina Department of Public Instruction. Dr. Weaver became an administrator in the community college system and wrote several guidebooks on adult education. (Courtesy Frank Byrd Weaver.)

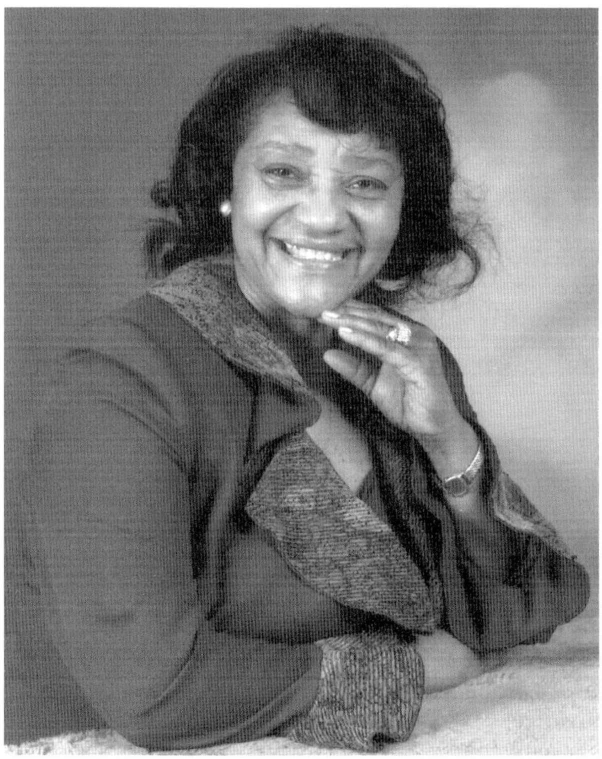

Evelyn Shaw Wilson
In 1990, Wilson became only the second African American to serve on the Edgecombe County School Board. Five years later, she became chair, a position she held until 2010 as the first African American Woman to guide the school system in the Twin Counties. She also won the distinguished service award for her work as county extension agent. (Courtesy Evelyn Wilson.)

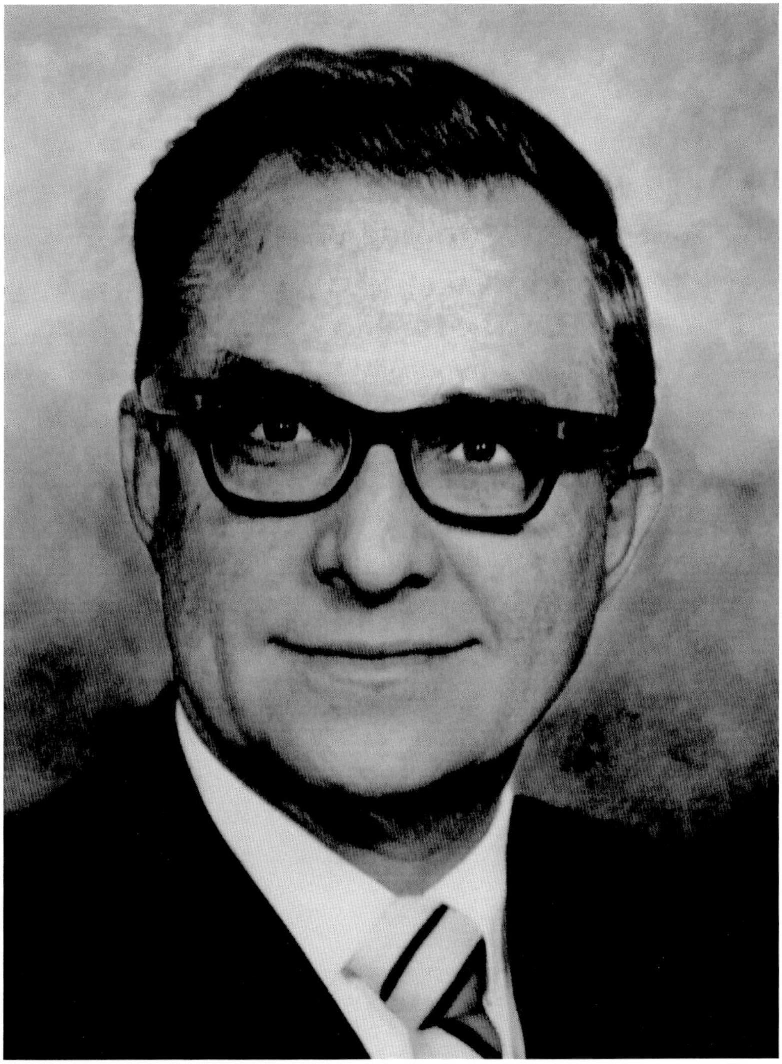

Rev. Thomas A. Collins Sr. and North Carolina Wesleyan College
NC Wesleyan opened in 1960, with Thomas Collins as its first president. The four-year, private, liberal-arts college is supported by the United Methodist Church. Actually, Rocky Mount had been on a list of locations considered for a new Presbyterian school in North Carolina, but it was not selected. Not to be defeated, local business leaders, including Billy Harrison, worked to get Rocky Mount considered by the North Carolina Conference of the United Methodist Church. Rocky Mount and Fayetteville were the two cities selected to be home to new colleges. A tract of land north of Rocky Mount was approved, and the Braswell and Pearsall families donated 125 acres and sold an additional 75 acres for a 200-acre campus. Three of the main buildings on the campus honor the family: Braswell Hall, Pearsall Classroom Building, and Elizabeth Pearsall Library. Arthur Tyler was selected as chairman to raise funds for the campus. The Rev. Thomas A. Collins came from Raleigh to lead the school, serving as president for the first 15 years of its development. Collins selected the faculty and served as spiritual leader of the college as well. After retiring from NC Wesleyan, Collins became assistant to the bishop in the area of church extension. Throughout his career, he led over 200 revivals and 80 seminars. As executive director for church extension, he assisted with the development of more than 70 churches. (Courtesy NC Wesleyan.)

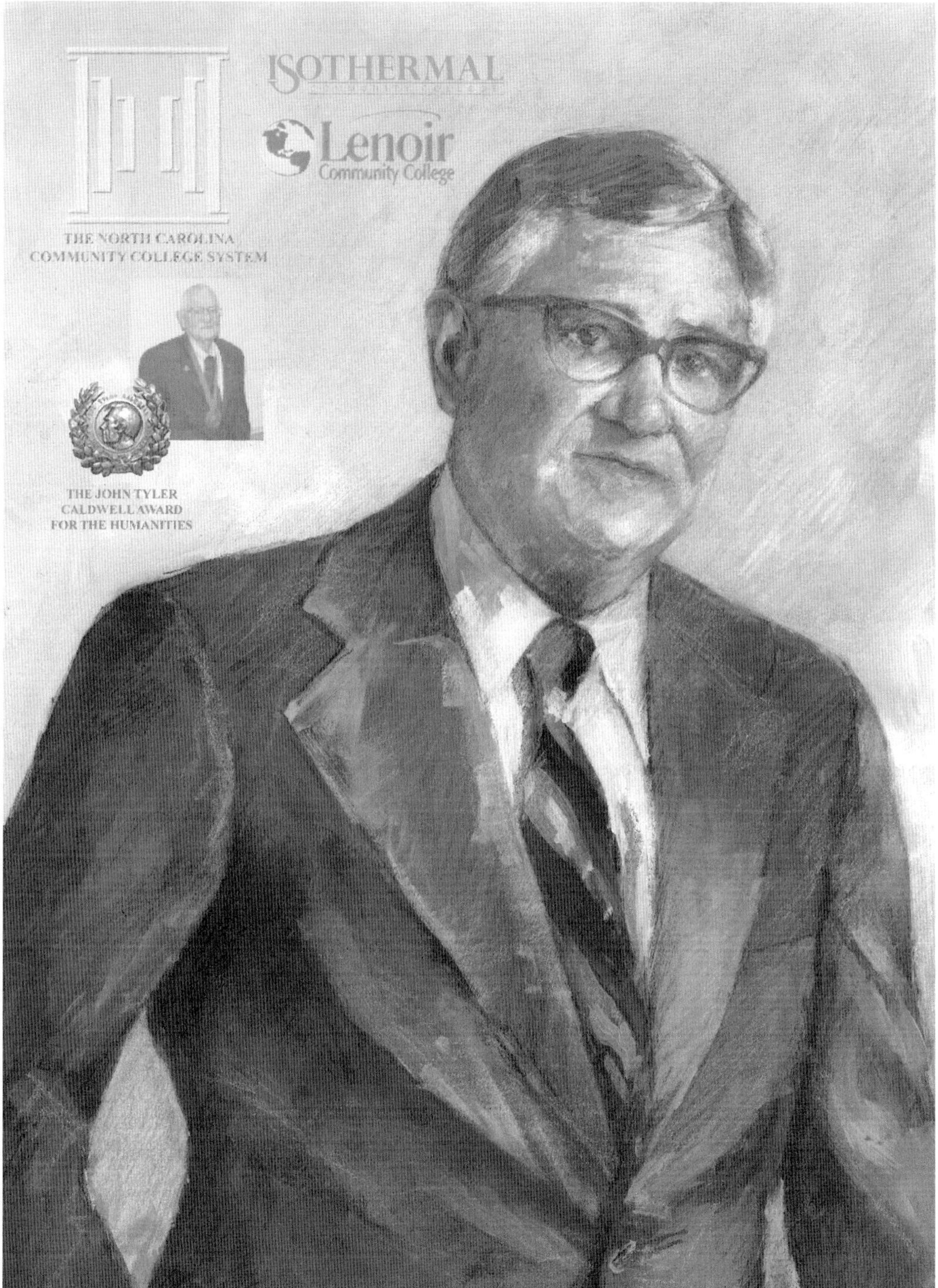
THE NORTH CAROLINA
COMMUNITY COLLEGE SYSTEM
ISOTHERMAL
Lenoir
Community College
THE JOHN TYLER
CALDWELL AWARD
FOR THE HUMANITIES

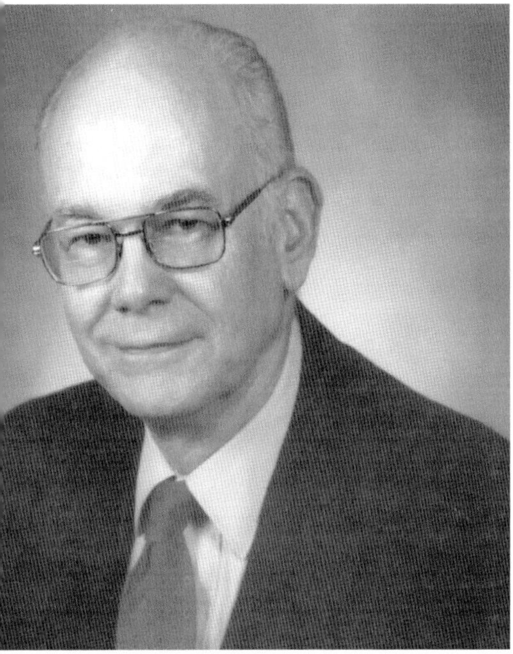

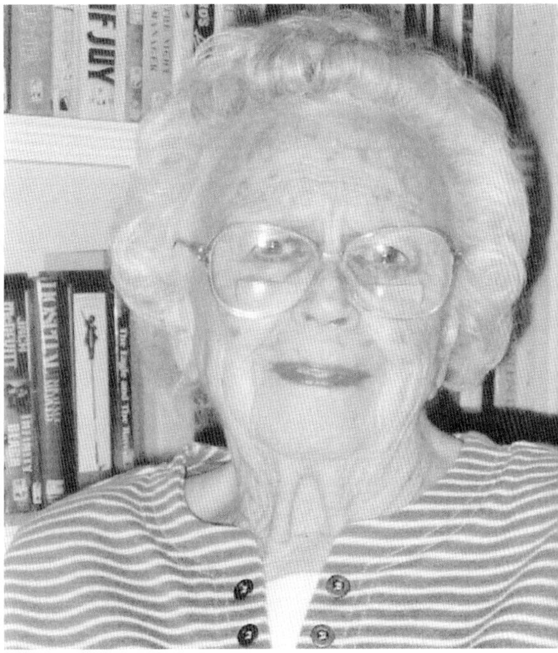

Dr. Thomas Fleming
A Tarboro dentist, Dr. Fleming was appointed to the board of trustees at Edgecombe Technical Institute in 1971. A decade later, he became the second chairman of the board, serving in that position until his death in 2007. During his time leading the board, the school grew from an institute to a community college. The arts and technology building on the Tarboro campus is named in honor of Fleming. (Courtesy ECC.)

Nina Walston Fountain
For over 40 years, Fountain (TCHOF 2006) was involved in education in Edgecombe County, influencing hundreds of students through her work as teacher, curriculum supervisor, and trustee of the Edgecombe Community College and its foundation. A dedicated community volunteer, Nina Fountain was a longtime participant in Relay for Life and served on numerous boards. (Courtesy Fountain family.)

Benjamin Eagles Fountain (OPPOSITE PAGE)
Ben Fountain (TCHOF 2007) was born on the Edgecombe side of Rocky Mount. An Eagle Scout, he credits his Scout leaders with helping him achieve his goals. He earned his bachelor of arts and master of arts degrees in education from UNC and served as a teacher and principal. After obtaining his doctorate of philosophy from UNC, he became an assistant professor at the school. He has served as president of both Lenoir Community College and Isothermal Community College. In 1971, Fountain was selected as president of the entire North Carolina community college system, the third largest in the nation. He served on the original committee to form the North Carolina Council for the Humanities. Fountain is an educational consultant and author of many educational and historical works. He is the recipient of the 2006 John Tyler Caldwell Award for the Humanities. (Portrait by Susan Fecho.)

Charles McIntyre

Charles McIntyre joined the administration of Edgecombe Community College in August of 1970; he would go on to lead the institution for 23 years. He guided its growth as it expanded from a renovated prison building with a few-dozen curriculum students to a two-campus, multimillion-dollar facility that reached thousands of community citizens in both curriculum and continuing education programs. A graduate of Wingate College, Charles McIntyre received his bachelors degree from NC State before entering the teaching field. He taught agriculture at North Edgecombe High School and pursued his masters of education degree at East Carolina University. He became the second president of the college, which was then called Edgecombe Technical Institute. McIntyre worked closely with the board of trustees, led first by Jack Havens and later by Dr. Thomas Fleming, to oversee the college's progression. One of his first duties upon joining Edgecombe was the dedication of a new vocational building, which housed classrooms and labs for the training of employees for the new Black & Decker plant, opening in 1971. He soon recognized a need to serve the residents in the western part of Edgecombe County and began working with the board of trustees to locate a site for a campus in Rocky Mount. In 1972, the old Rocky Mount Post Office became the first of several buildings acquired by the college. McIntyre dedicated the administrative building (which now bears his name) in Tarboro in 1977, the two-story Rocky Mount campus in 1987, and the library building in Tarboro in 1990. He was recognized as an outstanding college president and, in 1981, became president of the North Carolina Association of Community College Presidents. (Courtesy ECC.)

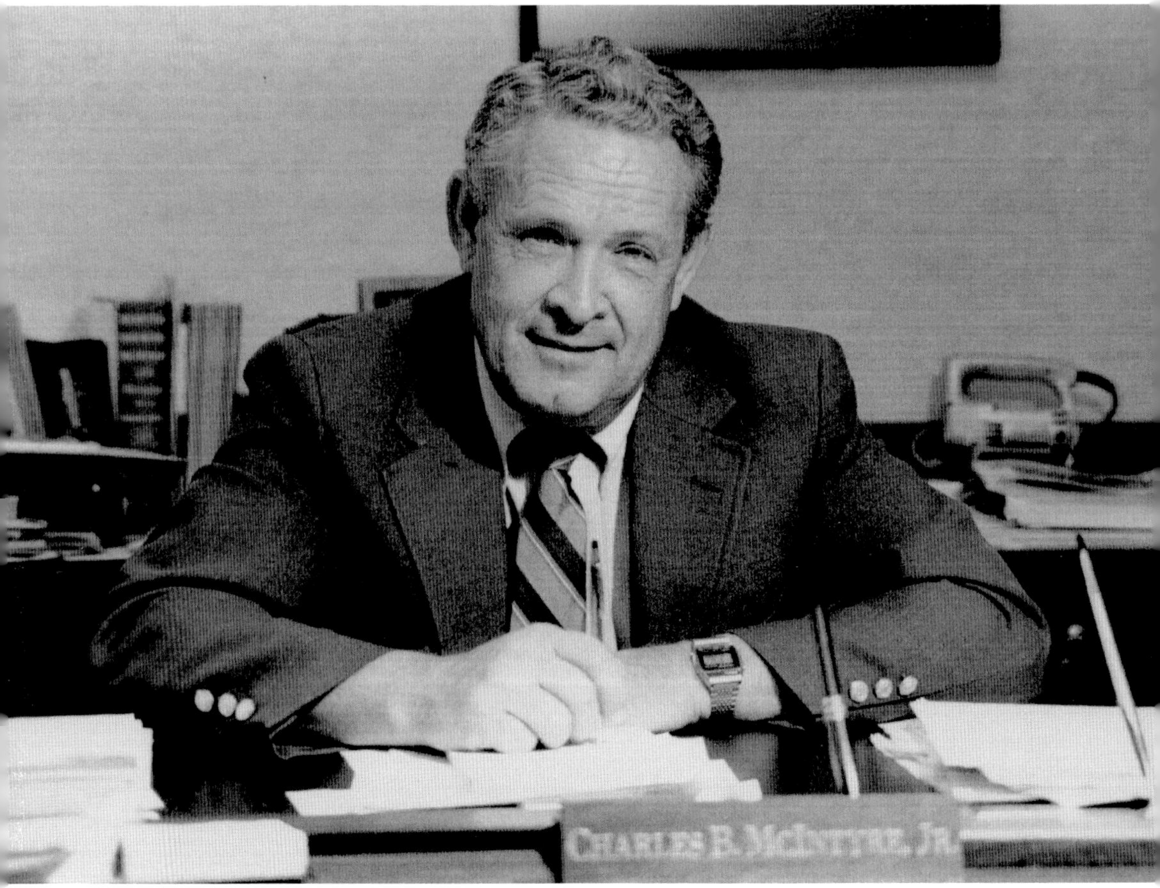

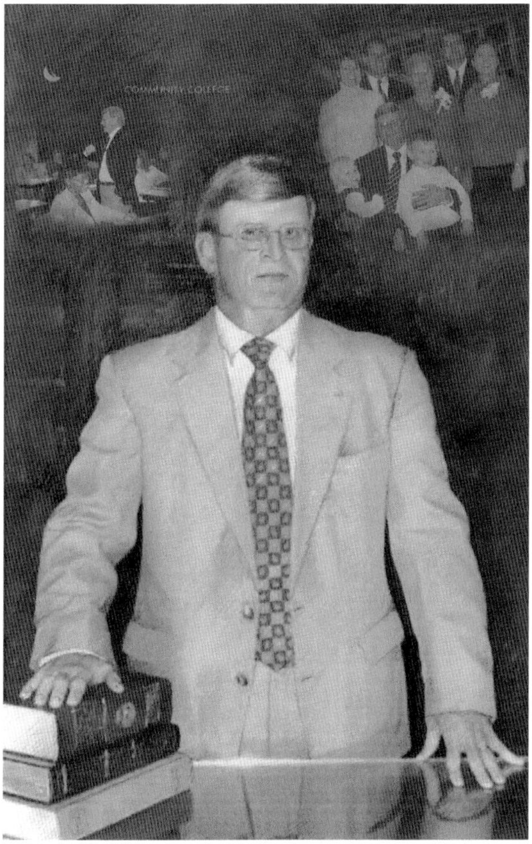

Hartwell Hight Fuller
Pinetops native Fuller (TCHOF 2011) attended South Edgecombe High School before earning a bachelor's degree from Atlantic Christian (now Barton) College in Wilson. He continued his education at East Carolina, where he received his master's degree, and then NC State, where he earned his doctorate of education. He spent his entire life devoted to education and to the improvement of the quality of life for the residents of the Twin Counties. He began teaching science courses at Rocky Mount Senior High, including biology, chemistry, and physics. In 1968, he joined the faculty of the newly organized Edgecombe Technical Institute, where he spent the next three and a half decades at this institution. He began as the director of adult education. In 1971, he was dean of instruction, a position he held until administrative reorganization in 1987, when he was named executive vice president. In 1994, the board of trustees selected him to become the third president of this college, a role he filled until his retirement in 2004. During his term as president, the college enrollment grew by almost 50 percent. Fuller expanded the school's program offerings to better meet the needs of local industry. He traveled to Japan and worked with officials there to build a plant near the campus, and he trained the first employees. He formed several partnerships to enhance the educational opportunities in the area. These included a teacher-education program; a collaborative effort to develop an early college high school; and a JobLink career center on the Tarboro campus, in a partnership with the Employment Security Commission. During his 36 years at Edgecombe Community College, Dr. Fuller was active in numerous community efforts, such as the Pinetops Lions Club, The Tarboro and Rocky Mount Chambers of Commerce, the local chapter of the American Cancer Society, and the Carolina Gateways Partnership. He was a member of the Pinetops Presbyterian Church and a 33rd degree Mason with Concord Lodge No. 58. His crowning achievement was the completion of the Fleming building in 2004, the left wing of which was, in 2008, named the Hartwell Fuller Center for Curriculum Instruction. (Portrait by Susan Fecho.)

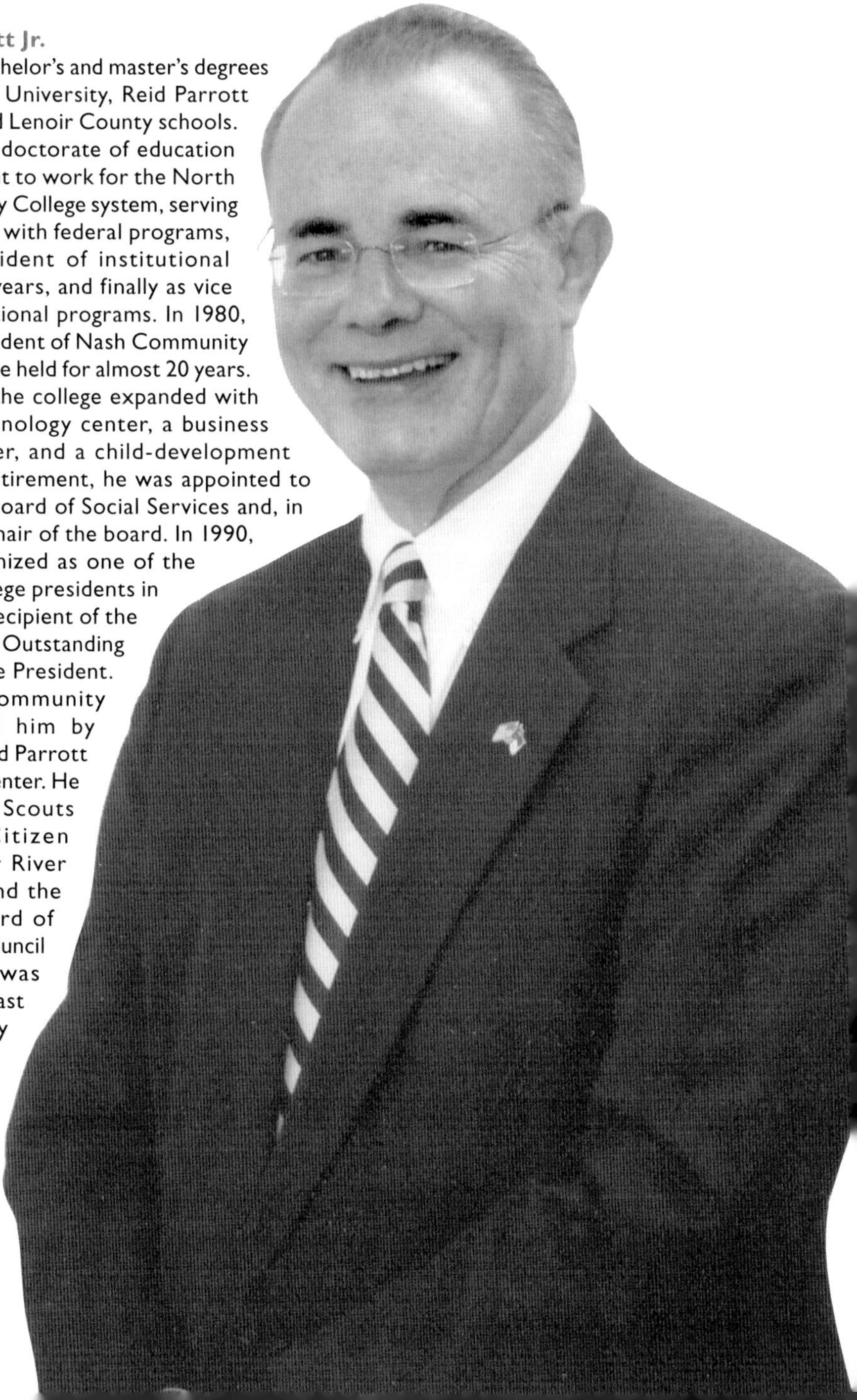

Jacob Reid Parrott Jr.

After earning his bachelor's and master's degrees from East Carolina University, Reid Parrott taught in Wayne and Lenoir County schools. After obtaining his doctorate of education at NC State, he went to work for the North Carolina Community College system, serving first as coordinator with federal programs, then as vice president of institutional services for three years, and finally as vice president of educational programs. In 1980, he became the president of Nash Community College, a position he held for almost 20 years. Under his tenure, the college expanded with a science and technology center, a business and industry center, and a child-development center. After his retirement, he was appointed to the Nash County Board of Social Services and, in 2011, became the chair of the board. In 1990, Parrott was recognized as one of the 10 outstanding college presidents in the state and was recipient of the I.E. Ready Award as Outstanding Community College President. In 2005, Nash Community College honored him by dedicating the J. Reid Parrott Jr. Administrative Center. He received the Boy Scouts Distinguished Citizen Award for the Tar River Council in 2004 and the Silver Beaver Award of the East Carolina Council in 2010. He also was honored with the East Carolina University Alumni Association Distinguished Service Award in 2010. (Courtesy of Parrott.)

CHAPTER FIVE

Government

Twin County residents have been active in politics since the American Revolution. Led by Elisha Battle, Nathanial Boddie and Duncan Lemon represented the area in the Provincial Congress in 1775 and 1776, when the Halifax Resolves was passed. The North Carolina General Assembly met in Tarboro in 1787 as the town was considered for the new state capital. Battle, William Fort, and Robert Diggs attended the State Ratification Convention in 1788 to debate the proposed US Constitution. Thomas Blount and Archibald Arrington were elected to the House of Representatives. Over the next two centuries, over a dozen men from the area have been elected to the US Congress. Others served in the state legislature, and during Reconstruction, African Americans from the Twin Counties served as both state and the federal representatives. Two men, Henry Toole Clark and Elias Carr, became state governors in the 19th century; two others, Elijah Longstreet Daughtridge and James Gardner, became lieutenant governors in the 20th century. In the 21st century, Mike Easley of Rocky Mount became the third governor from the Twin Counties. Two men, Maurice V. Barnhill and John Phillips Carlton, served on the state supreme court, and the current North Carolina Attorney General is from Rocky Mount. Locally, women were also active in politics, serving on county commissions and city councils. Several men had long service as mayors, especially during the tumultuous era of integration.

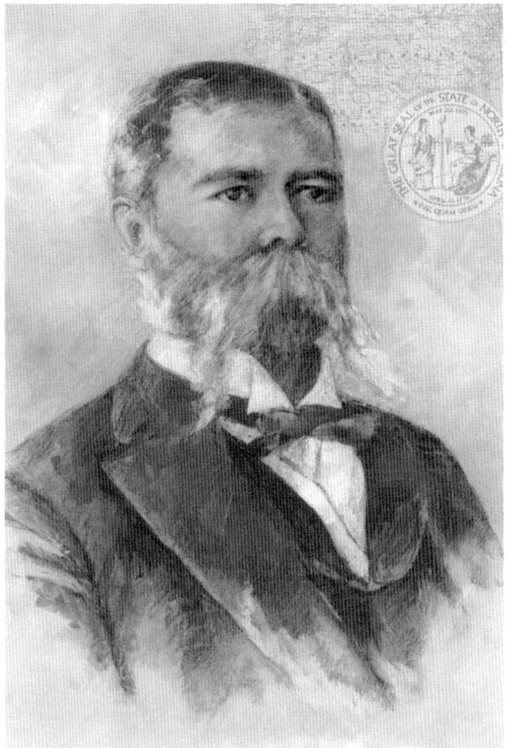

Elias Carr

Orphaned at age five, Edgecombe native Carr (TCHOF 2007) was raised by an uncle in Warren County. After the Civil War, he returned to claim his ancestral home and made it one of the finest farms in the state. He advocated diverse farming techniques and formed the Farmer's Institute of Edgecombe County to improve area farming. As delegate to the National Farmer's Congress in 1886, Carr gained political attention. In 1892, he was elected governor of North Carolina. (Portrait by Susan Fecho.)

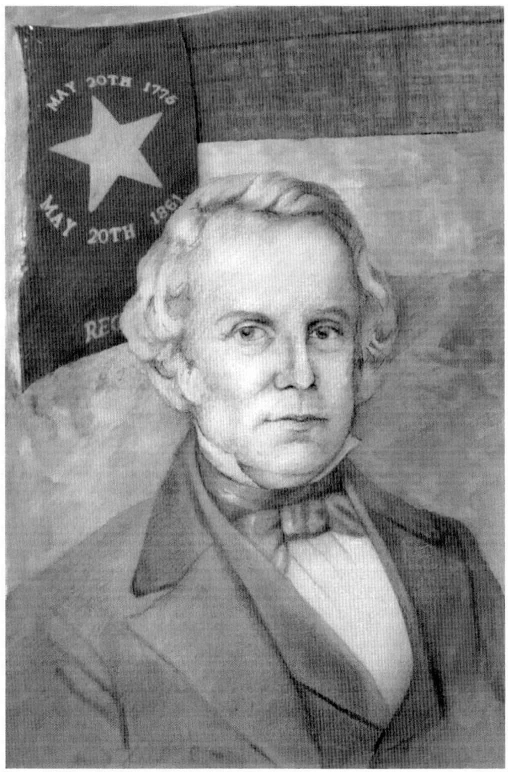

Henry Toole Clark

Son of congressman James West Clark, Henry (TCHOF 2011) graduated from UNC with an A.B. (artium baccalaureatus) degree at the age of 18. After earning a master of arts degree, Clark was admitted to the North Carolina Bar. In 1850, he was elected to the North Carolina Senate, where he served for a decade. Clark was selected to complete the term of Gov. John Ellis, who died in July 1861. He was reelected to the North Carolina Senate in 1866. His last public office was Edgecombe County Commissioner. (Portrait by Susan Fecho.)

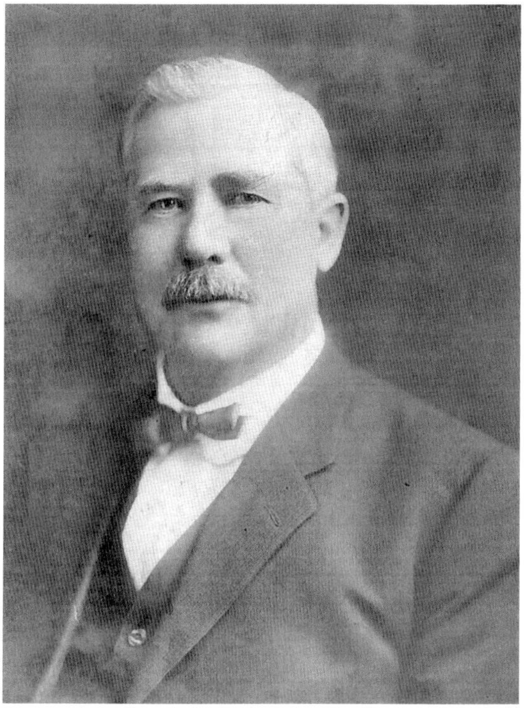

Elijah Longstreet Daughtridge
Businessman Elijah Longstreet Daughtridge's first elected office was that of Rocky Mount alderman, which he won in 1898. He served two terms in the North Carolina General Assembly and, in 1906, was appointed president of the North Carolina Fair Association. He was also active on the state board of agriculture. In 1912, he won the lieutenant governor's seat against county rival James Gaskill. (Courtesy Daughtridge family.)

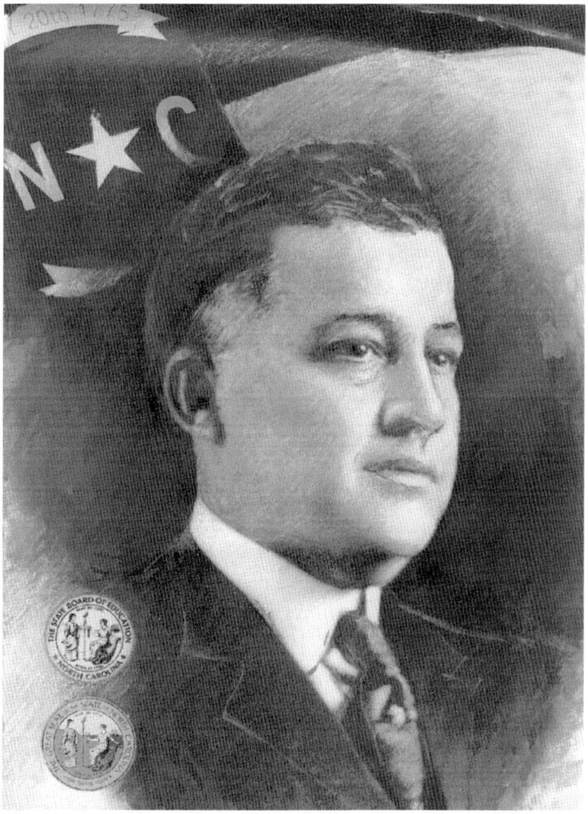

Richard T. Fountain
An Edgecombe County native, Fountain (TCHOF 2010) was born near Leggett in 1885 and received his law degree in 1907. He was appointed judge of the first municipal court established in Rocky Mount in 1911 and, in 1918, was elected to the first of five terms with the North Carolina House of Representatives, becoming speaker in 1927. Fountain served as lieutenant governor of North Carolina from 1928 until 1932. (Portrait by Susan Fecho.)

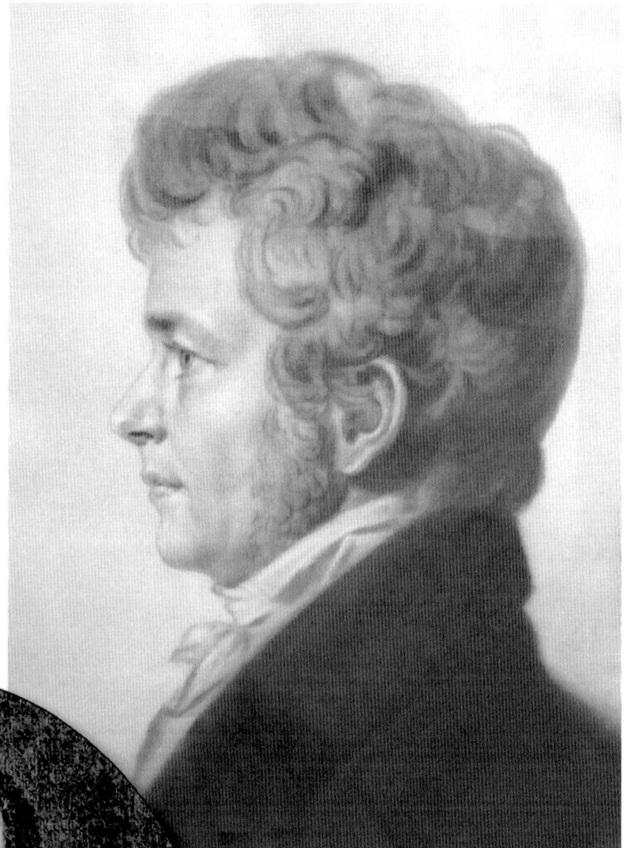

Thomas Blount
Blount, a member of a prominent North Carolina family, moved to Tarboro after serving in the American Revolution to operate a plantation and a shipping business with his brothers. He was a trustee to the University of North Carolina and helped plan the capital city of Raleigh. He served in the North Carolina General Assembly and was elected to the US House of Representatives for four different terms. (Courtesy BBH, original portrait in NC Museum History collection.)

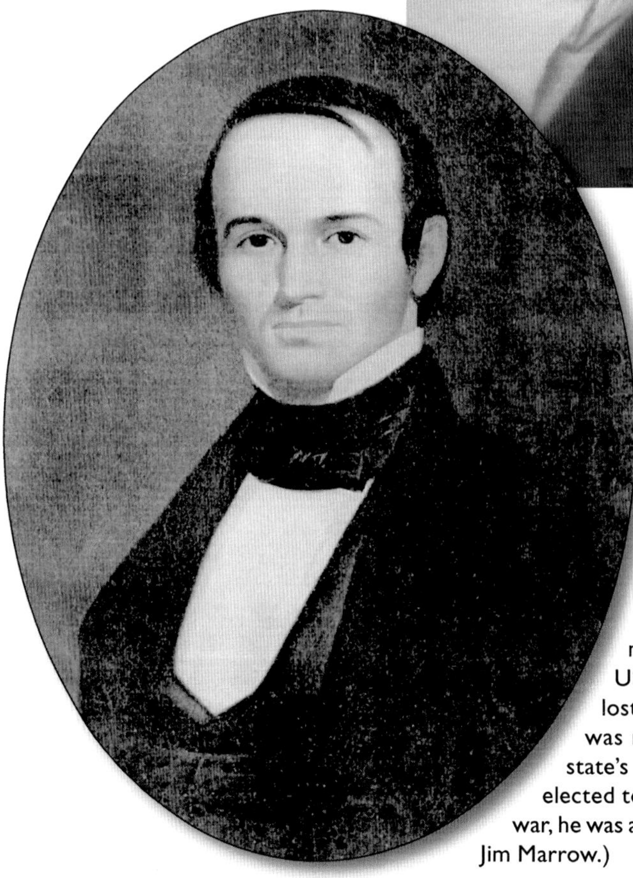

Archibald Hunter Arrington
A planter and lawyer from Nash County, Arrington managed a large plantation near Hilliardston. He was elected to the US House of Representatives twice but lost his third bid for office when the region was redistricted. He was a delegate to the state's secession convention and, in 1861, was elected to the Confederate Congress. After the war, he was a Nash County commissioner. (Courtesy Jim Marrow.)

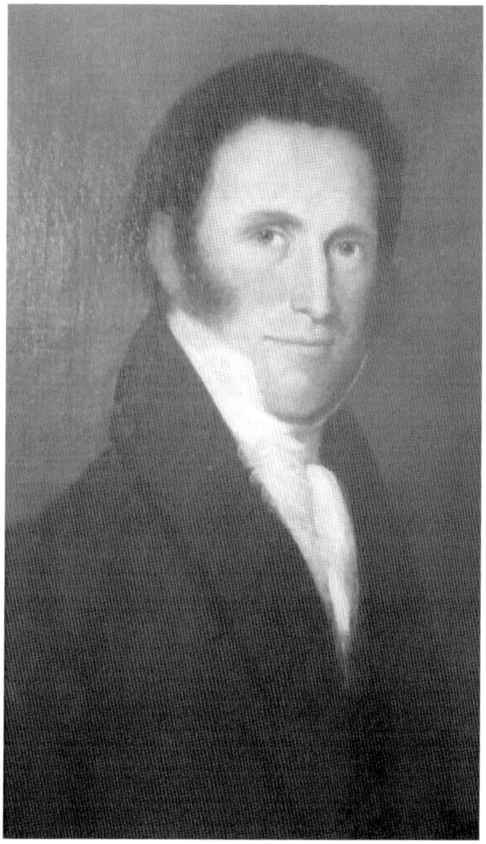

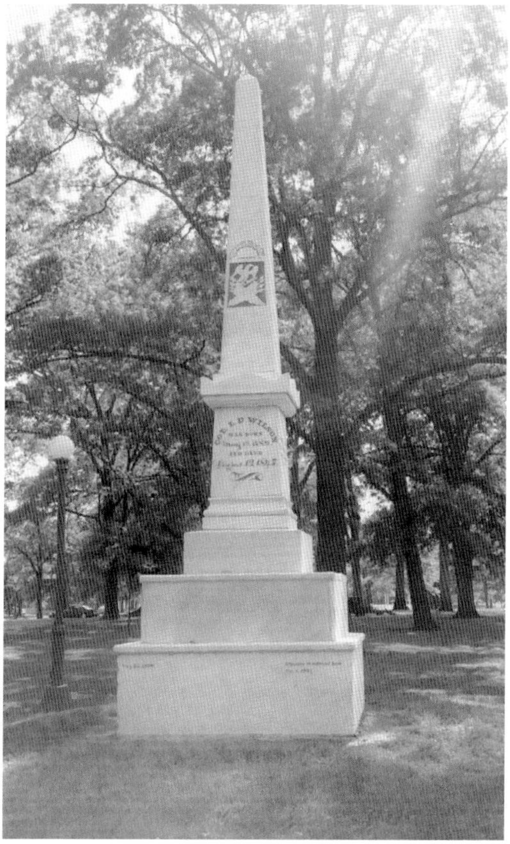

Louis Dicken Wilson

An Edgecombe native, Wilson served in the North Carolina House of Representatives and in the North Carolina Senate during various terms between 1814 and 1846. He was a delegate to the 1835 North Carolina Constitutional Convention where he advocated for public schools. He lost in his attempt to continue allowing free African Americans voting rights in the state. In 1846, at the age of 55, he resigned from the state legislature and raised two companies of men to fight Mexico for Texas. He died of yellow fever and was buried in Mexico in 1847. To honor its native son, Tarboro renamed a street for him and put up a monument on the courthouse square. His body was returned from Mexico in 1848, buried in the town cemetery, then moved to the family farm. In 1855, the state created the county of Wilson from parts of Edgecombe, Nash, and Johnston Counties. The monument was relocated to the town common in 1904, along with the body, which had been at a family graveyard. (Portrait courtesy BBH; photograph by the author.)

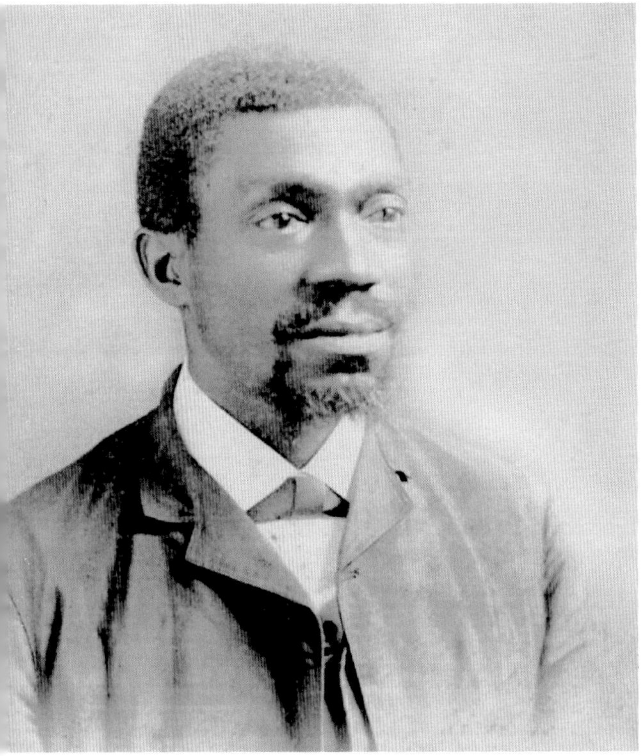

Dred Wimberly
Born a slave in 1848, Wimberly (TCHOF 2005) chose to continue working for the Battle family after the Civil War. He managed the Walnut Creek farm in Edgecombe County and later moved to Rocky Mount, where he was a carpenter. Elected to the North Carolina House of Representatives in 1879 and to the North Carolina Senate in 1887, he voted in 1889 to establish the North Carolina Agricultural and Mechanical School (now NC State). (Courtesy Wimberly family.)

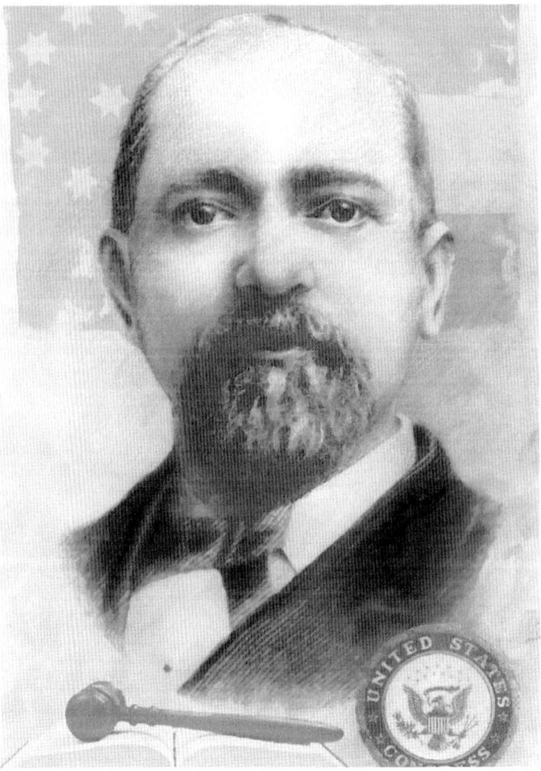

Benjamin Hickman Bunn
A member of the 47th North Carolina Regiment, Bunn (TCHOF 2011) was the only one of three brothers to survive the Civil War. He earned a law license and practiced for 40 years. He also led the incorporation of Rocky Mount and was elected its first mayor. Bunn served in the 1875 State Constitution Convention and was elected to three terms in the US House of Representatives. (Portrait by Susan Fecho.)

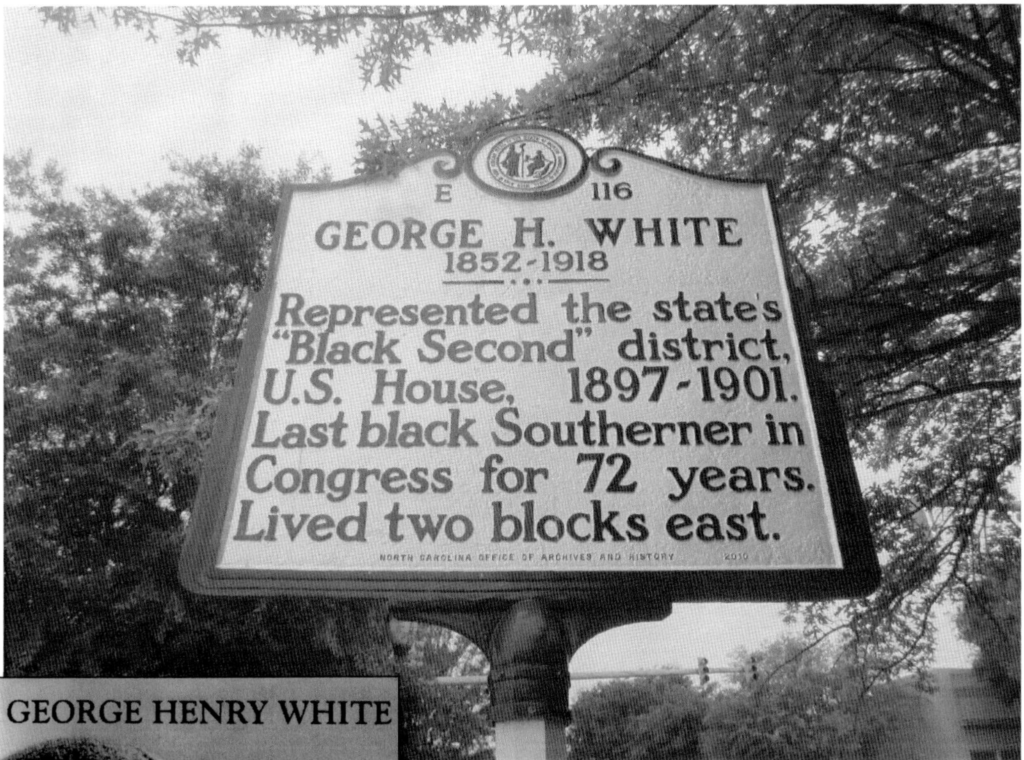

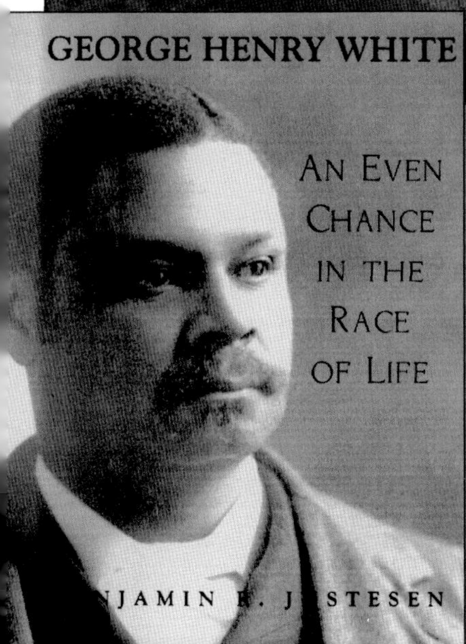

George Henry White

The son of a slave woman and a free mulatto father, White was born in Bladen County and was 13 years old when the Civil War ended. Over the next half century, he would leave legacies in New Bern, North Carolina, as a teacher, principal, and state legislator; in Tarboro as a lawyer; and, most significantly, in Washington, DC, as the last African American congressman to be elected during the 19th century. He was founder of the Ebenezer United Presbyterian Church in New Bern. While a member of the North Carolina House of Representatives, he proposed a bill mandating public education for all children in the state ages 6 to 18. He moved to Tarboro in 1887 after his marriage to Cora Lean Cherry. White was elected in 1896, and again in 1898, representing North Carolina's 2nd Congressional District. After his term in Congress, he moved north to Philadelphia, where he founded the first African American–managed bank in that city. He established an all-black community, Whitesboro, in New Jersey. In 2001, he was the subject of a biography by Benjamin Justesen, *George Henry White: An Even Chance in the Race of Life*. In 2005, the federal post office in Tarboro was renamed the George Henry White Post Office. (Portrait from Library of Congress, sign by the author.)

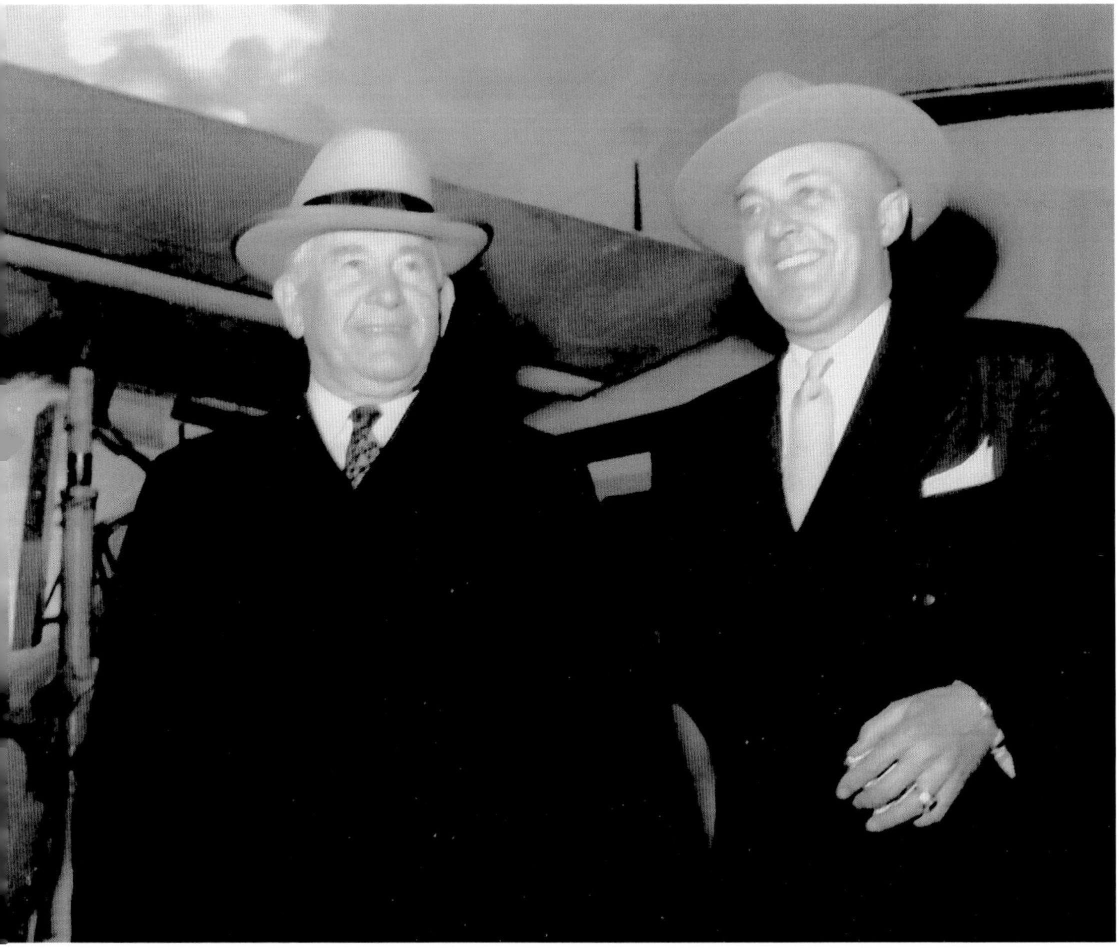

Harold Dunbar Cooley

A Democrat from Nashville, Cooley (TCHOF 2010) served in the US House of Representatives for 32 years. During World War I, he enlisted in the Navy and had ground training at the Naval Aviation Flying Corps in Massachusetts. In 1919, Cooley returned to Nashville to farm and practice law. In his first election in 1934, Cooley defeated five other candidates in the 4th Congressional District to begin his first term in the US Congress. As a farmer, he was on the House Committee on Agriculture. Thus, he was active in supporting President Roosevelt's New Deal program that controlled production and price supports. By 1949, Cooley had seniority. He is seen in this photograph with Vice Pres. Alben Barkley (left). The first chairman of the US House Committee on Agriculture from North Carolina in 104 years, Cooley played key roles in the development of the Farmers Home Administration, the Soil Conservation Service, the Crop Insurance Program, the Tobacco Program, and the Wheat and Cotton Program. He continued as chairman until his retirement in 1967, with the exception of a brief period when the Republicans were in majority. In 1961, as chairman under President Kennedy, he secured the Food for Freedom program, thus creating a foreign market for North Carolina. His travels in Europe and Asia fed his expanding interest in world agriculture and led to his involvement as a United Nations consultant. After 32 years in Congress, Cooley resumed his law practice in Nashville in 1967. For many years, he hosted speakers for the Harvest Festival, including Franklin Delano Roosevelt Jr. and future president Harry S. Truman. Cooley died in 1974. (Courtesy NCDAH.)

Lawrence H. "L.H." Fountain

Born in the Leggett community, L.H. grew up on a farm. He earned his A.B. (artium baccalaureatus) degree and juris doctor degree from UNC in the 1930s and began practicing law in Tarboro. He served in the US Army in World War II, leaving service as a major in the Judge Advocate General's Corps. Fountain continued in the Army Reserves, retiring as a lieutenant colonel. He was elected in 1947 to the North Carolina Senate, and in 1952 to the US House of Representatives. He would be reelected to congress for the next 14 terms, serving 30 years as the congressman from the second district. He introduced the bill to establish the Advisory Commission of Intergovernmental Relations to improve local, state, and federal government, and he served on the commission for 22 years. After a flood in Princeville in 1958, Fountain worked to get the Army Corps of Engineers to build a dike on the banks of the Tar River to prevent future disasters. He was appointed by President Johnson as a delegate to the United Nations. He also investigated programs in the Food and Drug Administration, and his work contributed to the recall of harmful pesticides and carcinogenic drugs. During his last terms in Congress, he served on the Committee of Foreign Affairs. He received numerous honors through his work with the East Carolina Council of Boy Scouts and the Kiwanis Club. In 2000, the state honored him by naming part of Highway 64 the L.H. Fountain Highway. Fountain was a trustee of the National Presbyterian Church in Washington, DC, and served as an elder in his home parish, Howard Memorial Presbyterian Church. He had perfect Sunday school attendance for 80 years. (Courtesy ECVMM.)

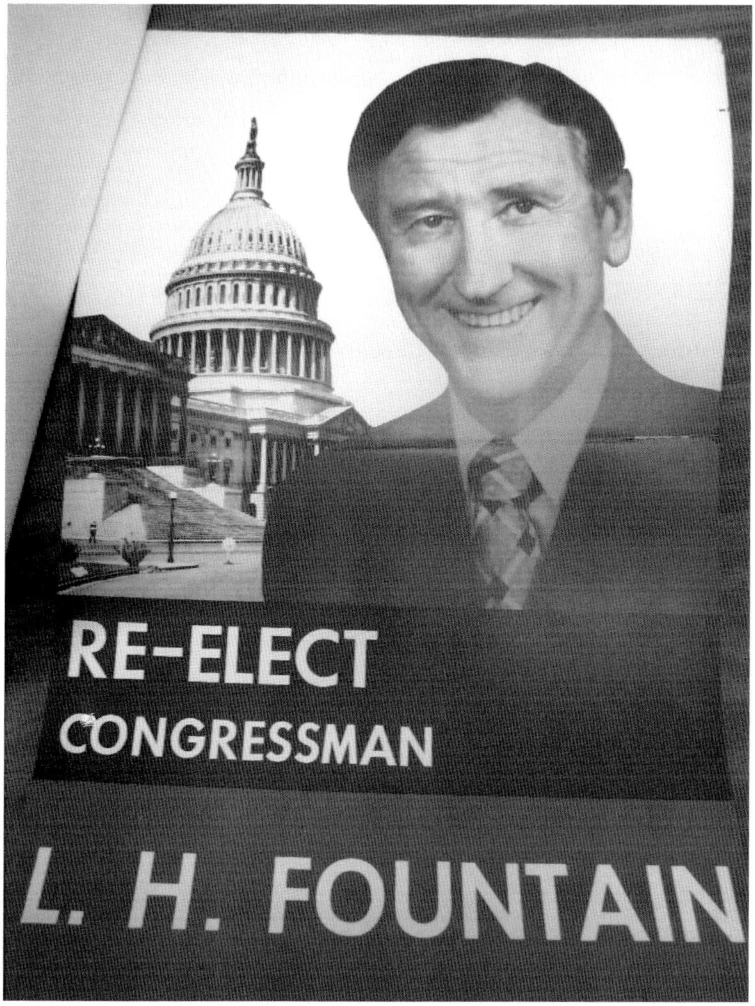

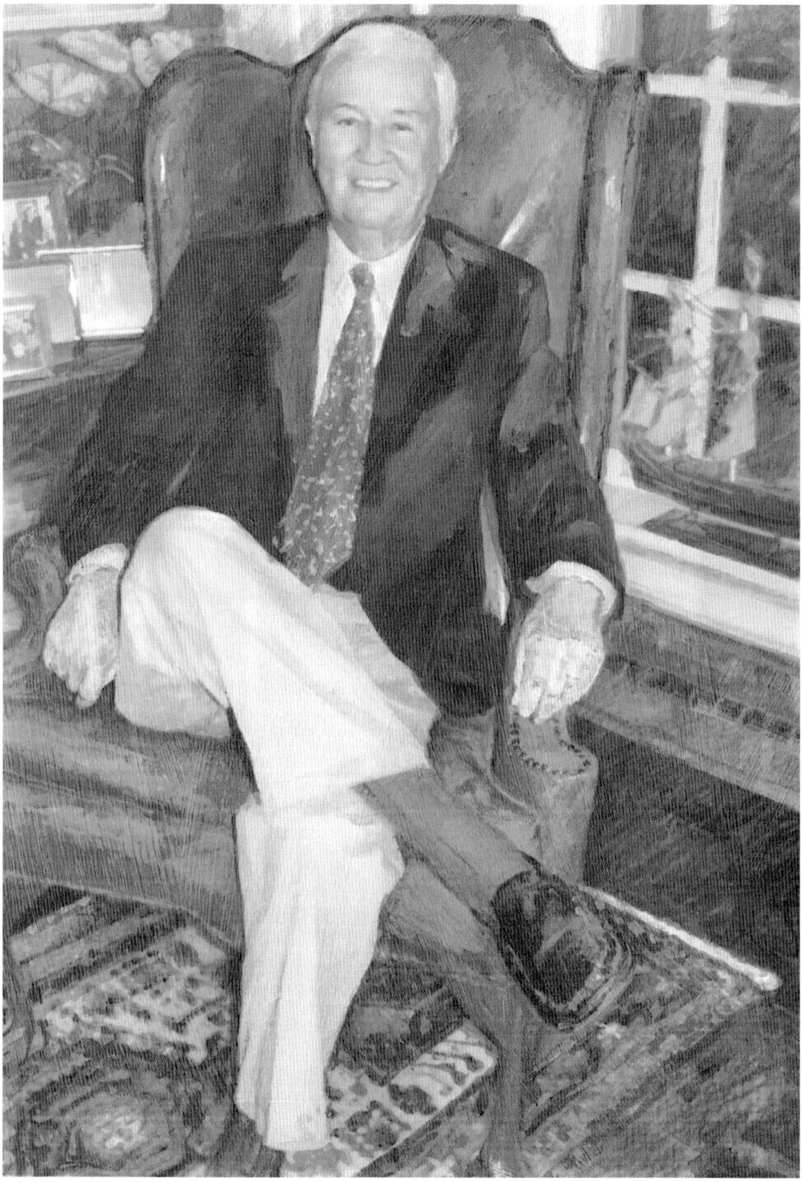

James "Jim" Gardner

Gardner (TCHOF 2005) grew up in Rocky Mount and attended Rocky Mount Public Schools before matriculating at NC State. Active in business in Nash and Edgecombe Counties, he was vice president of Gardner Dairy Products, cofounder of Hardee's Food Systems, and later established the chain of Gardner's Barbecue Restaurants. In 1966, he was elected to Congress, where he was an active member of the House Education and Labor Committees. Gardner was elected chairman of the North Carolina State Republican Party in 1965 and was elected lieutenant governor in 1988 (the first Republican to serve in that office since Reconstruction). Gardner was also president of the Carolina Cougars, the first professional basketball team based in North Carolina. Additionally, he also served as president and commissioner of the American Basketball Association. Gardner has been named "Tarheel of the Week" and "Outstanding Young Man of the South." (Portrait by Susan Fecho.)

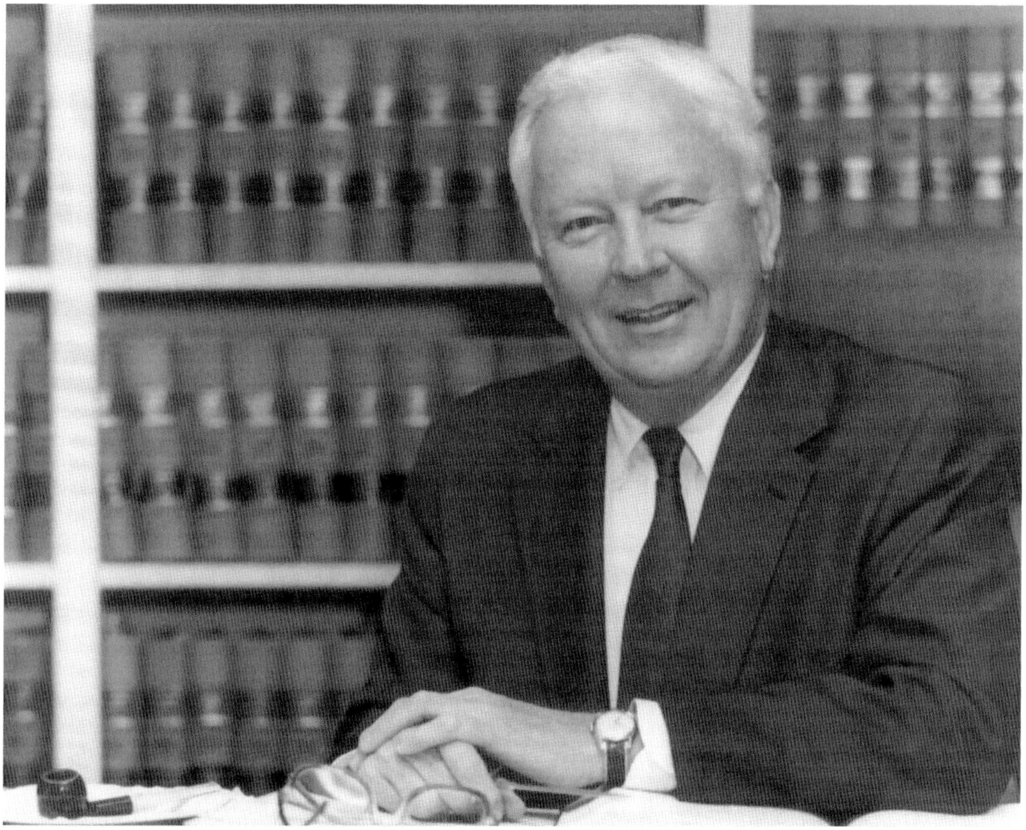

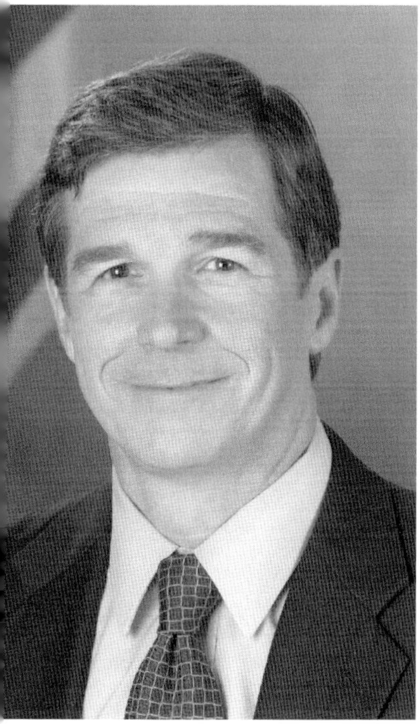

Itimous Thaddeus "Tim" Valentine Jr.
Nash County native Tim Valentine (TCHOF 2012) earned a bachelor's degree from The Citadel in Charleston, South Carolina, and served in the US Army Air Force during World War II. He earned a law degree from UNC Law School in 1952 and served in the North Carolina House of Representatives from 1955 to 1960. Valentine was elected as a US congressman for six terms, from 1982 to 1994. During his terms in Congress, Valentine was chairman of the Subcommittee on Technology, Environment, and Aviation. (Courtesy Itimous Thaddeus "Tim" Valentine Jr.)

Roy Asberry Cooper III
Nashville native Cooper was a Morehead Scholar at UNC, where he also earned his juris doctor degree. He was elected to two terms in the state House of Representatives and, in 1991, was elected to the North Carolina Senate. He was senate majority leader from 1997 to 2000 and today holds the position of North Carolina attorney general. (Courtesy the NC Attorney General's Office.)

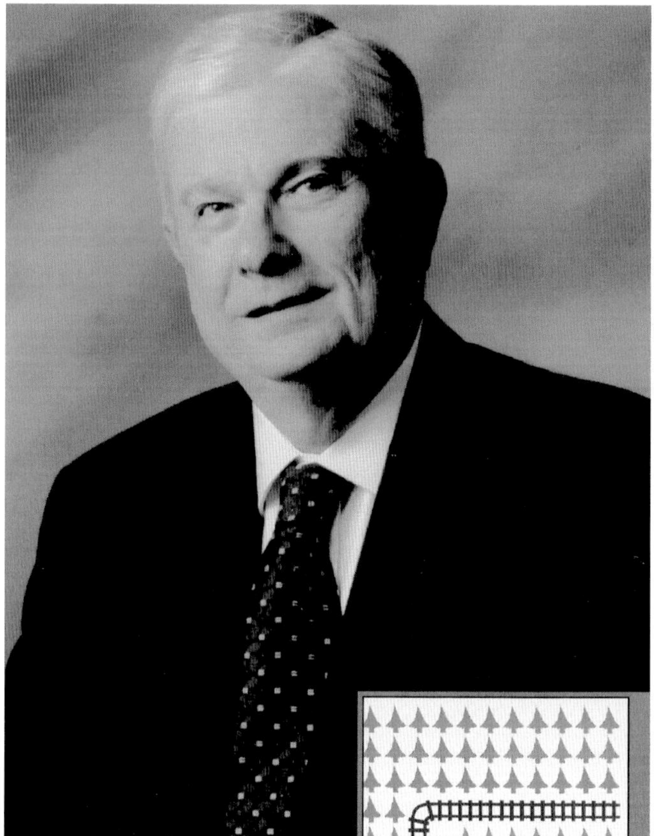

John Phillips Carlton
Edgecombe native Carlton (TCHOF 2007) graduated from NC State and earned his juris doctor degree from UNC Law School. He was the first chief district judge of the 7th Judicial District (Nash, Wilson, and Edgecombe Counties) and served on the North Carolina Court of Appeals in 1979. For four years, he was an associate justice of the state supreme court. Carlton has authored a book on the history of his hometown, *From Pine Tops to Pinetops*. (Courtesy Judge Carlton.)

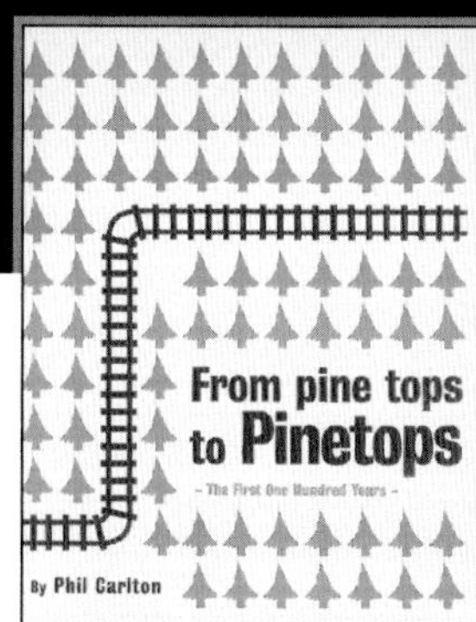

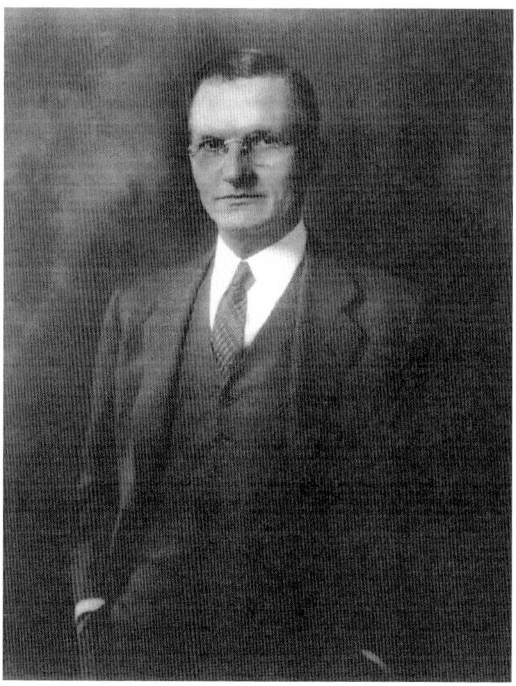

Maurice V. Barnhill
A native of Halifax County, Barnhill began practicing law in Rocky Mount in 1910, after graduating from UNC Law School. His practice lasted 27 years, during which time he was a superior court judge. In 1937, he was appointed to the North Carolina Supreme Court; he became chief justice in 1951. (Courtesy NCDAH.)

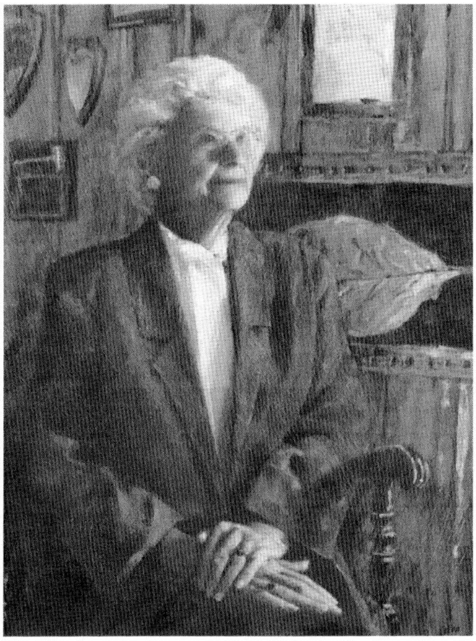

Ruth Cherry
The first woman to hold the office of Edgecombe County Commissioner, Cherry (TCHOF 2005) has served as state president of both Farm Bureau Women and the North Carolina Extension Homemakers Association. She was a founding member and president of West Edgecombe Ruritanettes. Cherry is active with 4-H and also volunteers with numerous organizations, including the Hospice Foundation of Edgecombe County, Edgecombe County Council on Aging, Volunteers Offering Independent Care for the Elderly, and the Ruritan Club. (Portrait by Susan Fecho.)

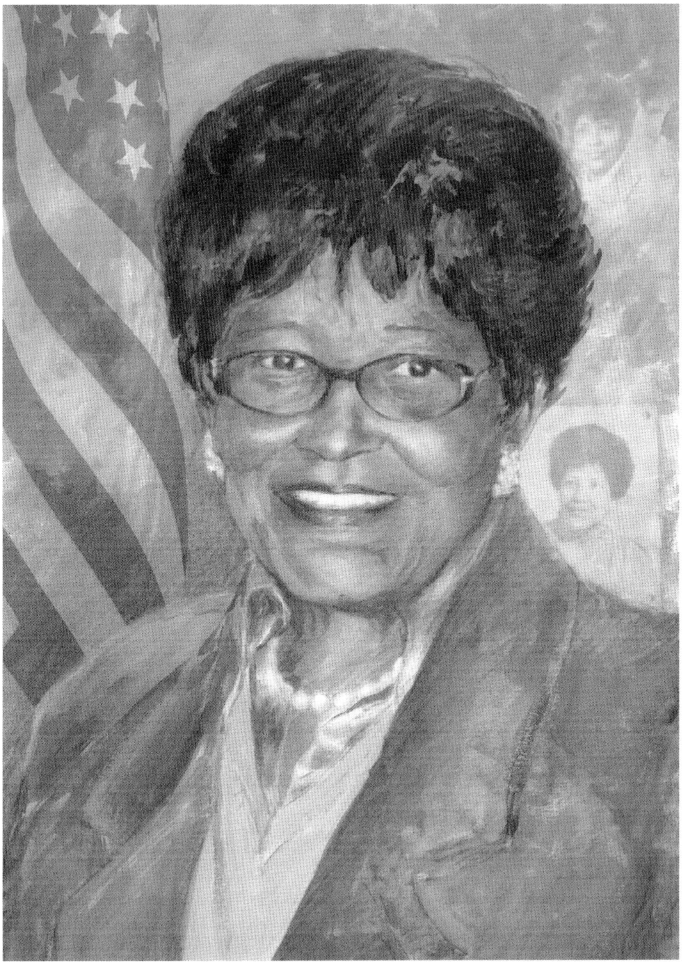

Helen Parker Gay
The first African American woman elected to the Rocky Mount City Council, Gay (TCHOF 2006) served on the council for 20 years. She was employed for 37 years by the Employment Security Commission and set up the Household Training Institute. Active in various community programs, Gay was part of the Nash County Development Commission and Rocky Mount Chamber of Commerce. On the state level, she served on the North Carolina Business Council of Management and Development. (Portrait by Susan Fecho.)

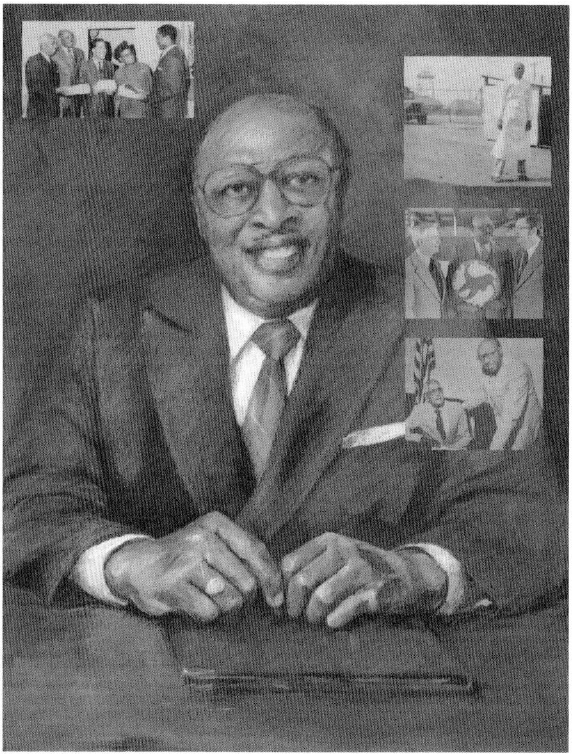

Moses A. Ray

Dr. Ray (TCHOF 2007), born in Clinton, North Carolina, earned his doctorate in dentistry from Howard University. He came to Tarboro in 1946 to open a dental practice and quickly became involved in his community. Dr. Ray was elected to the Tarboro Town Council and became the first post-Reconstruction African American mayor of Tarboro, a position he held from 1987 until his death in 1995. During his tenure as mayor, Tarboro earned the All-America City designation. (Portrait by Susan Fecho.)

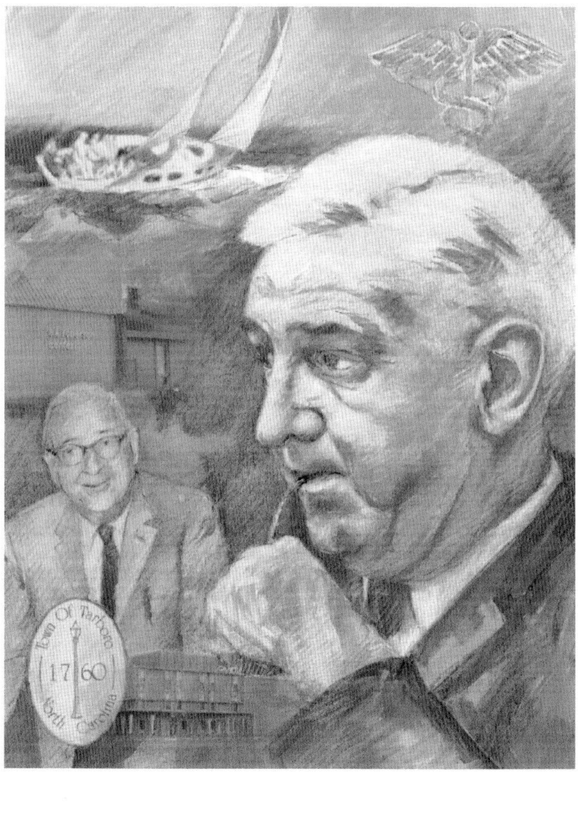

Edward L. Roberson

Born in Tarboro, Roberson (TCHOF 2008) earned his bachelor of science degree from Davidson College and his doctorate from the University of Maryland. He also became a doctor of medicine in 1936. He served four years in the Navy during World War II. "Dr. Ed" served as president of the Tarboro Clinic and as chief of staff and chief of surgery at Edgecombe General Hospital. He was also Tarboro's mayor for 14 years (1961–1975), leading the area through desegregation and the civil rights movement. (Portrait by Susan Fecho.)

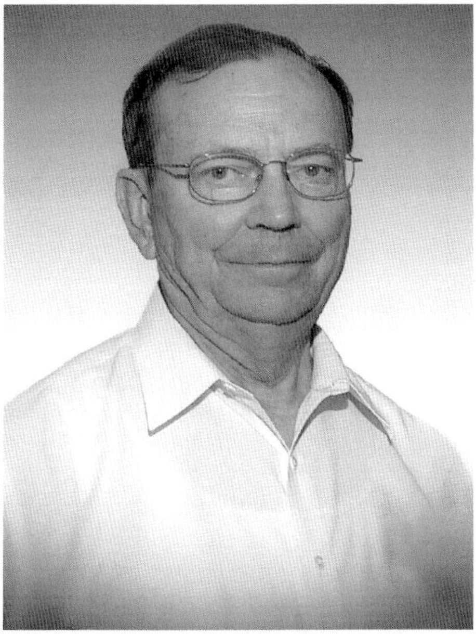

John Vines Cobb Jr.
A graduate of the business program at UNC, Cobb served in the Air Force for two years. He returned home to Pinetops to manage the Peoples Bank and Trust Company (later Centura) for 35 years. He was an Edgecombe County commissioner for 12 years and served 8 years on the county board of education. In 1999, he was elected mayor of Pinetops, a position he still holds. (Courtesy Cobb family.)

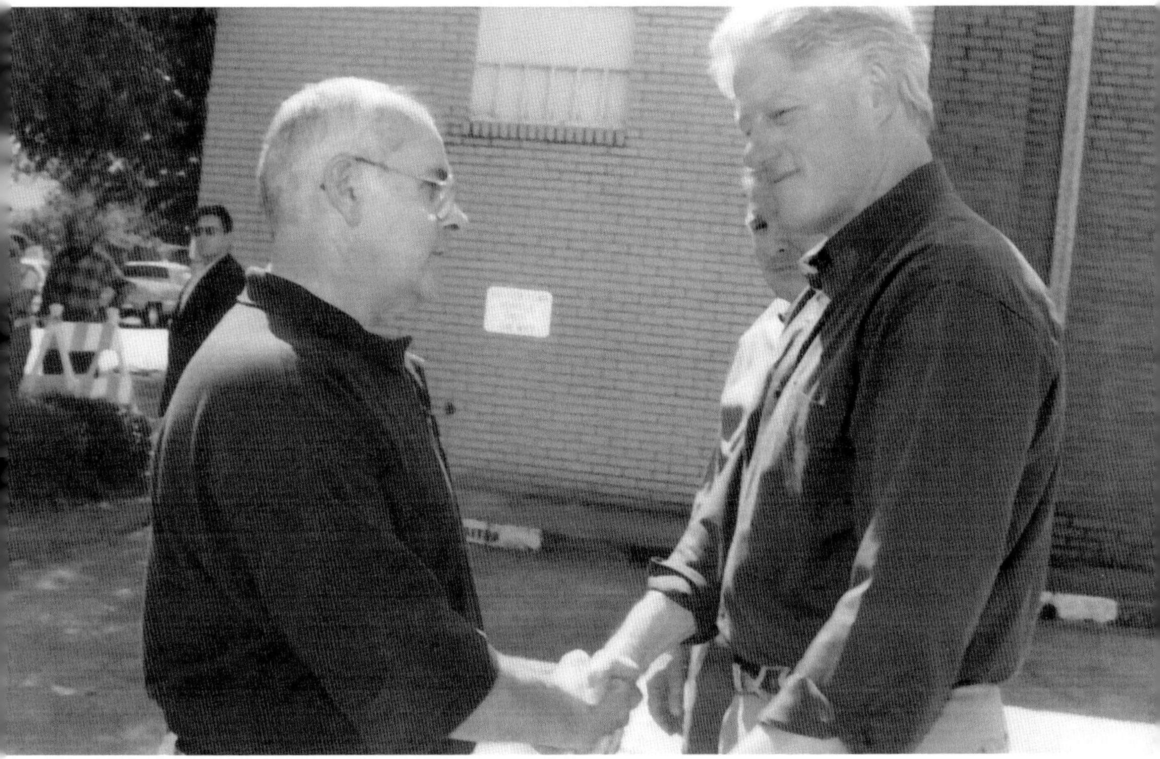

Donald Morris
Retired from work at Simmons Furniture Company, Morris has been mayor of Tarboro since 1995. He is an active member of the Golden K Kiwanis Club. He led Tarboro through the recovery after Hurricane Floyd and the resulting flood. He is pictured here with Pres. Bill Clinton, who visited Tarboro in September 1999 to offer support during the recovery. (Courtesy Donald Morris.)

Frederick Turnage

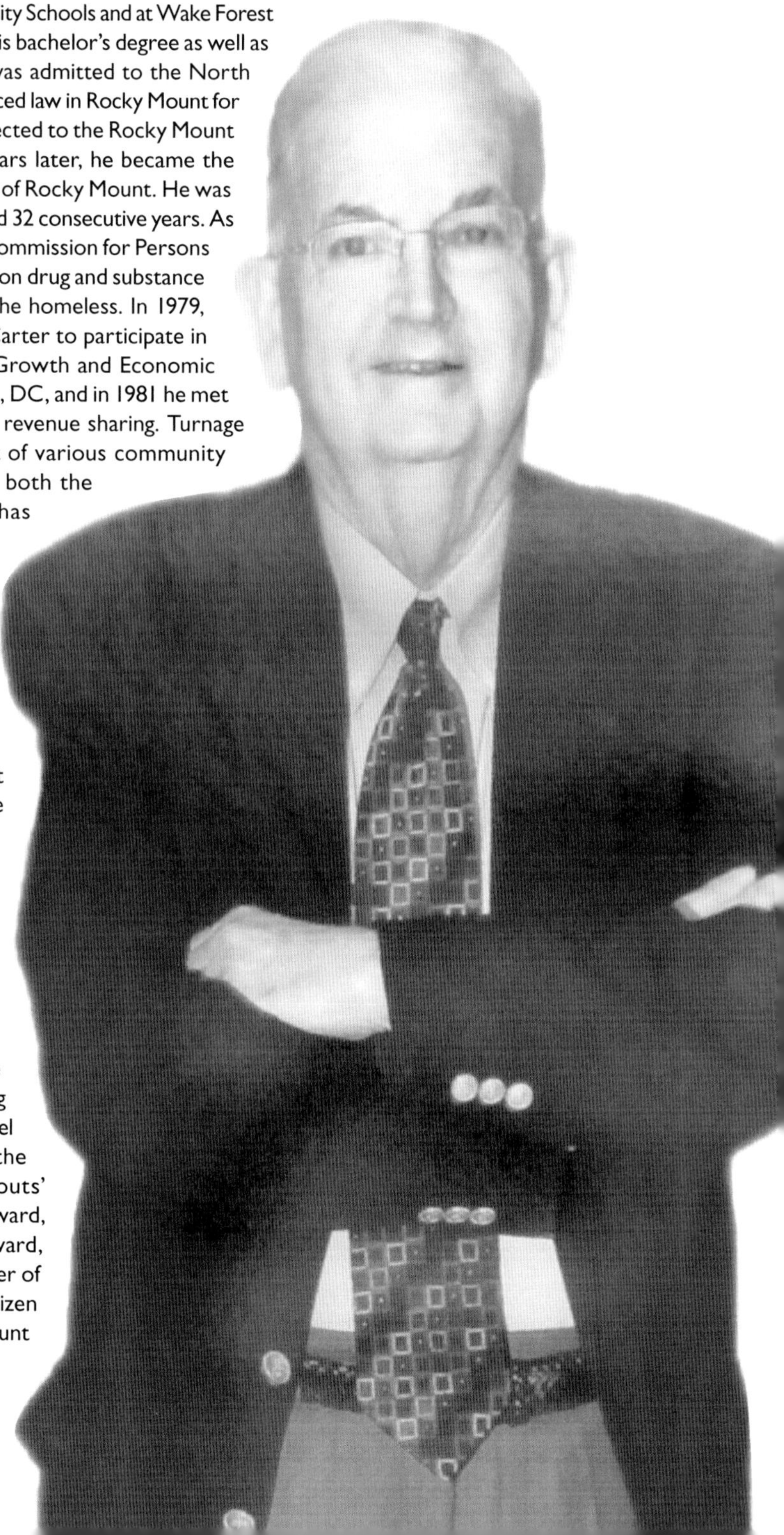

Rocky Mount native Fred Turnage (TCHOF 2005) was educated in the Rocky Mount City Schools and at Wake Forest University, where he earned his bachelor's degree as well as his juris doctor degree. He was admitted to the North Carolina Bar in 1961 and practiced law in Rocky Mount for over 40 years. Turnage was elected to the Rocky Mount City Council in 1971; two years later, he became the youngest mayor in the history of Rocky Mount. He was reelected nine times and served 32 consecutive years. As mayor, Turnage created the Commission for Persons with Disabilities, a committee on drug and substance abuse, and a committee for the homeless. In 1979, he was named by President Carter to participate in a conference on "Balanced Growth and Economic Development" in Washington, DC, and in 1981 he met with President Reagan about revenue sharing. Turnage served as chair or president of various community boards and organizations at both the local and state levels. He has been a member of the Rocky Mount Board of Elections, the Nash–Edgecombe Civil Defense Agency, the Rocky Mount Business Development Authority, the North Carolina Local Government Commission, and the Local Government Advocacy Council (of which he was the first vice chairman). He was commissioner for North Carolina Eastern Municipal Power Agency for over 20 years and a member and past president of ElectriCities of North Carolina. Among the honors that Turner has received are the Jaycee Award for Outstanding People in Government, "Tarheel of the Week" designation, the Eastern Council of Boy Scouts' 1994 Distinguished Citizen Award, the Rotary Club Aluhsen Award, and the Rocky Mount Chamber of Commerce Distinguished Citizen Award. (Courtesy Rocky Mount Chamber of Commerce.)

CHAPTER SIX

Medicine and Science

Physicians have been in the Twin Counties since before the Civil War. Several served in the war as company surgeons, and a couple managed the local wayside hospitals created near the railroad to care for wounded soldiers. The first hospitals in the area included Pittman Sanatorium, founded by Dr. Newsome J. Pittman of Tarboro, and the Atlantic Coast Line Hospital of Rocky Mount, built by the ACL railroad for it employees. The Rocky Mount Sanitarium opened in 1913, and two years later, Parkview Hospital was built in Rocky Mount. In 1919, Edgecombe County had the first health department in the state. In the 1920s, Bass Memorial Hospital opened in Tarboro, and eventually the Pittman Hospital became Edgecombe General. After World War II, Dr. Quigless opened the first black hospital in the area. In the 1950s, Edgecombe General expanded to a new facility on north Main Street in Tarboro, and the Tarboro Clinic also relocated from downtown. In 1971, Nash General opened as the major hospital in Rocky Mount, and two older hospitals—Parkview and Sanitarium—closed. In 1972, Rocky Mount was the base for one of the first area health education centers in North Carolina, Area L-AHEC. The AHEC program was a coordination of five counties, including Nash and Edgecombe, with the UNC Medical School to provide educational programs for medical professionals. Tarboro closed Edgecombe General and opened Heritage Hospital in 1985, and the new facility soon became a part of University Health Systems of Greenville and associated with Pitt Memorial Hospital and the East Carolina University School of Medicine. In 2012, Heritage and all the affiliated clinics became known as Vidant Health Systems. The area also had numerous satellite clinics in the smaller towns of Pinetops, Macclesfield, Princeville, and Whitakers. In addition to its success in medicine, this area also produced people of science and technology. Curtis Satterthwaite is a senior logistician at the Kennedy Space Center. Nuclear physicist Harold Denton has consulted on nuclear reactors around the globe. Spencer K. Fountain was a creative inventor in the region.

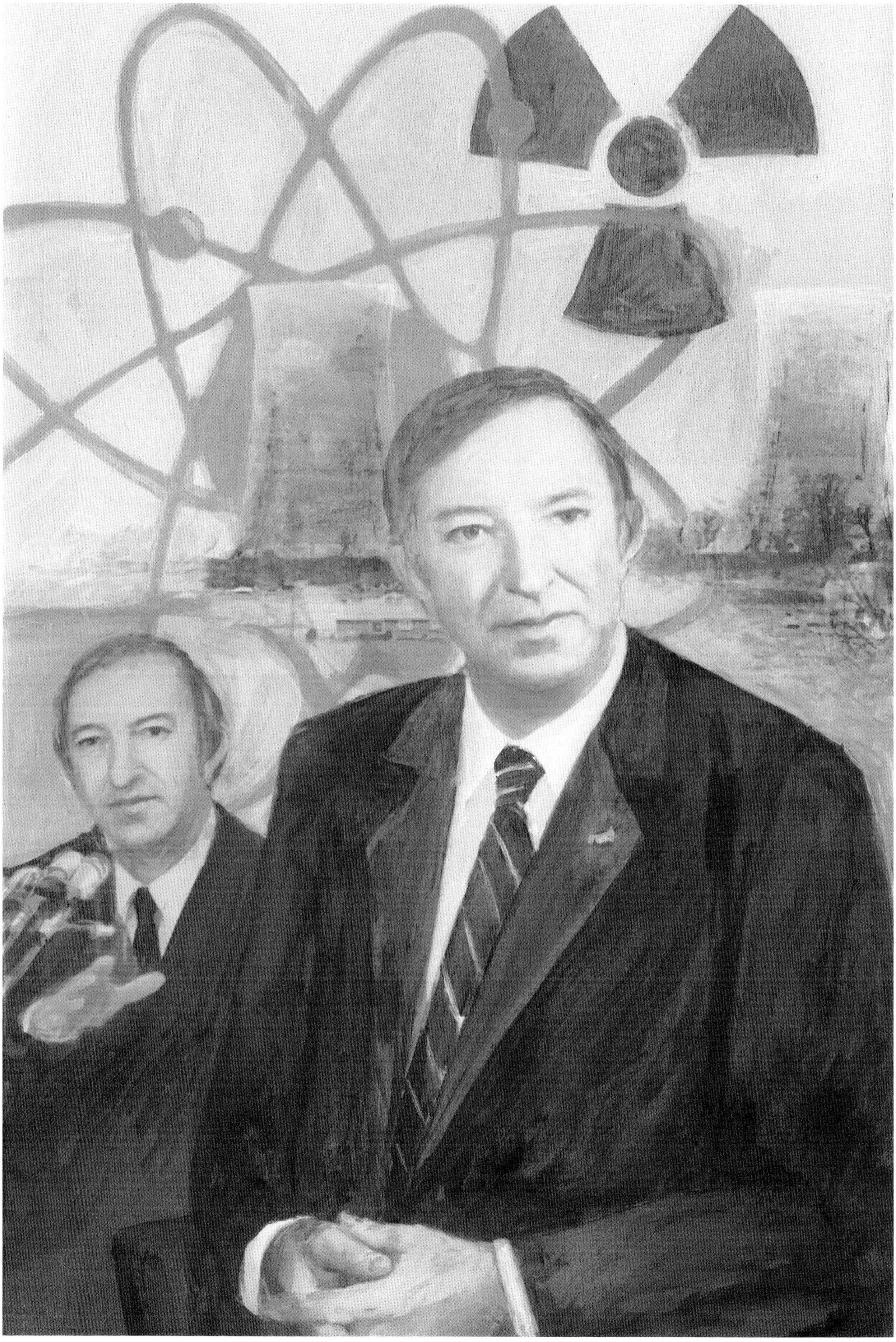

Harold Ray Denton (OPPOSITE PAGE)
Born in Rocky Mount, Nash County, Denton (TCHOF 2004) attended Battle Elementary School and was in the first class to graduate from the "new" senior high school in 1954. He earned a bachelor of science degree in Nuclear Engineering from NC State and did graduate work at the University of Maryland. An internationally recognized nuclear physicist, Denton was former director of the Office of Nuclear Reactor Regulation. Following the Three Mile Island incident, he was President Carter's personal on-site representative at the nuclear facility. He is the recipient of the Presidential Distinguished Executive Award from Presidents Carter and Reagan. He was also consulted by Japan on the stability of their nuclear reactors after the 2011 earthquake. He is a frequent lecturer at engineering schools on nuclear safety issues. (Portrait by Susan Fecho.)

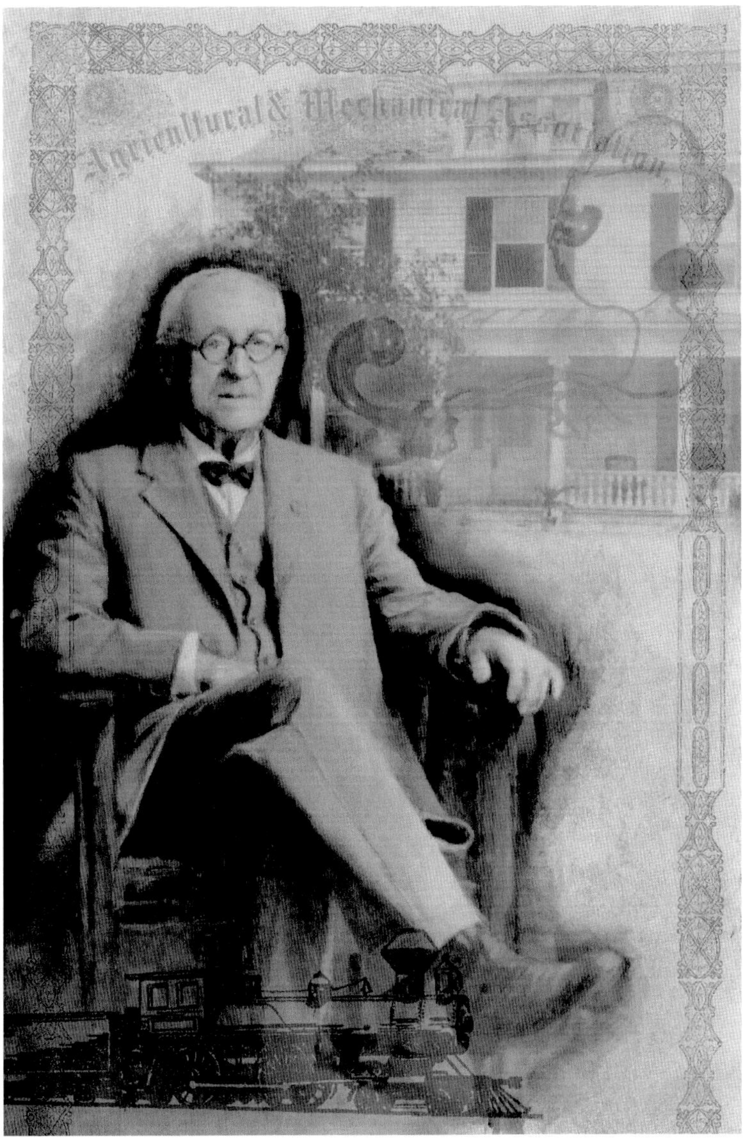

Spencer K. Fountain
An inventor and communications pioneer, Spencer K. Fountain (1848–1931; TCHOF 2004) supervised installation of the first telegraph line from Rocky Mount to Wilmington. He designed and made the necessary components and was key in establishing the first voice communication from the train depot to Rocky Mount Mills, from Rocky Mount to Tarboro and to Wilson. He was instrumental in starting the first agricultural fair, and the Carolina Cotillion Club. In addition to working for the Atlantic Coast Line Railroad for 54 years, he operated a foundry, a machine shop, and planning mill where he devised the necessary parts for his many technological innovations. (Portrait by Susan Fecho.)

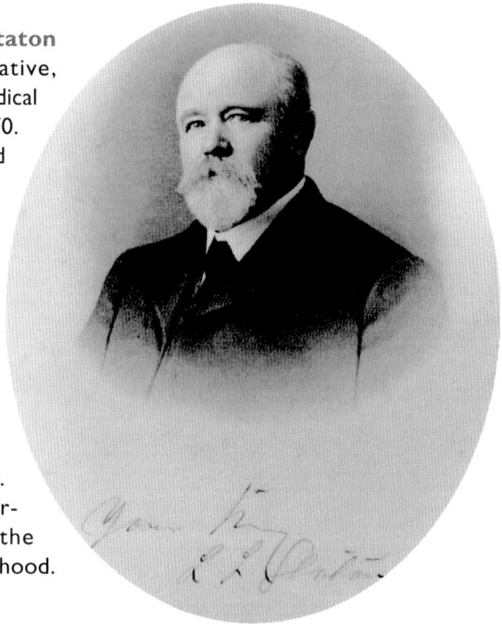

Dr. Lycurgus Lafayette Staton
An Edgecombe County native, Staton graduated from the Medical College of New York in 1870. He opened his practice and became a partner in Staton & Zoeller Drugstore. In 1880, Dr. Staton is credited with performing the first successful gastrostomy in America. According to a 1984 article in the *Surgery, Gynecology and Obstetrics Journal*, patients died in all previous abdominal surgery attempts by other physicians. Staton's patient, eight-year-old Lewis Lyon, survived the operation and lived into adulthood. (Courtesy BBH.)

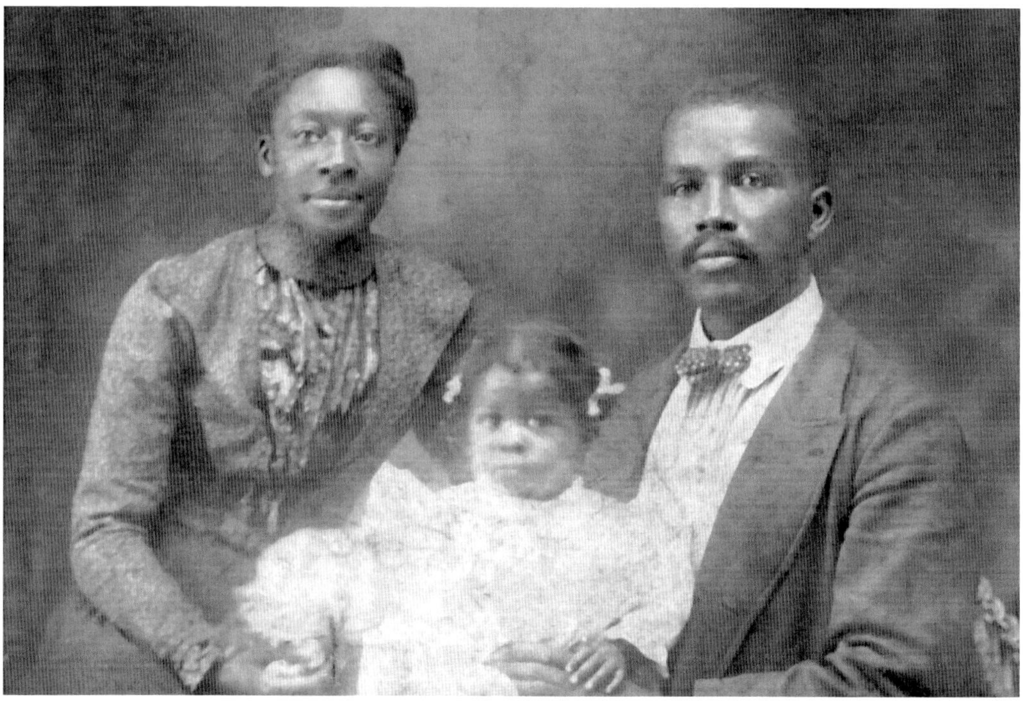

Dr. Alexander Sidney McMillan
One of 13 children born to slaves, McMillan was born free. He graduated from the Leonard Medical School at Shaw University in March 1898. Two months after getting his state medical license, he opened a practice in Tarboro, becoming the first African American physician in Edgecombe County. He became president of the Old North State Medical, Dental and Pharmaceutical Society. McMillan is pictured here with his wife, Viola Gray, and their daughter Viola. (Courtesy BBH.)

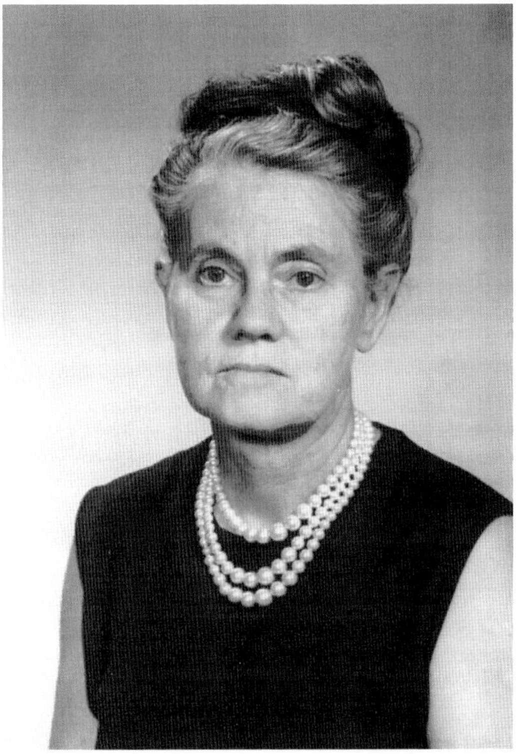

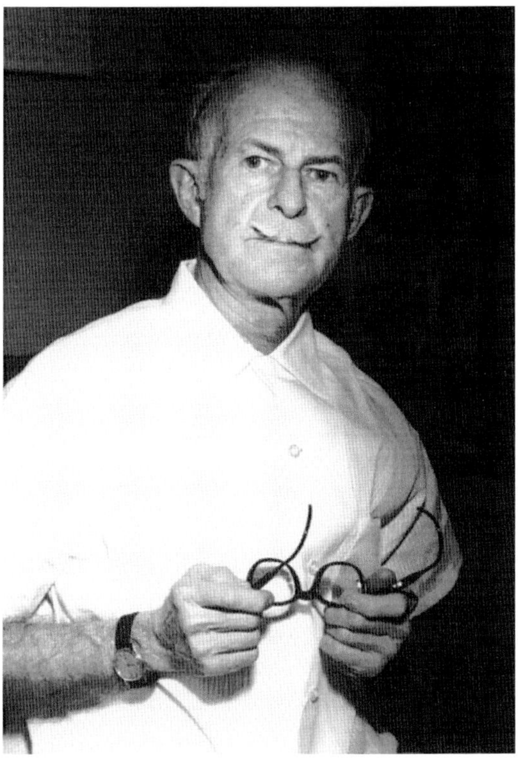

Dr. Margaret White Battle and Dr. Newsome Battle
A native of Michigan, Margaret White graduated from the University of Michigan Medical School. She came to Rocky Mount in the 1930s to work at Parkview Hospital, the first female physician in Rocky Mount. In 1937, she married Dr. Newsome Battle, a surgeon at Parkview. She practiced gynecology and obstetrics for 50 years. Together, the Battles worked to have Nash General Hospital built. She was active with the local Red Cross and in local and state medical societies. She also loved history and, after her retirement, became very active with the Nash County Historical Association, which she helped found in 1970. She worked with others in the organization to record lost cemeteries. She also worked to get Stonewall—an 1830 plantation house that was the first brick home in the Twin Counties—restored and open for public tours. (Both, courtesy Nash General Hospital.)

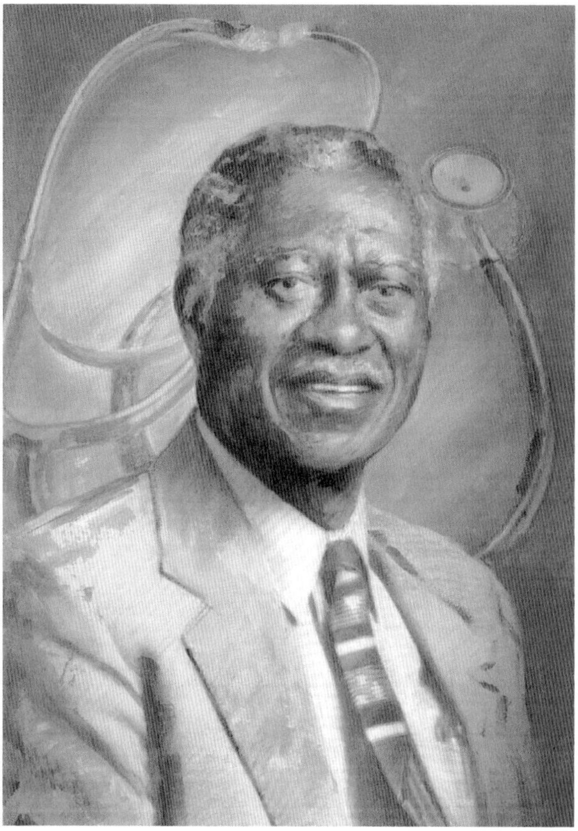

Dr. James Edward Bryant
A graduate of the North Carolina Agricultural and Technical State University, Bryant (TCHOF 2006) obtained his medical degree from Howard University in 1960 and practiced medicine for 40 years. He was the first African American physician to have hospital privileges at Park View and Nash General Hospitals. He was active in medical associations and served in the Rocky Mount chapter of the NAACP, the Rocky Mount Chamber of Commerce, and his college alumni associations. (Portrait by Susan Fecho.)

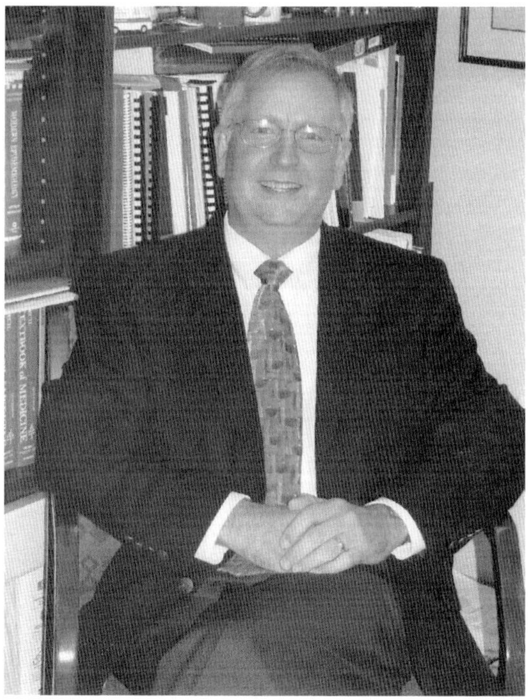

Dr. David Calvin Goff Jr.
A Rocky Mount native, Goff was educated at Duke University, the UNC School of Medicine, and the Queen Mother's Hospital in Glasgow, Scotland. He is director of the Center of Health Care Research and a professor of public health at Wake Forest University School of Medicine. Goff is considered an expert in heart disease and has written numerous articles for medical journals. (Courtesy Goff.)

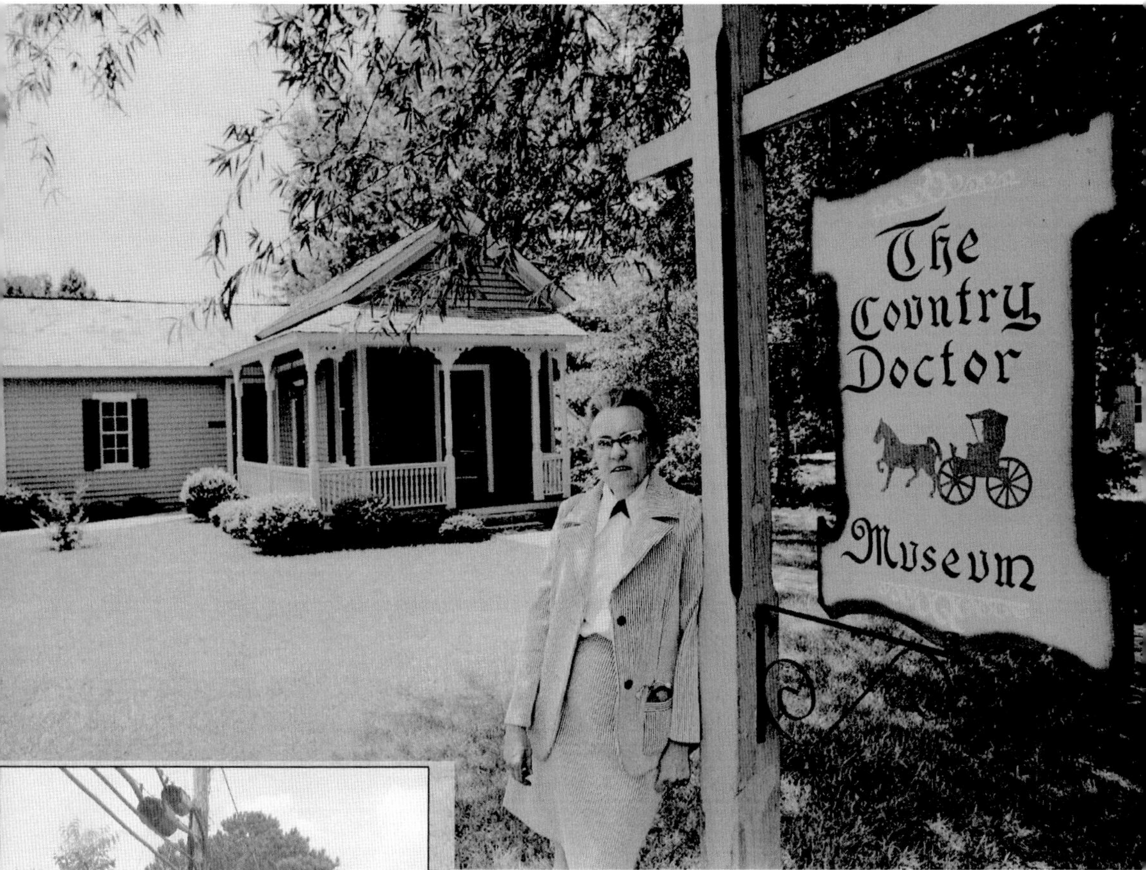

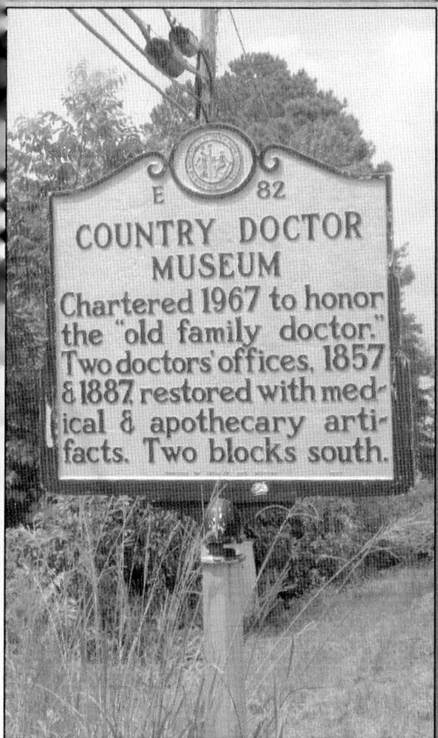

Dr. Josephine E. Newell and the Country Doctor Museum
Her father's family had seven generations of doctors, so it was only natural that Newell (TCHOF 2012) wanted to keep the family tradition going. She grew up in Vance County and earned a chemical engineering degree at the age of 16 from the University of South Carolina. She then attended the University of Maryland School of Medicine. She began her practice in Bailey in 1951 as one of the first female physicians in Nash County, where she treated patients for the next 23 years. Dr. Newell was involved in numerous state health care projects and is one of the founders of the Country Doctor Museum in Bailey, which opened in 1967. It is the oldest museum in the country for rural health care. Newell managed the museum for 30 years. Today, the more than 5,000 medical artifacts are managed by the Medical Foundation of East Carolina University. (Above, courtesy Country Doctor Museum; left, photograph by author.)

Dr. Milton Douglas Quigless Sr.

A native of Mississippi, Quigless (TCHOF 2004) came to Tarboro in 1936 to treat the African American population in the area. After World War II, he established the first African American hospital in the Twin Counties in an old garage using military surplus medical materials. Eventually, he had a two-story hospital with a surgery room, as he was not allowed in some of the area general hospitals. The hospital remained open until 1973, but the downstairs clinic area, which had served both black and white patients since the 1940s, remained in operation until Quigless's death in 1996. Dr. Quigless was also a community activist who worked to improve relations within the area. The former Quigless Hospital now features a museum exhibit and is operated by his daughter as a health therapy center. (Portrait by Susan Fecho.)

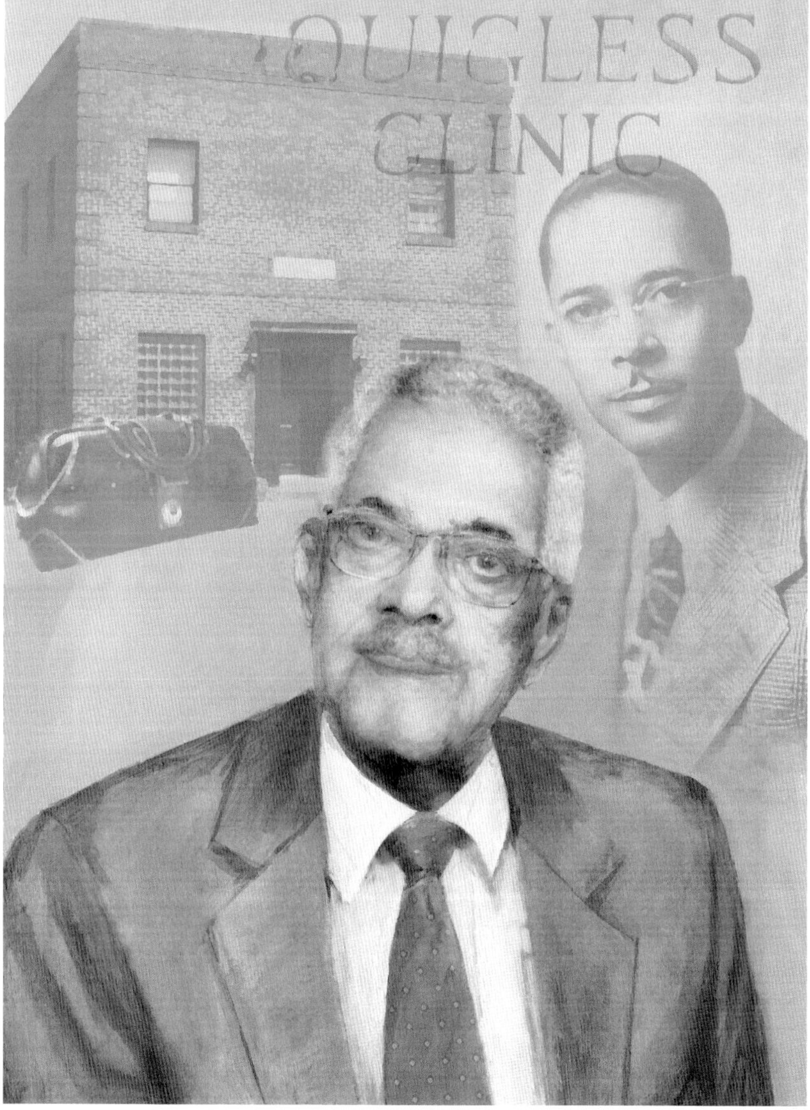

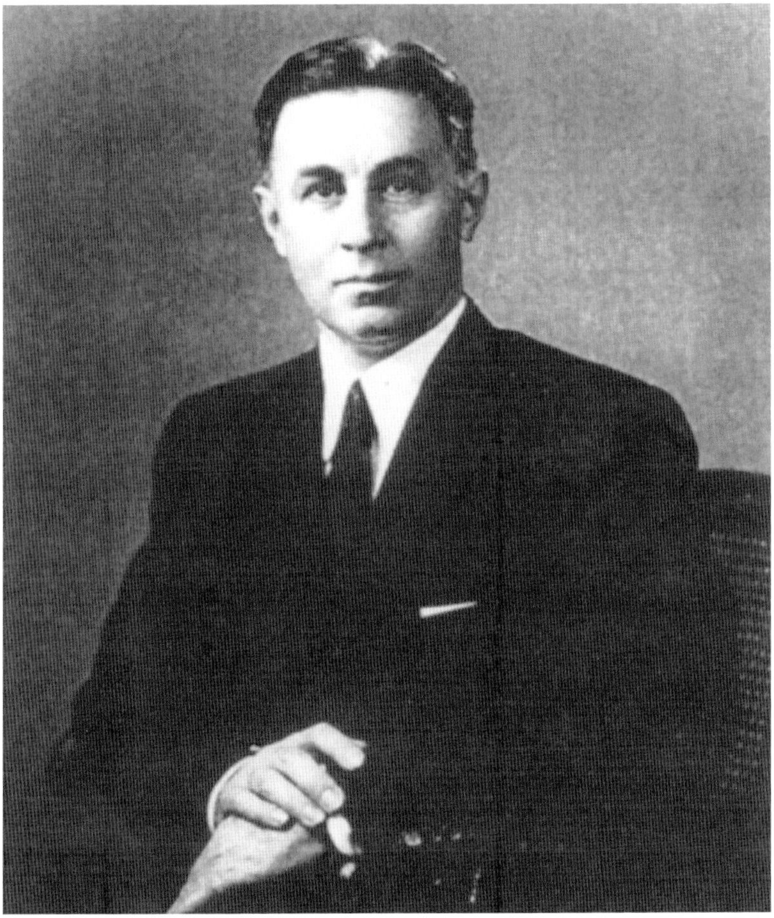

Dr. James Allen Whitaker
Nashville native Whitaker (TCHOF 2006) earned his doctor of medicine degree from Temple University in 1933 and graduated from the UNC School of Public Health in 1934. His medical career began with a decade-long position as a health officer in Rocky Mount. He then served in various Rocky Mount area hospitals as an urologist from 1948 until his retirement in 1987. Concerned about public health, Dr. Whitaker introduced many programs that are still active today. He died at the age of 101. (Courtesy Dr. Whitaker.)

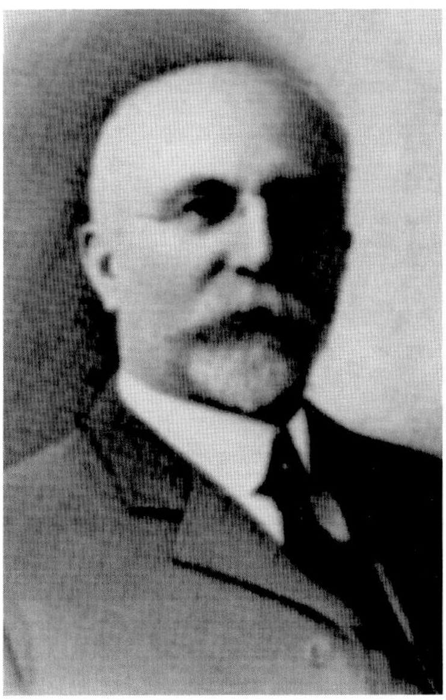

Dr. William H. Whitehead
A graduate of the University of Maryland Medical School, Dr. Whitehead opened his practice in his hometown of Battleboro. He soon became the chief of staff at the new Atlantic Coast Line Hospital that opened in Rocky Mount. Along with practicing medicine for 36 years, Dr. Whitehead served as president of the North Carolina Medical Examiners Association and as a member of the North Carolina State Board of Heath. (Courtesy University of Maryland.)

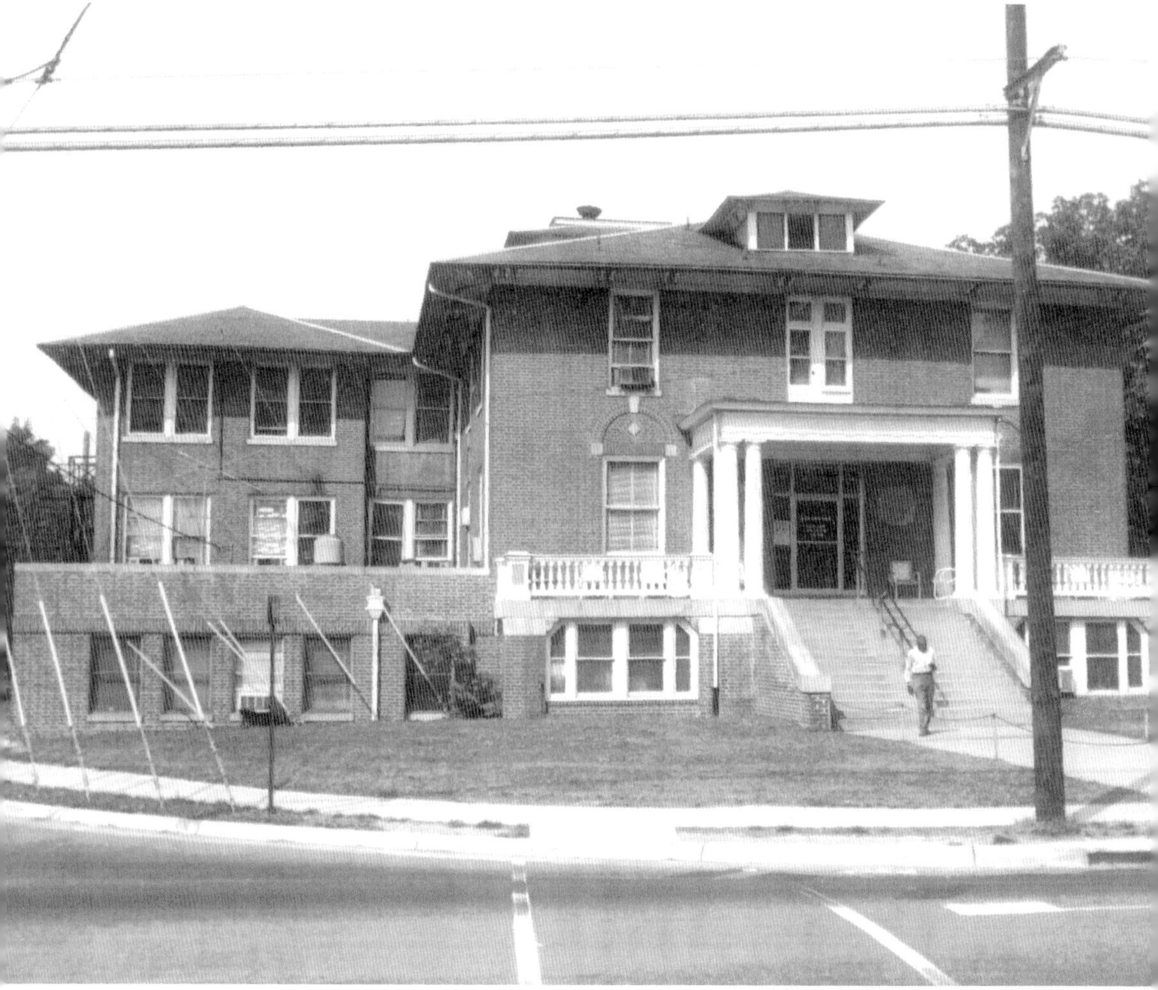

Parkview Hospital and Boice-Willis Clinic

In 1914, Drs. Joseph Whitehead, Edmund Boice, Byrd C. Willis, Ivan P. Battle, E.P. Quillen, and Richard Speight formed the Park View Hospital Group. Whitehead was the son of Dr. William Whitehead, chief surgeon of the ACL Hospital. Dr. Joseph Whitehead had attended the University of Maryland Medical School like his father. He practiced for 27 years and was also active in the North Carolina State Medical Society and the Nash County Medical Society. Drs. Boice and Willis had relocated to this area from Richmond, Virginia. In addition to being surgeons on the staff at Parkview, they formed a specialty clinic in 1915, which operates today as the Boice-Willis Clinic. Dr. Boice maintained his medical practice for 50 years and was a charter member of the Rocky Mount–Nash chapter of the American Cancer Society. Dr. Byrd C. Willis worked for 45 years at Parkview and at the Boice-Willis Clinic before retiring and returning to his native Virginia. (Courtesy Nash General Hospital.)

CHAPTER SEVEN

Military

Men of the Twin Counties have served in the US armed forces since the American Revolution. They have been in every major conflict that followed the formation of this country, serving in the War of 1812, the Mexican War, the Civil War, the Spanish-American War, World War I, World War II, Korea, Vietnam, the Gulf War, Iraq, and Afghanistan. Even during the Seven Years' War (or French and Indian War) of the 1750s, a government report indicated that Edgecombe County had more than 1,300 men eligible to serve in a militia if needed. State records mention that Ned Griffen of Edgecombe County, a slave, dutifully served his country and, in return, was freed after the American Revolution. While most have served as enlisted men, there have been several notable officers in the Civil War, World War II, and beyond. Memorials honoring the many area veterans can be found in most towns in the Twin Counties. Local women began participating in the military by World War I, some serving as nurses in the Red Cross or the Army. By World War II, the role of women had expanded to all branches of service, and they were no longer serving strictly as nurses. It is estimated that over 5,000 men and women from this area served in the armed forces in World War II. One Tarboro native, Willie H. Fuller (TCHOF 2012), flew 76 combat missions as a Tuskegee Airman. Some families had several members enlisted, and not all returned home. The monuments and the memorials are the citizens' thank-you to the many who did serve the call of their country. One of the first memorials was a Memory Chapel in the Old Town Cemetery in Tarboro. In addition to the monuments, the Edgecombe County Veterans' Military Museum opened in 2005. There is a monthly flag raising hosted by the Golden Kiwanis Club that honors an Edgecombe County veteran. ROTC groups from the area high schools participate in every ceremony.

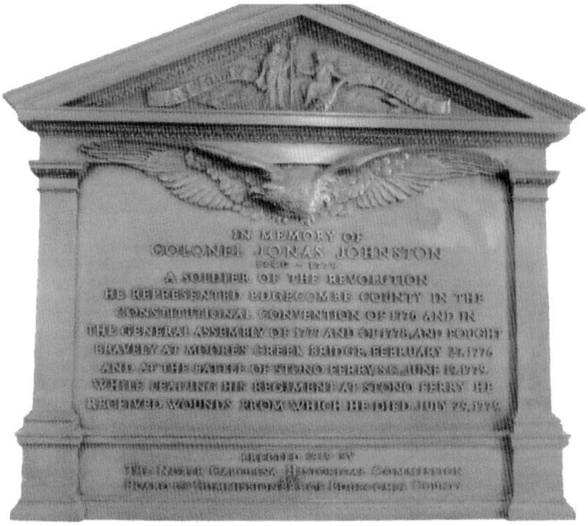

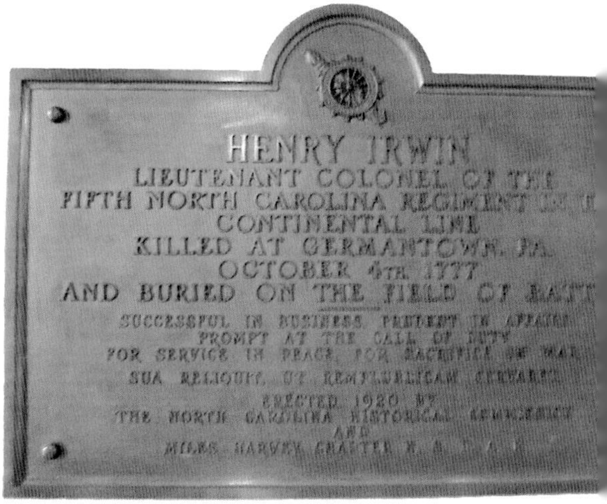

Jonas Johnston and Henry Irwin
It is not known exactly how many men served in the American Revolution, either in Washington's Continental Army or in the state militia, but it is known that two local sons were killed while fighting for independence. Jonas Johnston led a company of militiamen at the Battle of Moore's Creek Bridge, and he later commanded a militia unit in South Carolina. He died somewhere in South Carolina. Henry Irwin was a lieutenant colonel of the 5th North Carolina Regiment of the Continental Line. He was killed at Germantown. Plaques honoring these two men are in the Edgecombe County Courthouse. (Photographs by the author.)

Josiah Solomon Pender (OPPOSITE PAGE)
Pender, a cousin of Gen. Dorsey Pender and son of local merchant Solomon Pender, had attended a military academy for a short time before deciding that the structure was not to his liking. He went to Europe and studied art, becoming a painter. Pender's first military experience was in the Mexican War. Seen here in his Army uniform, Pender soon came into a disagreement with his commanding officer and was dishonorably discharged. He challenged the charges and was reinstated by President Polk. He resigned his commission at the end of the war. He married and moved to Beaufort, where he operated the Atlantic House, a hotel on the waterfront. With his own company of men, the Beaufort Harbor Guards, Pender led the capture of Fort Macon in April 1861 without authorization from the governor. When the Union occupied the coast, Pender lost his business. He was later assigned to Fort Macon as part of the 10th North Carolina Regiment. His wife, Maria, was ill, and he requested leave. He was denied leave, but, according to records, he returned to Beaufort to care for her. His wife died in December 1861, and he was dishonorably discharged from the Confederate army for being absent without leave, receiving his discharge on the day of her funeral. He brought his nine children home to Tarboro for relatives to look after them and became reacquainted with a cousin, Laura Melvina Pender. The couple married on September 23, 1862, and Josiah took Laura to Bermuda, where he was part of a blockade-running operation, smuggling goods into the port of Wilmington for the Confederate cause. Laura became pregnant and wanted to return home to Tarboro to have her baby, but Josiah had to go to England to get more goods. He put Laura on a ship with orders that the captain take the ship into Wilmington. As the ship neared port, Union ships tried to capture it. The captain was ready to surrender until Laura Pender persuaded him (some say with a pistol) to escape the blockade. The ship arrived safely in Wilmington, and Laura took the train home to Tarboro. Two weeks later, on October 19, 1863, she delivered Josiah Keon Pender. Unfortunately, the elder Josiah Pender died of yellow fever 1864, never making it home to see his son. Pender was buried beside his first wife in the Old Burying Ground in Beaufort. (Courtesy John Pender.)

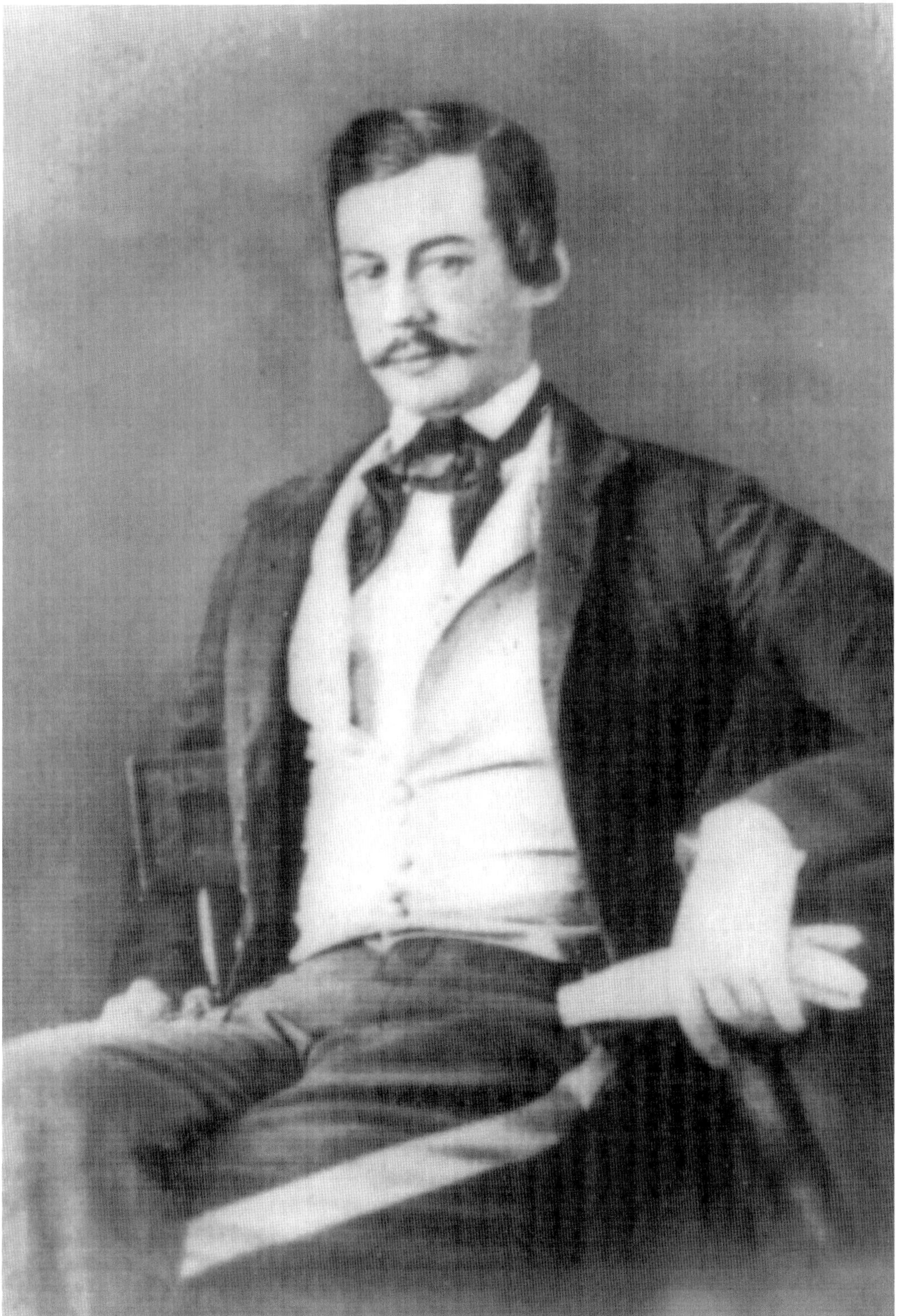

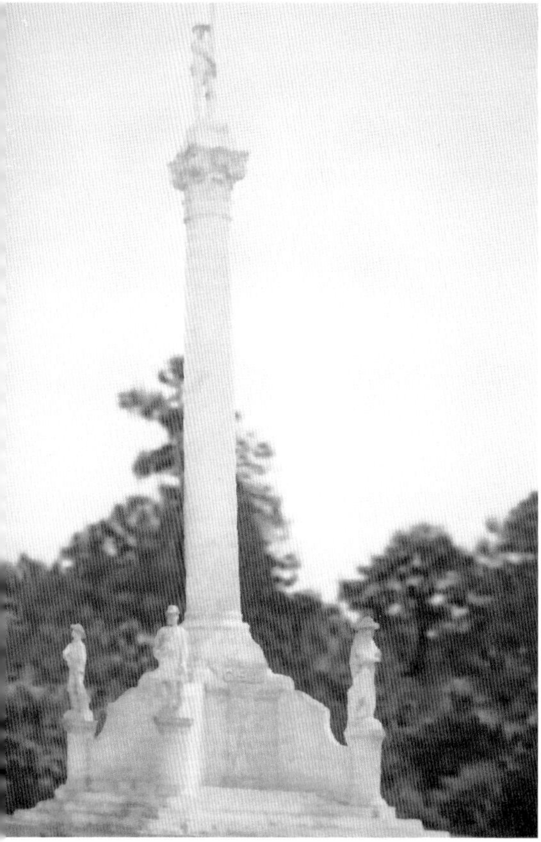

Civil War Monument in Rocky Mount

Several members of the 1st North Carolina, known as the "Bethel Regiment," were from Rocky Mount. One of the members was Robert H. Ricks. He became a successful businessman after the war and personally paid for this monument to be built at Battle Park in Rocky Mount. Over the years, vandals have damaged the statues on the corner pedestals. (Courtesy Braswell Library.)

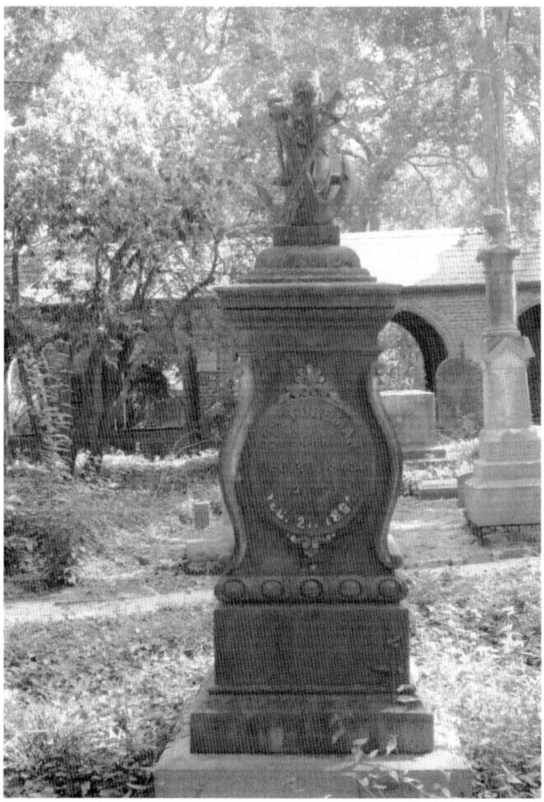

Ivey Foreman

The only naval officer in the Twin Counties to serve in the Civil War, Foreman was enrolled at the US Naval Academy when the war began but resigned to join the newly forming Confederate States Navy. He saw action at the Battle of the Ironclads in March 1862. Foreman contracted a fever and died one day after his 21st birthday. He was sent home to be buried in Calvary Episcopal Churchyard. (Photograph by the author.)

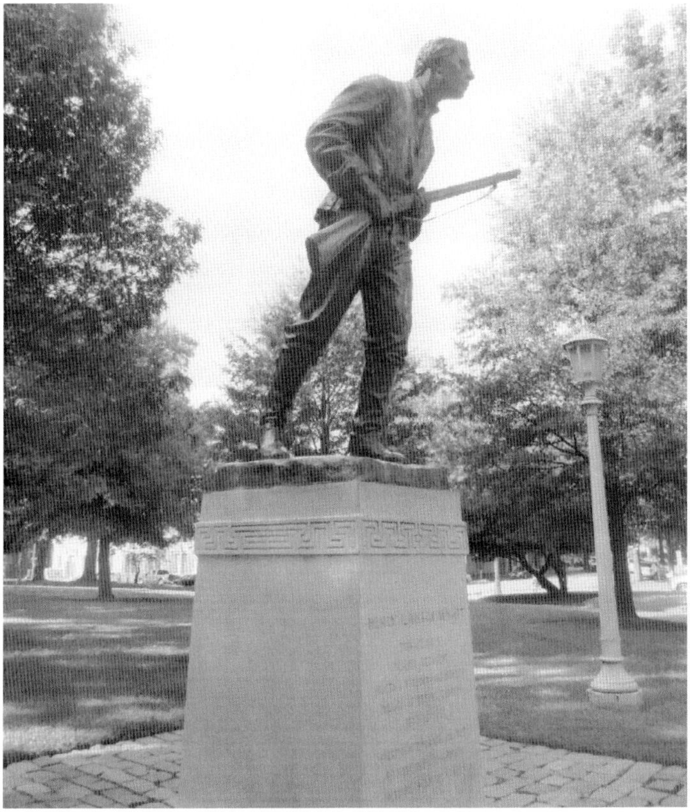

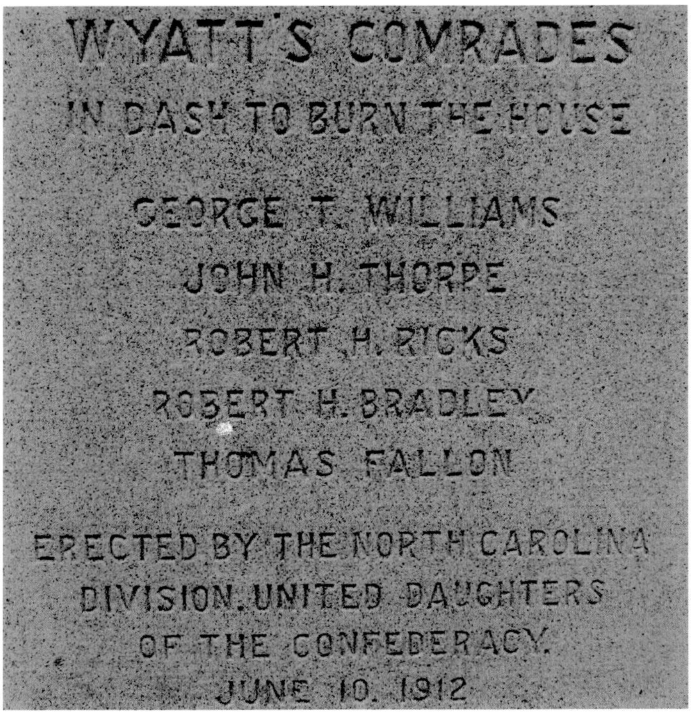

Henry Lawson Wyatt
Henry Lawson Wyatt was a carpenter's apprentice in Tarboro when the Civil War began, and he volunteered to join the militia of Colonel Bridgers, which soon became the 1st North Carolina Regiment. Wyatt was just 19 years old when he trained with his unit before being sent with them to an area near Yorktown, Virginia. He and a few others in his company volunteered to go after a sniper in a house at the Battle of Bethel Church in Virginia on June 10, 1861. Wyatt was shot in the head, and, for the past 150 years, North Carolina has claimed its fallen son to be the first to die in combat during this war. A statue was put up on the Capitol Grounds in Raleigh. One side tells Henry's story, and the other side lists his comrades that were with him that fateful day. (Photographs by the author.)

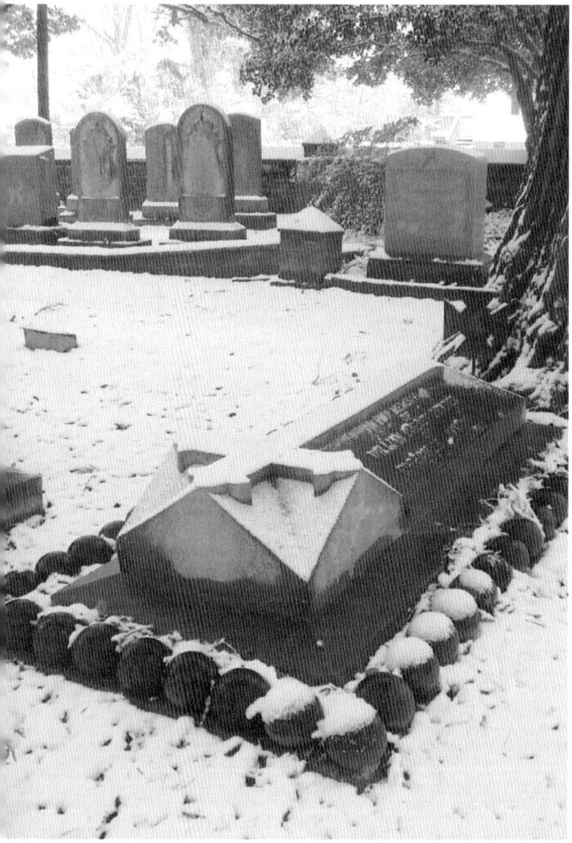

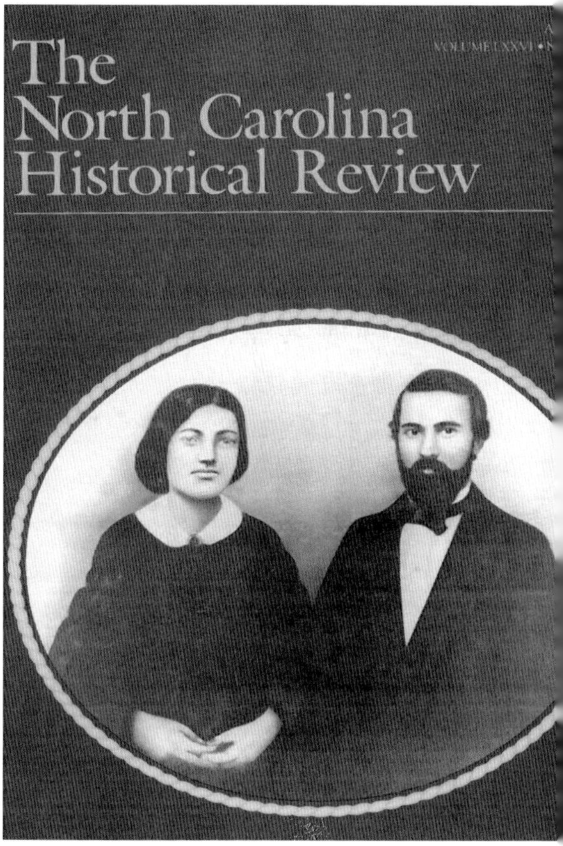

Gen. William Dorsey Pender
West Point graduate Dorsey Pender was the first commander of the 13th North Carolina Regiment. The son of James Pender, he was one of nine children and the only son not to follow his father into farming or to become a merchant. Born in 1834 in what is now Wilson County, Pender had decided at a young age that clerking a store was not for him. He graduated from West Point in 1854, and served in the US Army until the Civil War, whereupon he resigned his commission in the Union Army and joined the Confederate army. Just before the war, Pender married Mary "Fanny" Shepherd, the sister of one his West Point classmates. Pender and Fanny had one son when the war began, with a second on the way. Pender's love for his wife has been preserved in a series of letters that she kept, which were published in the book *The General to His Lady* almost 150 years after his death. Pender was wounded twice in 1862, both times recovering from the wounds and returning to duty. He was not so fortunate at Gettysburg. On the second day of the campaign, he was hit with shrapnel and received a serious wound in his thigh. He was removed from the field against his protests and eventually taken to a hospital in Staunton, Virginia. He developed gangrene, and even though his leg was amputated, the infection spread. He died, two weeks after the battle, on July 18, 1863. His family had been notified of his injury, so his brother David was with him when he died and brought his body home to be buried in Calvary Episcopal Churchyard. A stack of cannonballs marked the grave. Years later, a granite marker in the shape of a cross was placed there, with the cannonballs surrounding it. His wife raised their three sons and was buried beside him in 1922. (Left, photograph by the author; right, courtesy Mrs. William C. Pender, published by NCDAH.)

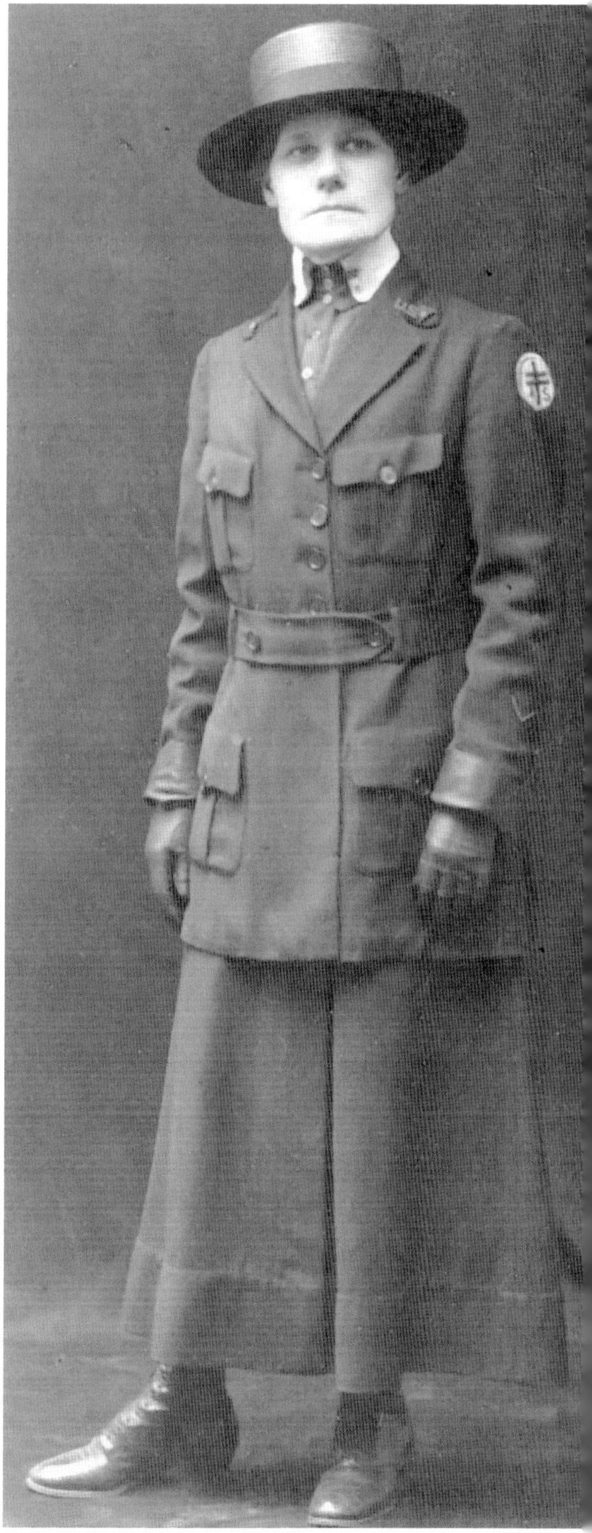

"Miss Mattie" Shackleford

Mattie Shackleford was not an Edgecombe County native, but she spent the last half of her life serving its people. Originally from Virginia, Miss Mattie received her nurse's training in Norfolk. She moved to Tarboro in the early 1900s to work at Pittman Hospital. She volunteered in World War I as a nurse, and it was this experience, perhaps, that led to her strong dedication to helping servicemen and veterans. After the war, she returned to Tarboro, where she was an active Red Cross member all of her life. Her patriotism never waned, and she was the first woman to serve as commander of the local American Legion chapter. She built the Memory Chapel in the Old Town Cemetery (behind Howard Memorial Church) to honor the veterans of the county, and she led parades and programs on Memorial Day, Flag Day, and Independence Day. (Right, courtesy ECML; below, photograph by the author.)

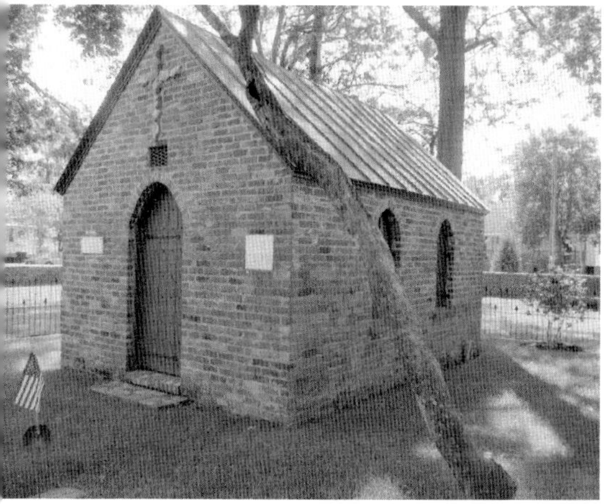

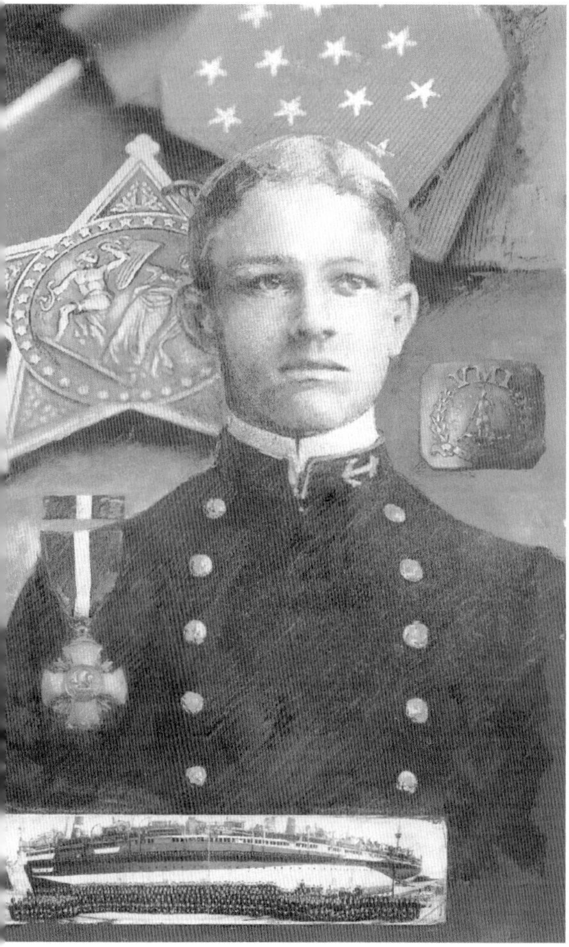

Adm. Aldolphus Staton
The son of a doctor, Staton (TCHOF 2010) went to the Virginia Military Institute for his advanced education. He then transferred to the US Naval Academy, where he graduated in 1902. In 1915, Staton was awarded the Congressional Medal of Honor for "distinguished conduct in battle, engagement of Vera Cruz, 22 April 1914." He served in World War I and retired, but was recalled for World War II. (Portrait by Susan Fecho.)

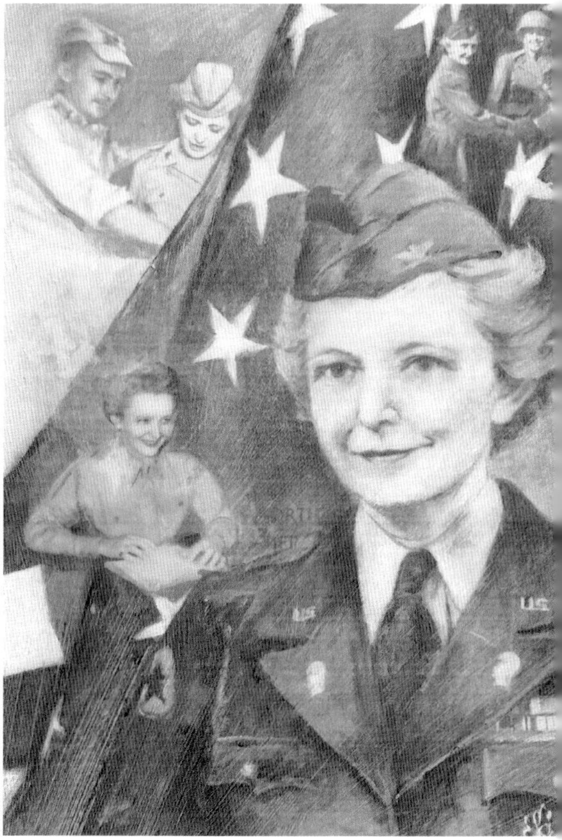

Westray Battle Boyce Long
Volunteering for service in 1942, Westray Battle Boyce Long (TCHOF 2005) earned the rank of colonel before becoming director of the Women's Army Corps (WACS) in 1945. She retired from the WACS in 1947, having won the Legion of Merit and the War Department General Staff Badge. During her military service, she was the highest-ranking woman in the military. Following retirement, Colonel Long spent 25 years in the US Army Officers Reserve Corps. (Portrait by Susan Fecho.)

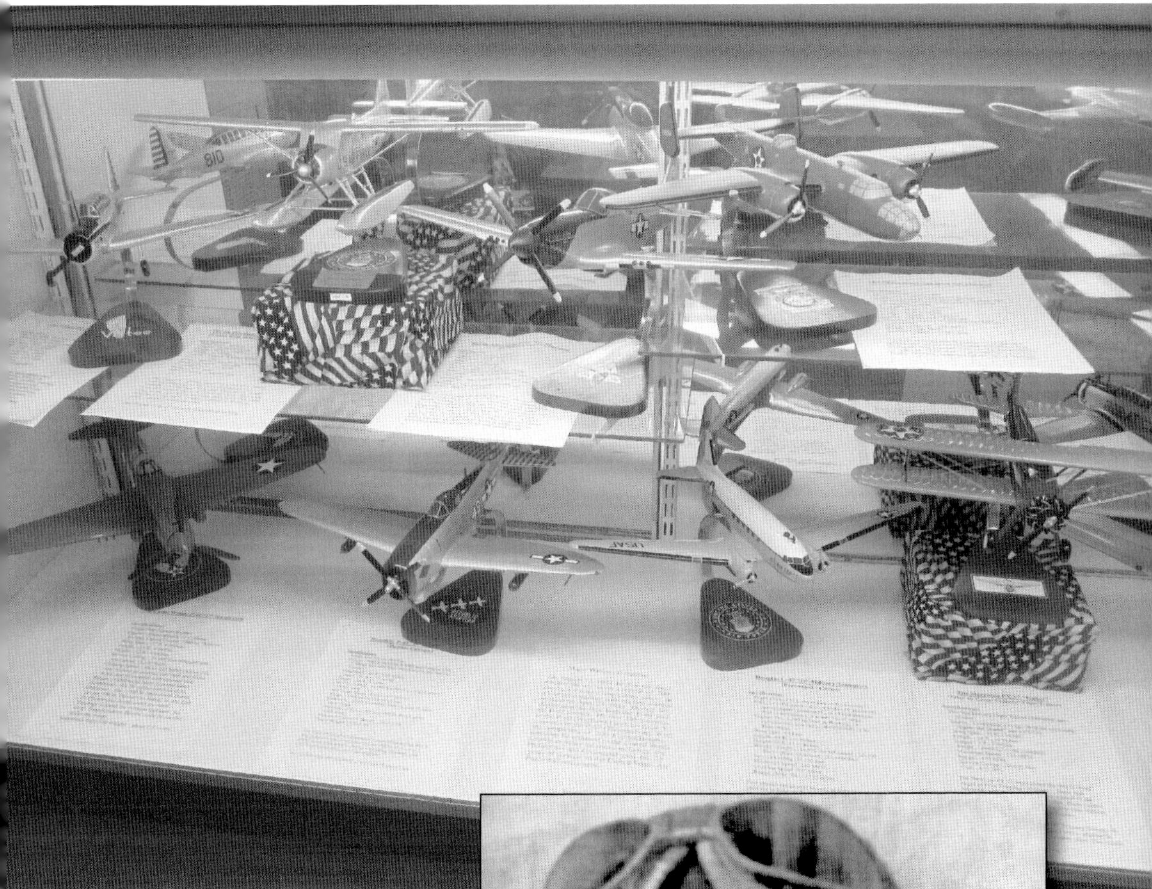

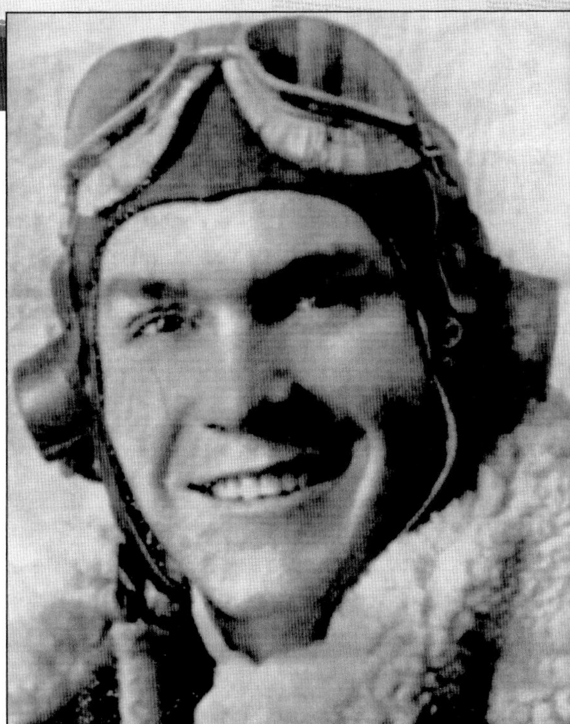

William David Gatlin
Gatlin served 25 years in the Air Force. He enlisted in World War II and set a record of 200 consecutive fighter-bomber missions in Africa, Italy, and southern France. He flew a variety of aircraft including P-40s and P-47s. After the war, he was stationed around the world, including a stint in the Philippines. He retired as a major in 1964. The Edgecombe County Veterans' Military Museum has a special display of models by Gatlin of the various planes he flew and details about his missions. (Above, photograph by the author; right, courtesy ECVMM.)

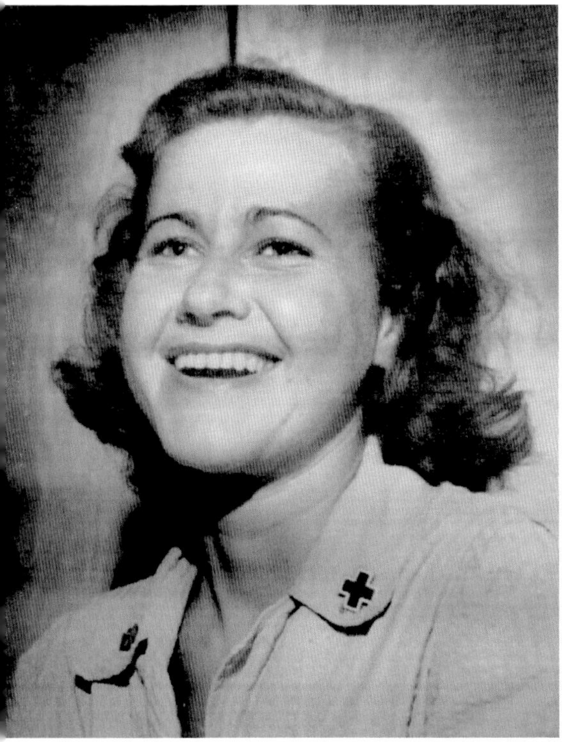

Mary Ferebee Howard
In January 1942, Howard left Tarboro to volunteer her services in the war effort. She ended up in the South Pacific serving at New Caledonia and Guadalcanal, where she worked in service clubs. She met First Lady Eleanor Roosevelt. After the war, she came home and taught school for more than 30 years. She retold her experiences in *No Drums, No Trumpets*, published in 1992. (Courtesy ECVMM.)

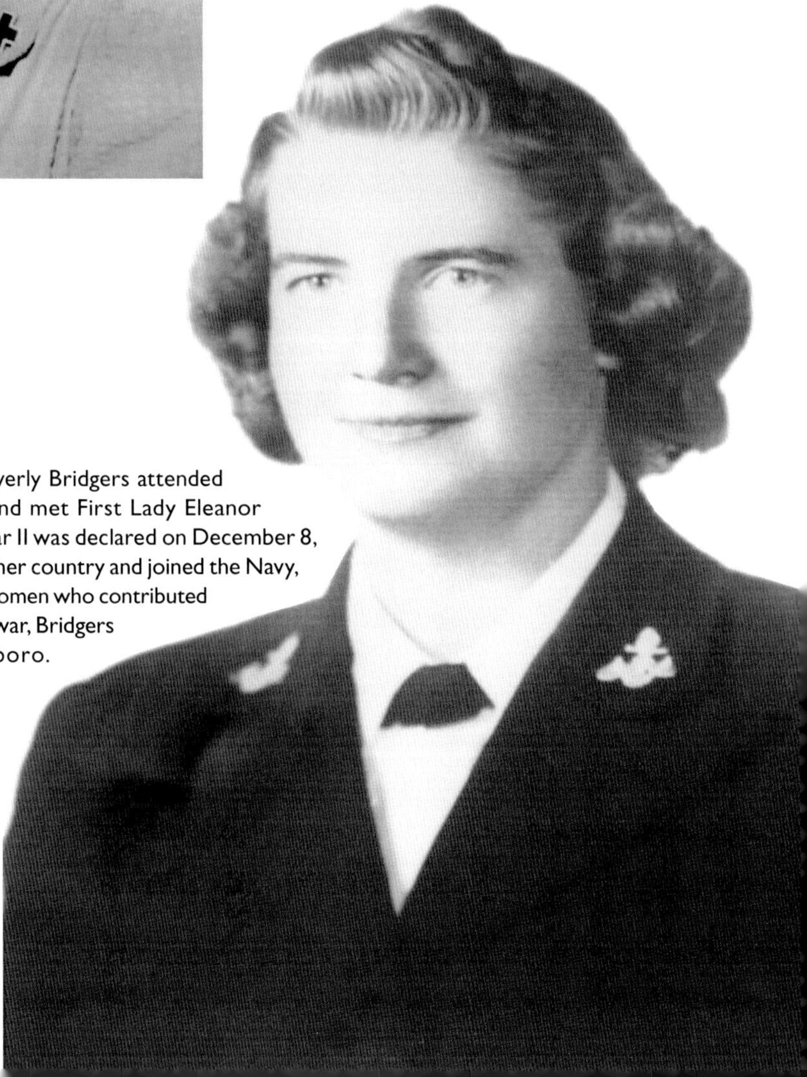

Beverly Bridgers
On December 5, 1941, Beverly Bridgers attended a program in Greenville and met First Lady Eleanor Roosevelt. After World War II was declared on December 8, Beverly decided to support her country and joined the Navy, becoming one of the many women who contributed to the war effort. After the war, Bridgers returned home to Tarboro. (Courtesy ECVMM.)

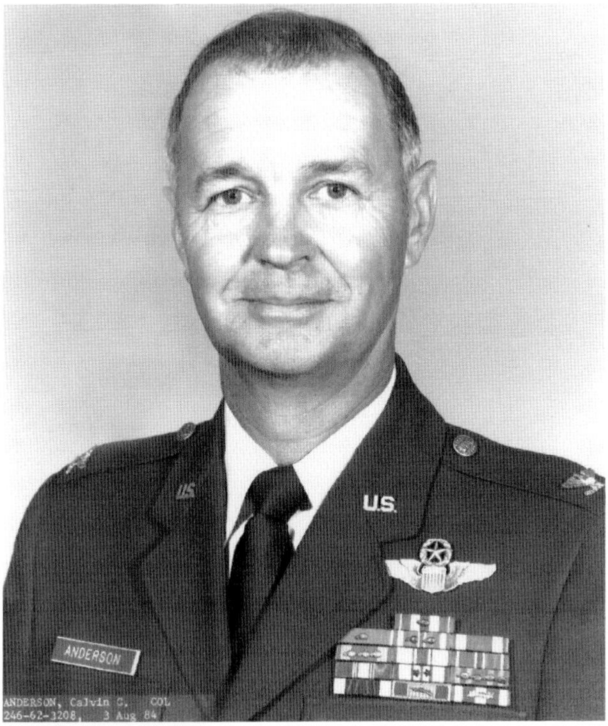

Calvin Anderson
Anderson spent 28 years in the Air Force, including service as a pilot in Vietnam. He has been active with the creation of the Tarboro Veterans Memorial and the Edgecombe County Veterans' Military Museum. He serves as chairman of the museum's board. Anderson also served 12 years as an Edgecombe County commissioner. (Courtesy ECVMM.)

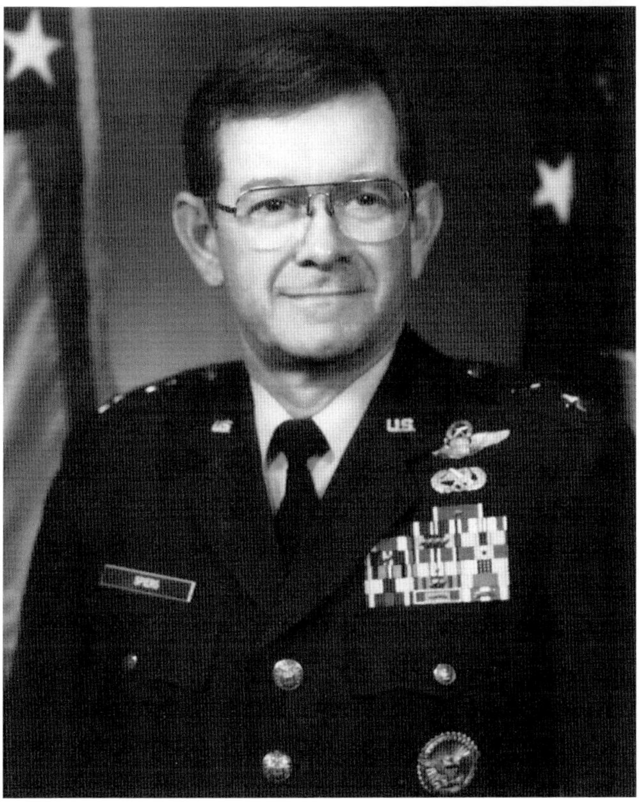

Gen. Joseph Speirs
Tarboro High graduate Speirs already had a pilot's license before he went off to college at NC State, where he enlisted in the ROTC. Upon graduation from college, he was sent to flight school in Texas and eventually became a flight instructor. He flew over 100 combat missions in Vietnam and has been stationed all over the United States. He was presented the Legion of Merit and Distinguished Flying Cross. Speirs retired as a major general. (Courtesy ECVMM.)

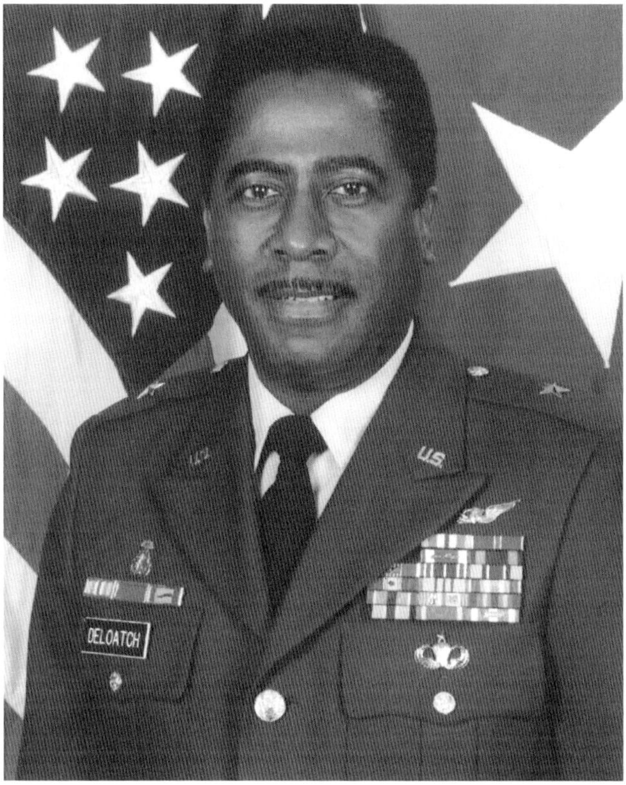

Gen. Vonaree Deloatch
The first person in his family to ever attend college, Deloatch went to the North Carolina Agricultural & Technical State University and enrolled in the ROTC. He served in Vietnam, Bosnia, Sarajevo, Saudi Arabia, and Kuwait. After his tour in Vietnam, he earned a master's degree in public administration from Howard University and joined the Army Reserves, where he spent the next 23 years. Deloatch spent 35 years in the military and retired as a brigadier general. (Courtesy ECVMM.)

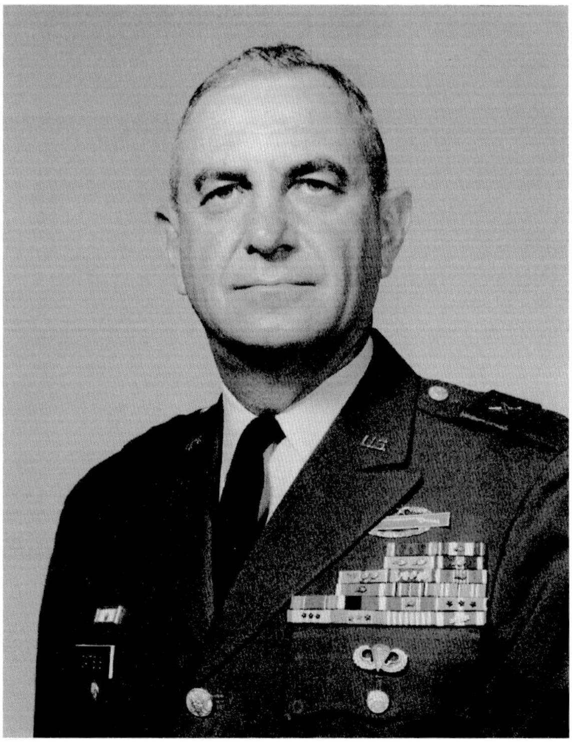

Gen. Andrew John Gatsis
Gatsis spent 36 years in the US Army and had several overseas assignments. A native of Alabama, Gatsis attended West Point, graduating in 1945. He was a paratrooper and served in the Korean War, where he received the Distinguished Service Cross. He also spent two tours in Vietnam. Gatsis received every major decoration of valor, including two Silver Stars, two Bronze Stars, 27 Air Medals and two Purple Hearts. He retired to his wife's hometown of Rocky Mount as a brigadier general. (Courtesy Gatsis family.)

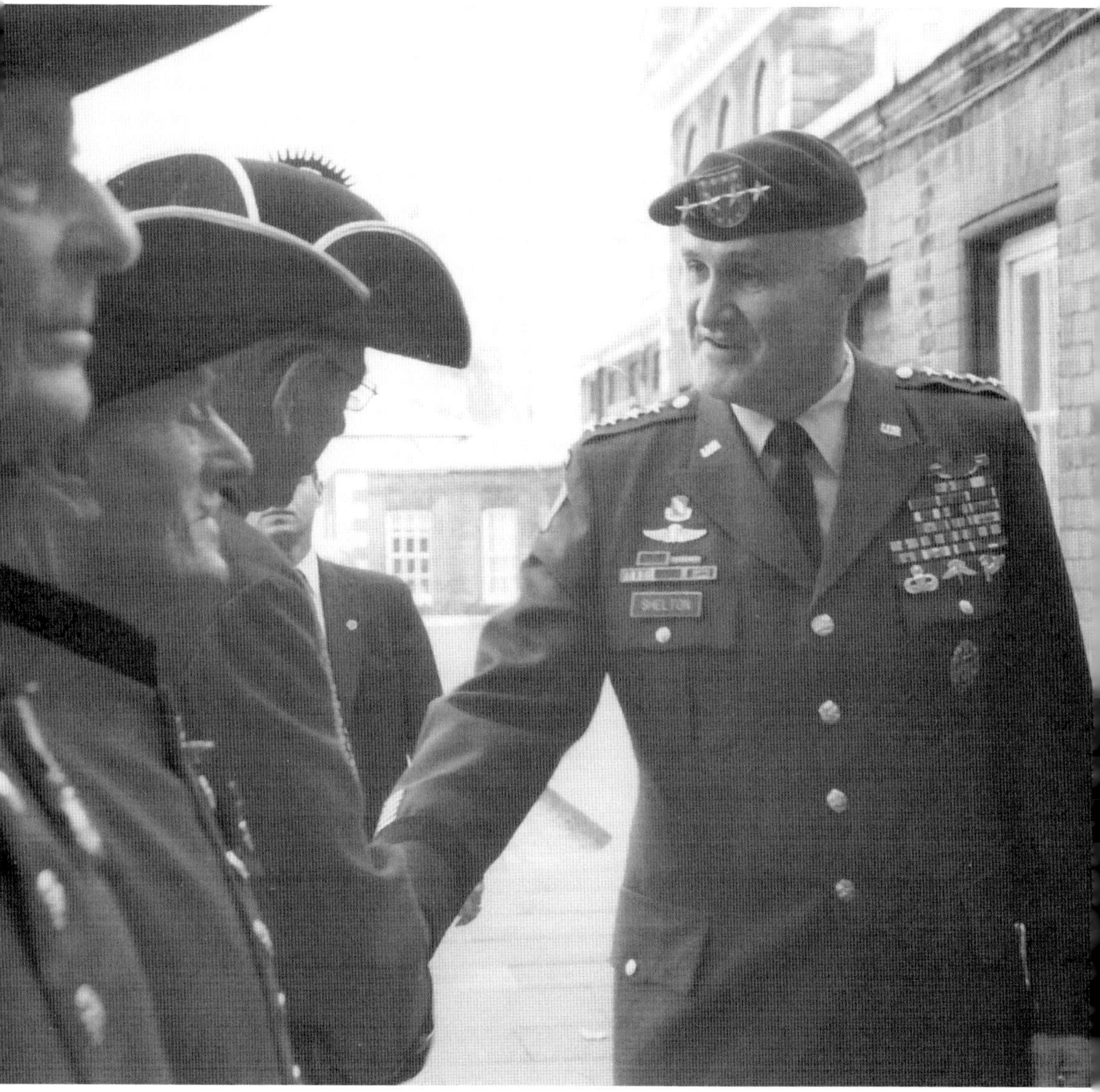

Gen. Henry Hugh Shelton

General Shelton (TCHOF 2004) is a former chairman of the Joint Chiefs of Staff under Presidents Clinton and Bush (1997–2001). He has received the Congressional Gold Medal, the Defense Distinguished Service Medal, Legion of Merit, Bronze Star, Purple Heart, and Meritorious Service Medal, and he has been knighted by Queen Elizabeth II. Shelton was born in Tarboro, North Carolina, on January 2, 1942, and graduated from North Edgecombe High School in 1959. He received his bachelor's degree from NC State in 1963 and his master's degree from Auburn University in 1973. He graduated from the National War College in 1983. (Courtesy General Shelton.)

Rocky Mount Veterans Memorial

The Veterans Memorial at Jack Laughery Park in Rocky Mount was dedicated on Veterans Day in 2007. It is located on the site of the first Hardee's restaurant. Laughery, a veteran, was chief executive officer of Hardee's. The memorial was funded by contributions made by local individuals and businesses to the city. In addition to the marble monument with the flags, there are two granite posts with bronze plaques honoring two Congressional Medal of Honor recipients: Aldophus Staton, of Edgecombe County, and Harold Bascom Durham Jr., of Rocky Mount. The memorial is "in honor of all men and women who served their country in the United States armed services." (Photograph by the author.)

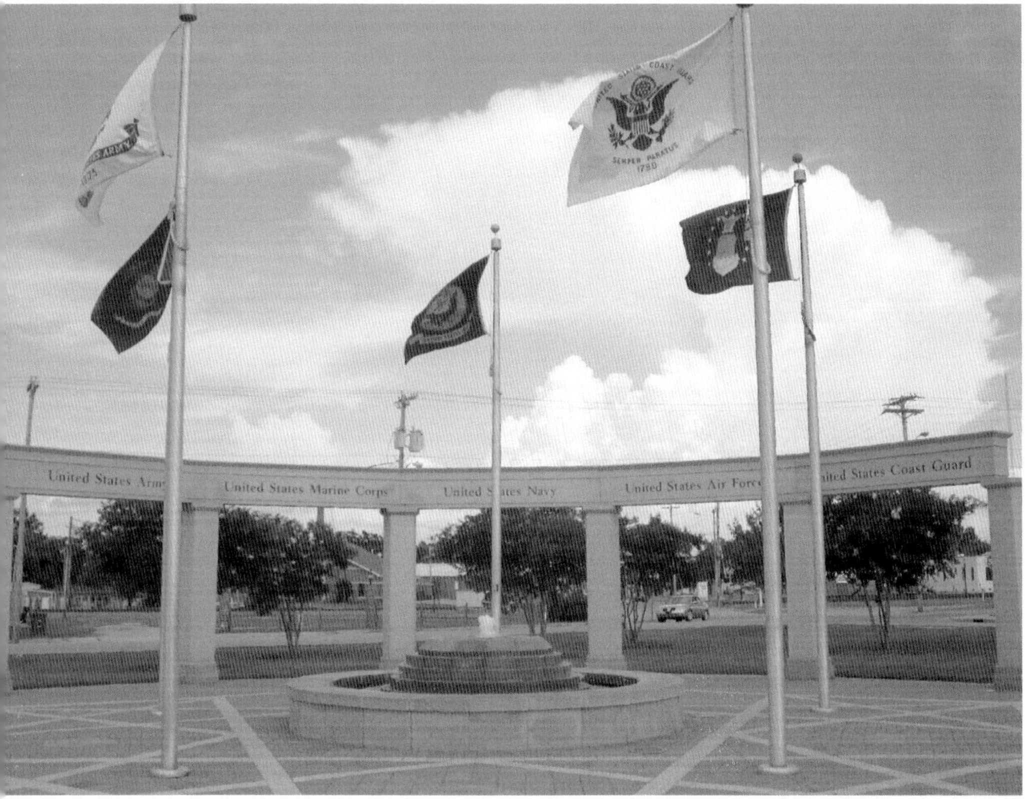

Tarboro Veterans Memorial (OPPOSITE PAGE)

Joel Bourne led a campaign along with Col. J.W. Wood to construct a memorial on the Tarboro Town Common where other military memorials stand. They were successful in raising $80,000 for the granite memorial, which features six flagpoles—one for each branch of the military, with the central pole for the American flag. The memorial was dedicated on Veterans Day in 2002 and includes benches and plaques around the base. Each month, the Golden K Kiwanis Club has a flag raising in honor of a local veteran. Family members of the selected veteran watch as a flag is raised, and the audience hears about the military service of the individual. A special display table with the veteran's photograph and memorabilia is set up at the Edgecombe County Veterans' Military Museum. (Photograph by the author.)

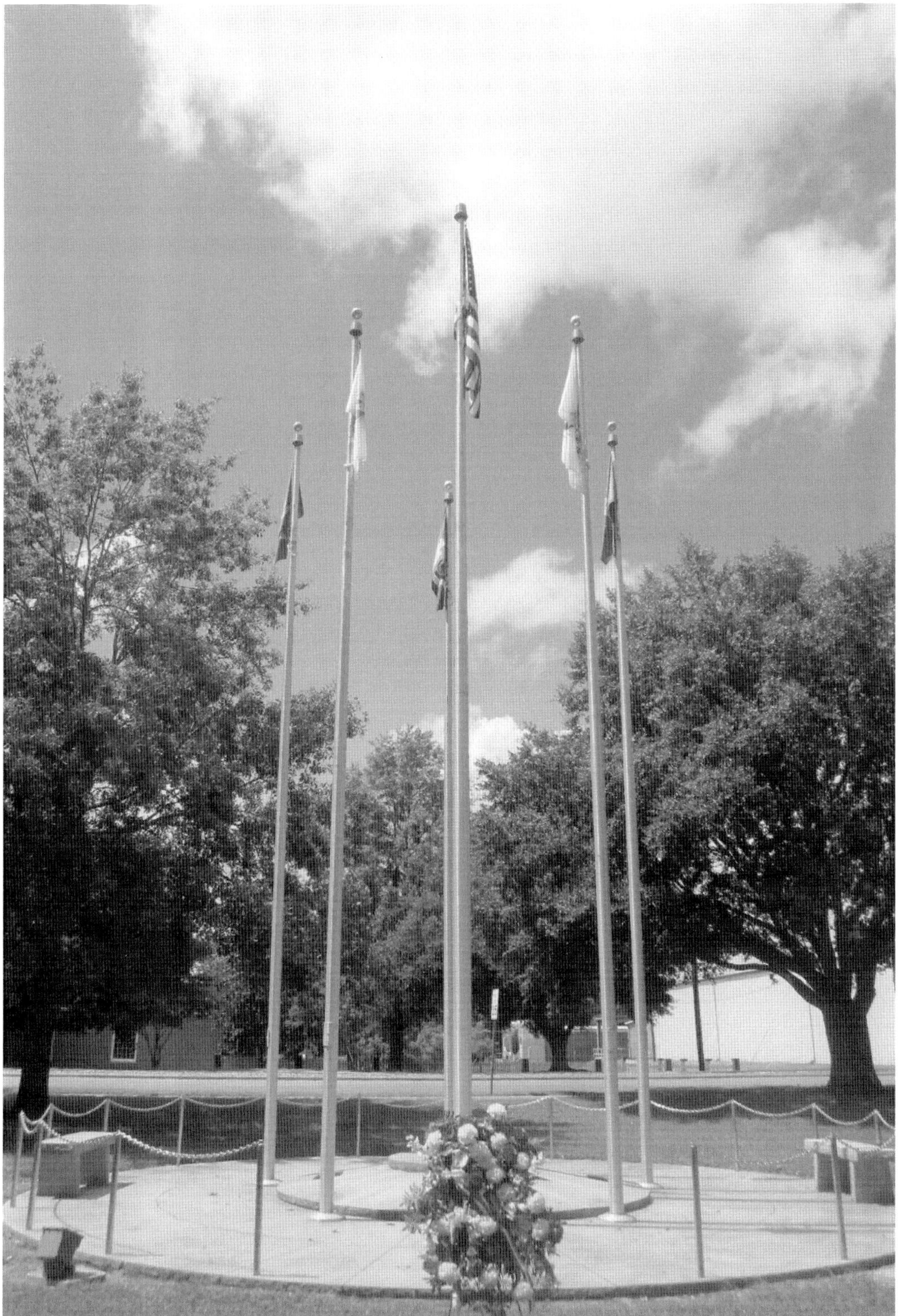

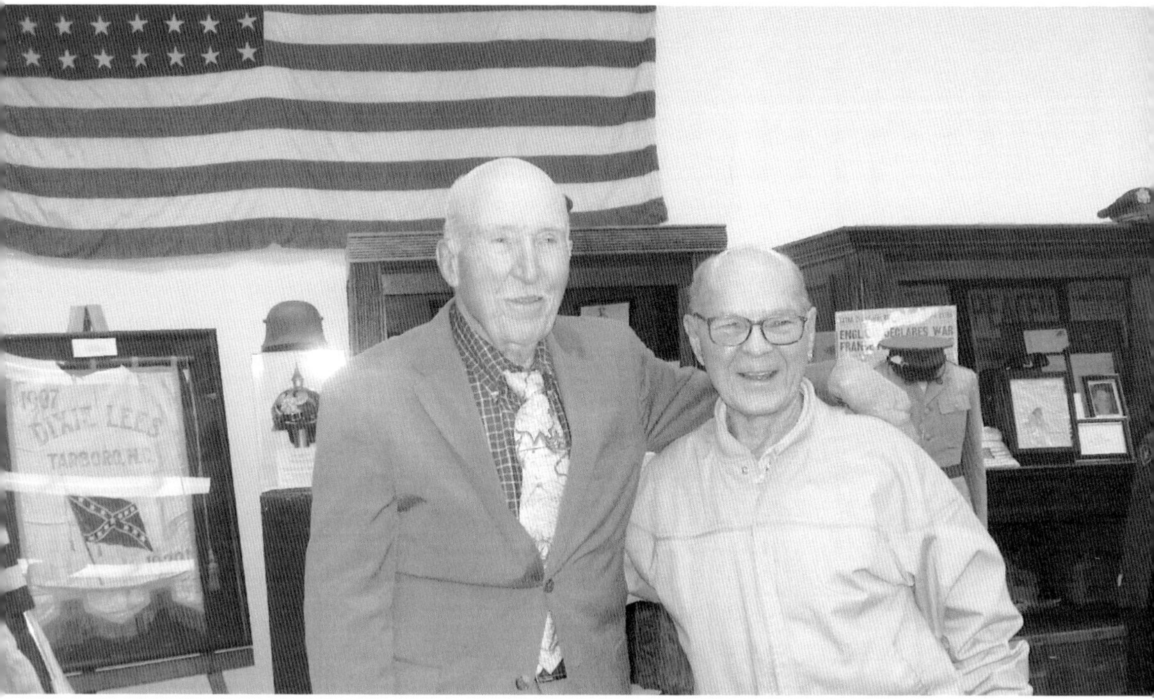

Joel Bourne and Edgecombe County Veterans' Military Museum

Bourne (TCHOF 2008) grew up in Edgecombe County and graduated from Tarboro High School in 1942. He served with the US Marines in the Pacific during World War II. After the war, Joel earned his law degree from UNC and returned to Tarboro, where he practiced for 30 years. In retirement, Joel continued to manage his farm and began a second career in community service. He was founder of the Edgecombe Forestry Club, a charter member of the Edgecombe Beekeeper Association, and warden at Calvary Episcopal Church. He also volunteered with the local Red Cross chapter, Habitat for Humanity, and at Heritage Hospital. Bourne gave land to the Town of Tarboro for its athletic complex and led the campaign for the Edgecombe Livestock Arena (he donated land for that facility, too). Perhaps his most notable legacy is in his recognition of veterans. He led successful campaigns for a veterans' memorial and museum, bringing about the Edgecombe County Veterans' Military Museum. Located on Church Street in Tarboro (in the old police department), the museum has photographs of more than 800 veterans and artifacts including uniforms, military tools, weapons captured from enemies, and even a restored jeep. The organization recognizes veterans from all branches of service, and it is staffed entirely by volunteers. Joel purchased the old 1919 Colonial Theatre, got others involved in its restoration, and then donated the building to the Veterans' Military Museum. In this image, Bourne (right) is showing National Park Historian Emeritus (and fellow World War II veteran) Ed Bearss around the museum. (Photograph by the author.)

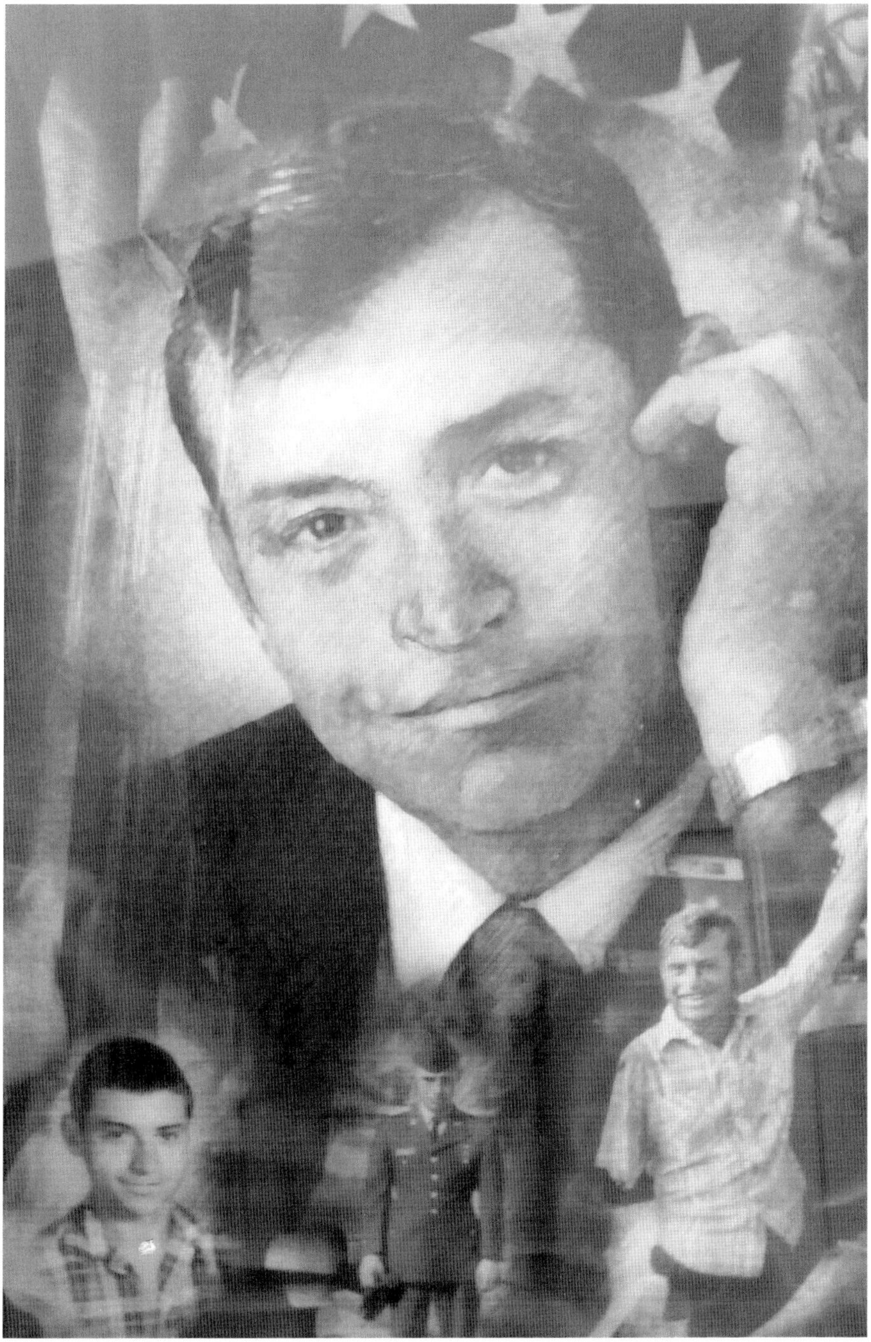

James Edwards "Butch" Robbins

Butch Robbins (TCHOF 2012) grew up on a farm in southern Edgecombe County. Robbins joined the US Army in 1967 and was sent to Vietnam. In 1968, he stepped on a mine and lost both legs and an arm. He returned to North Carolina to the farm life he knew well. Later, he became an auctioneer with Goins and Harris. In 1993, he began his own auction firm. Robbins wrote *So You Think Times Are Tough!* and became a motivational speaker, encouraging others to succeed as he has. (Portrait by Susan Fecho.)

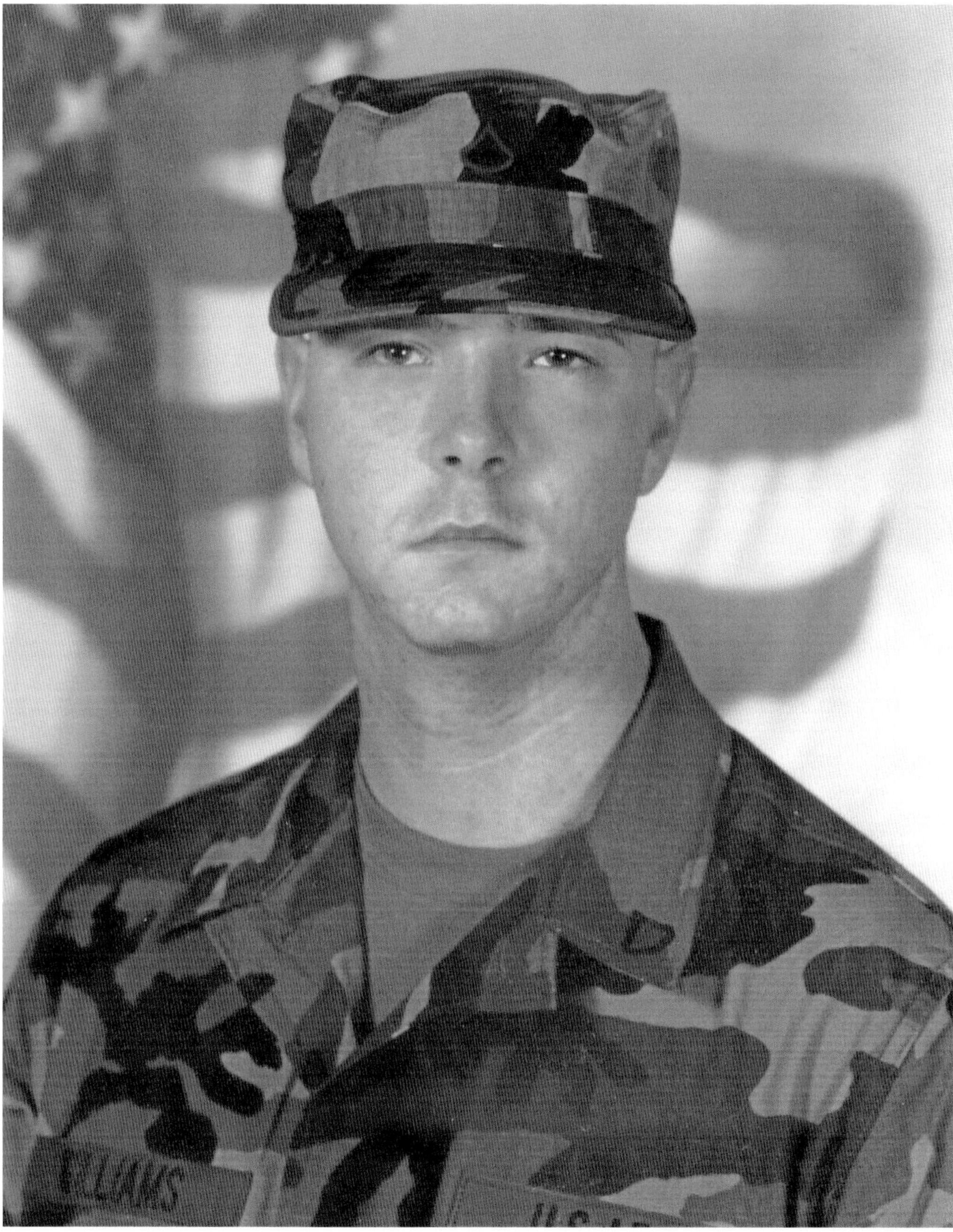

Sgt. David Blake Williams
A 2000 graduate of Tarboro High School, Blake Williams joined the National Guard in 2003. He served in the 1132nd Military Police Company based at the National Guard Center in Rocky Mount. He served one tour in Iraq and was awarded the Combat Action Badge and the Army Commendation Medal. Sergeant Williams served a second tour in 2008. He was killed, along with two others, when a roadside bomb exploded near his Humvee. Williams was the first—and, to date, only—Edgecombe soldier to die in Iraq or Afghanistan. He was 26 years old. (Courtesy ECVMM.)

CHAPTER EIGHT

Sports

An appreciation for athletes has been part of Twin County history since the beginning of the 20th century, when both Rocky Mount and Tarboro had minor-league baseball teams. The Rocky Mount Leafs and the Tarboro Tars were part of the Coastal Plains Division. The sport was so popular that, at one time, there was a diamond on the Tarboro Town Common to support youngsters playing baseball. Today, both Rocky Mount and Tarboro have city ballparks for Little League and community teams. In addition to baseball, golf has been a popular activity in the area since one of the first nine-hole courses in the state opened in Tarboro in 1899. Today, there are at least five golf courses in the Twin Counties. But most athletic recognition appears on the high school level, and the area high schools have produced some exceptional athletes. Some were recognized as outstanding players in college, while others went on to careers with professional teams. Three athletes competed in the Olympic Games. It is not just the players who are recognized, though. There have been some outstanding coaches who have taken teams to state championships again and again—Sandra Langley in girls' basketball and Herman Boone, Raymond Cobb, and Jeff Craddock in football. The book *The Blackbirds* described the outstanding seasons at Rocky Mount High in the 1960s in multiple sports. Not all the players were in the big three sports of football, basketball, and baseball. Harvie Ward was a championship golfer. Lee Carrol and Michael Stokes won state wrestling titles and competed on the national level in college.

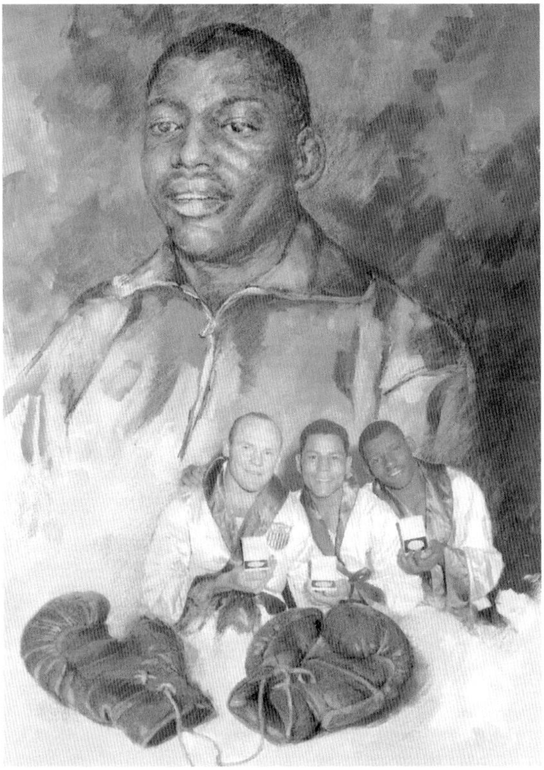

Olympian James Boyd
James Boyd (TCHOF 2009) of Rocky Mount joined the Army after graduating from Booker T. Washington High School. While in the Army, he qualified for the 1956 Summer Olympics (held in Melbourne, Australia), where he won a gold medal in the light heavyweight class. (Portrait by Susan Fecho.)

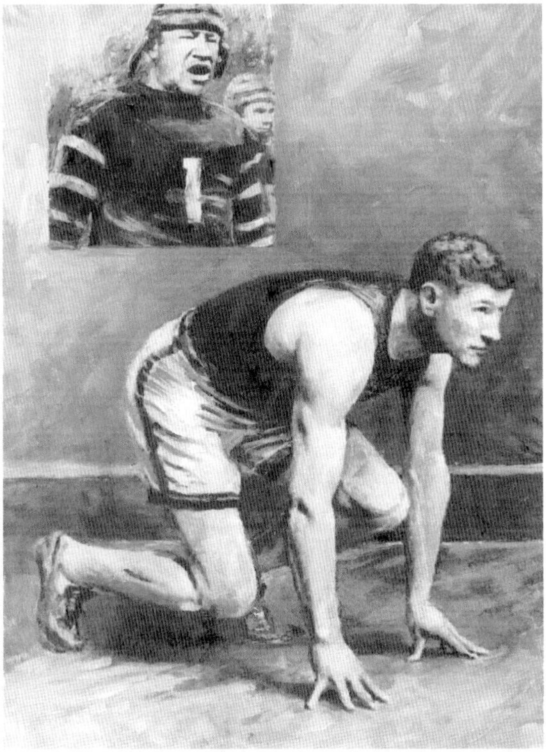

Olympian Jim Thorpe
Olympic gold medalist James "Jim" Thorpe (TCHOF 2005) was born in Oklahoma Indian Territory. He is the only person ever to win both the Olympic pentathlon and the decathlon. He also played major-league baseball and professional football, for which he was the first premier player. Thorpe served as the first president of the American Professional Football Association (now the NFL). Thorpe played baseball for a Rocky Mount minor-league team before his appearance in the 1912 Olympics, and his medals were stripped but later reinstated. (Portrait by Susan Fecho.)

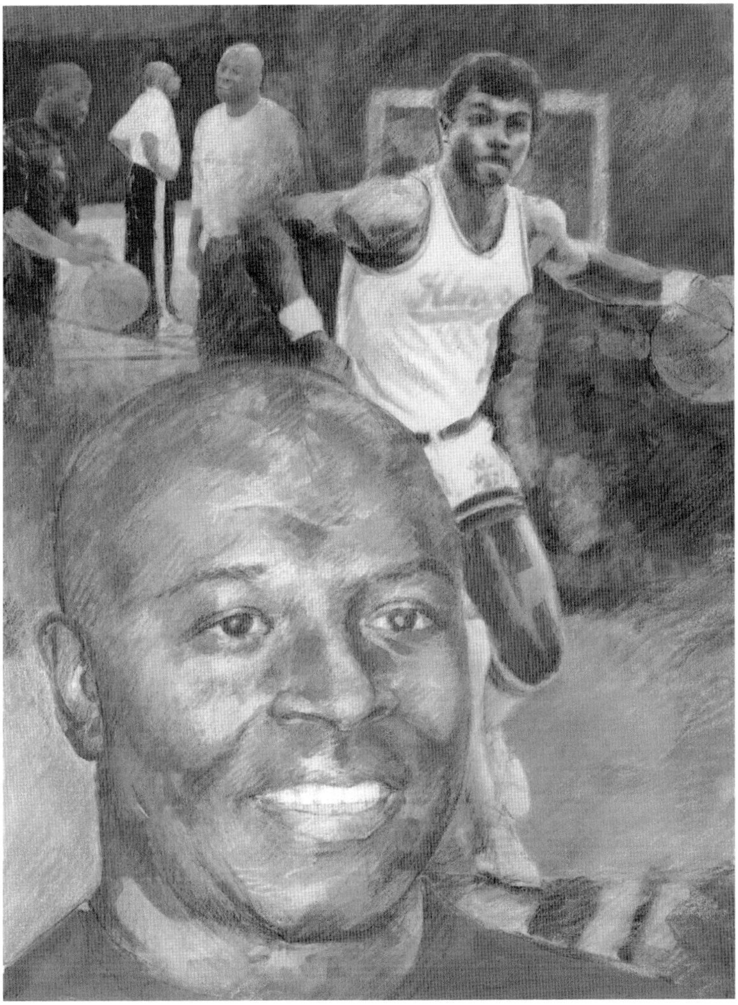

Phil Ford

Phil Ford (TCHOF 2008) graduated from Rocky Mount High in 1974. At UNC, he scored 2,290 points—an all-time basketball record. He won a gold medal in the 1976 Olympics as a member of the US Basketball Team. In 1978, he was the ACC Player of the Year; he was also named the "National Player of the Year" by the US Basketball Writers Association, the National Association of Basketball Coaches, and *Sporting News*. (Portrait by Susan Fecho.)

Charles Linwood "Buck" Williams

Williams (TCHOF 2006) led his Rocky Mount High School team to the 4A state championship in 1978. He played three years for the University of Maryland, leading the ACC in rebounds. Williams played professional basketball for 17 years with the New Jersey Nets, the Portland Trailblazers, and the New York Knicks. During that time, he played in three all-star games. He retired in 1999 after scoring 16,000 points in his career. Williams also served as president of the NBA Players Association. (Portrait by Susan Fecho.)

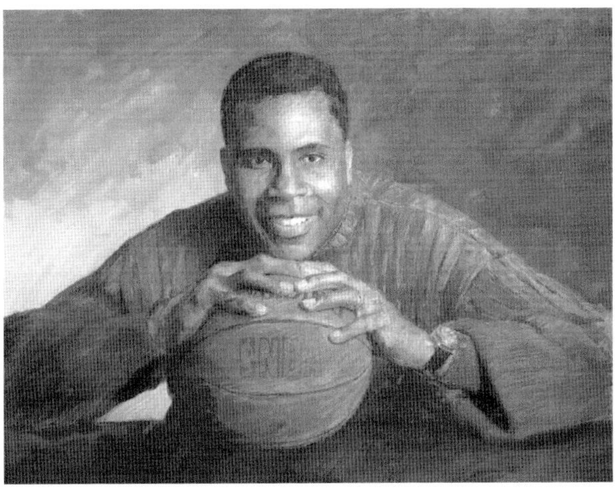

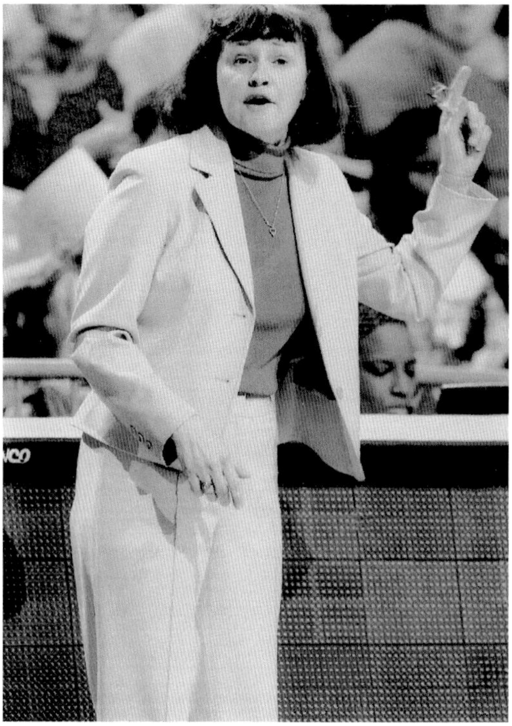

Sandra Langley

Langley (TCHOF 2005) graduated from South Edgecombe High School, Atlantic Christian (now Barton) College, and East Carolina University. She was elected to the Barton College Athletic Hall of Fame in 1992. She has been athletic director at SouthWest Edgecombe High since 1991, where she has coached the girls' basketball team to four state championships. She is the only coach to be named "North Carolina Coach of the Year" by the Associated Press four times, and she has more wins than any other women's basketball coach in North Carolina, according to the North Carolina High School Athletic Association. (Courtesy Sandra Langley.)

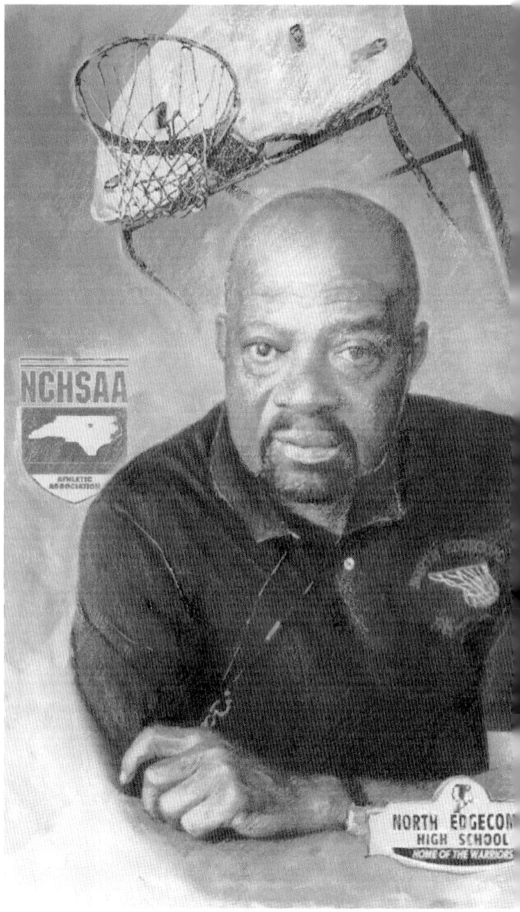

Warren Ray Jones

A lifetime member of the North Carolina Coaches Association, Jones (TCHOF 2010) coached basketball for 30 years and took his teams to six conference tournament championships, as well as 14 consecutive state playoffs. He had an overall record was 491 wins and 291 losses and was honored as "Coach of the Year" four times. He taught for 36 years in Edgecombe County, and the North Edgecombe Gym has been named in his honor. (Portrait by Susan Fecho.)

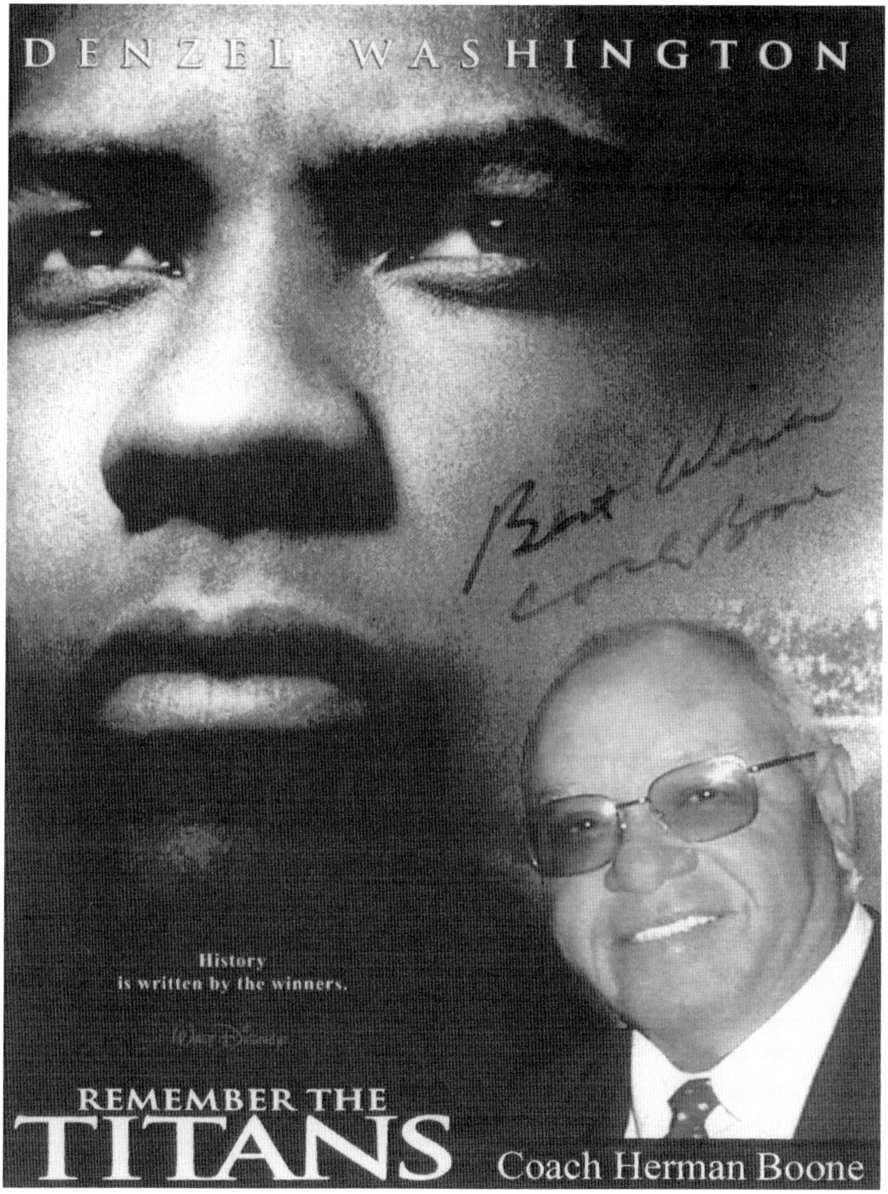

Herman Ike Boone
One of 12 children of Frank and Daisy Boone, Herman Boone (TCHOF 2006) graduated from Booker T. Washington High School in Rocky Mount. After graduating from North Carolina Central University with both a bachelor's and a master's degree, Boone began his teaching and coaching career in Virginia. He returned to North Carolina in 1961 as a coach in Williamston. In nine years, Coach Boone had five regional championships and two state championships. In 1971, he went to Alexandria, Virginia, where he became the head coach of an integrated high school football team, leading them to a 13-0 record, state championship victory, and a second-place national ranking. These successes are depicted in the film *Remember the Titans*. Boone is a generous contributor, both in supporting youth and addressing other community needs. (Courtesy Herman Ike Boone.)

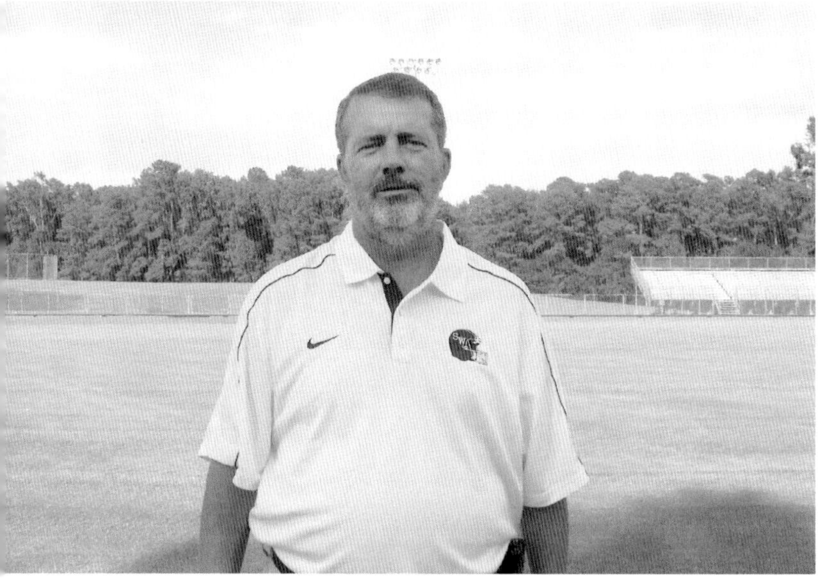

Raymond Vines Cobb
Sometimes called a football legend, Cobb coached the sport for 25 years in Edgecombe County. His teams won two state championships while he was at North Edgecombe. His overall record is 253-79, covering his years at both North Edgecombe High School and SouthWest Edgecombe High School, the latter of which he retired from at the end of the 2012 football season. (Photograph by Sandra Langley.)

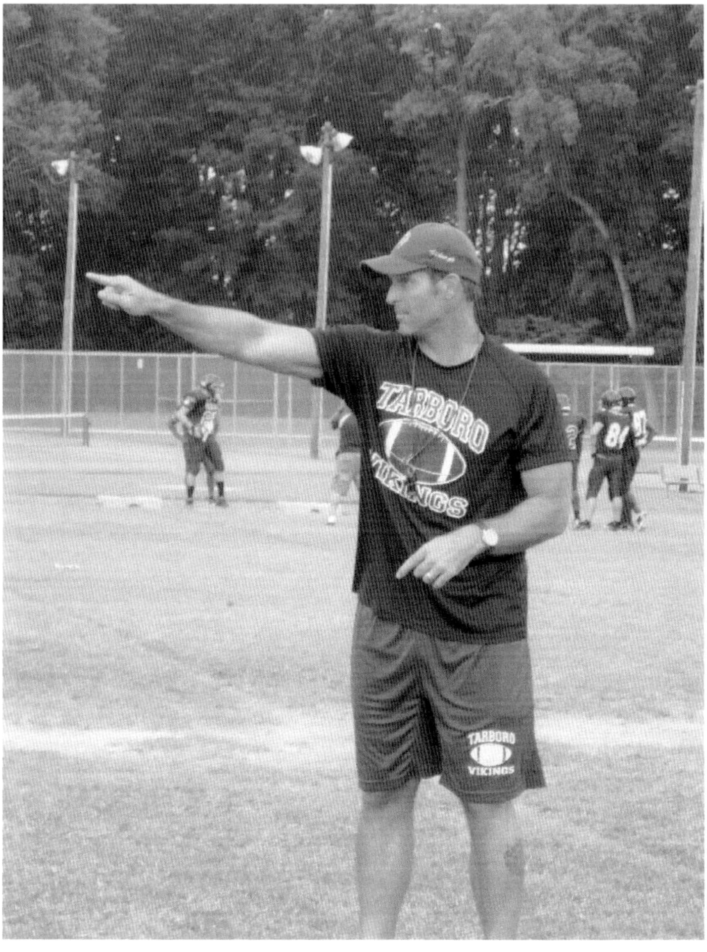

Jeff Craddock
Tarboro High football coach Craddock led his teams to five consecutive North Carolina High School 2A state championship games, winning three back-to-back titles. He has had a winning record of 72-6 since 2008. He was named the Edgecombe County "Coach of the Year" in 2011 and was second in votes for the Associated Press "Coach of the Year" in North Carolina in 2011. (Photograph by the author.)

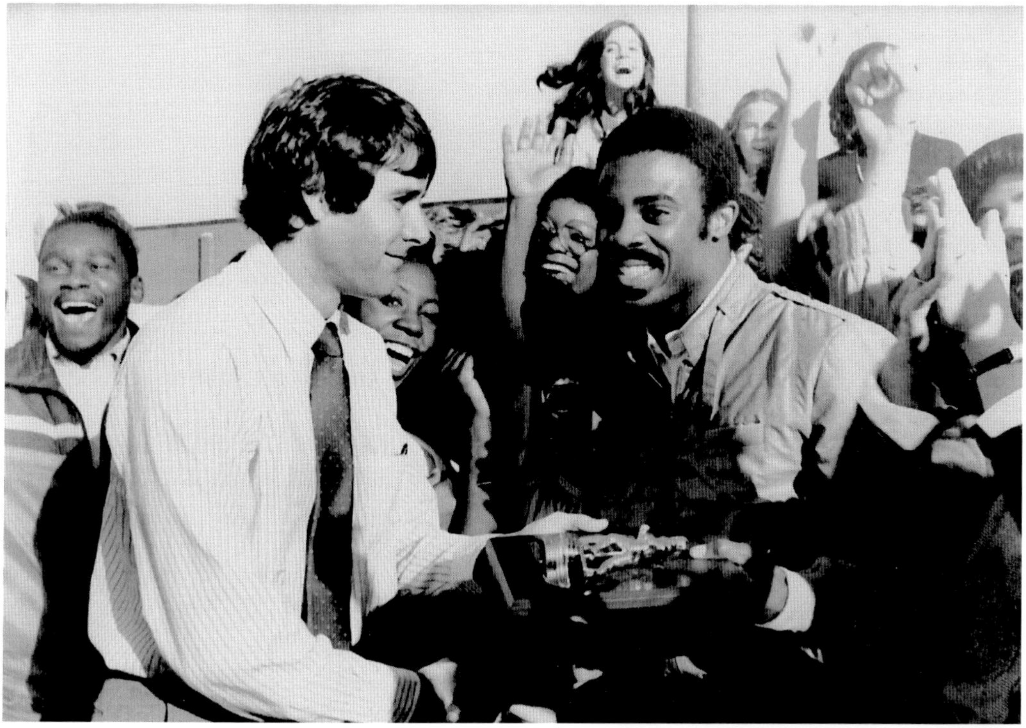

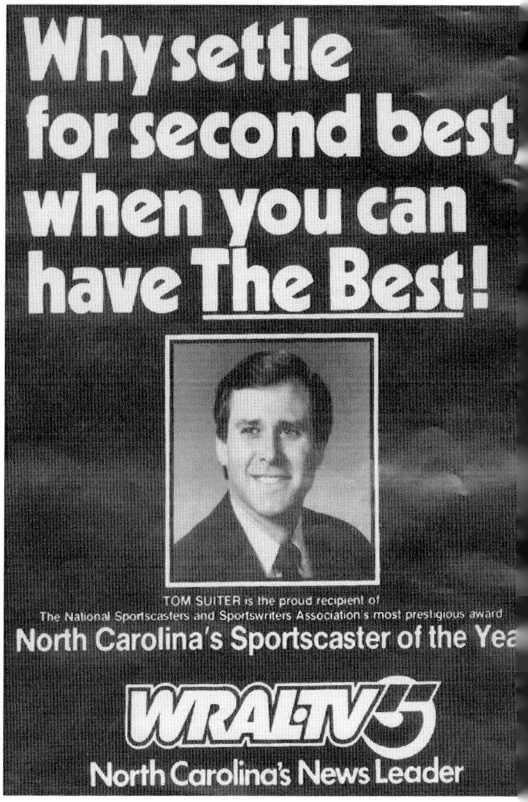

Tom Suiter

Born and raised in Rocky Mount, Suiter majored in history at Erskine College in South Carolina. His enthusiasm for athletics, however, had him playing basketball and writing for the campus newspaper. He joined WRAL-TV in Raleigh in 1971, where he did the weekend and morning news. In 1981, Suiter became sports anchor, and the station sought a new promotion to encourage viewership. The Extra Effort Award was launched, and for 30 years, it has continued to recognize high school athletes who have special qualities or who stand out off the playing field as well as on it. In the first year of the Extra Effort Award, Suiter presented the trophy to wide receiver Ken Weaver of Rocky Mount Senior High. Suiter also launched "Football Friday," a special broadcast that reviews area high school games after the late news and has been airing for 32 years. He has won two Emmy awards out of 17 nominations and was inducted into the North Carolina High School Athletic Association Hall of Fame. In 1987, Suiter was recognized by *Radio TV Age* magazine as one of the three best local sports anchors in the nation. He was named "North Carolina Sportscaster of the Year" in 1990. (Both, courtesy Tom Suiter.)

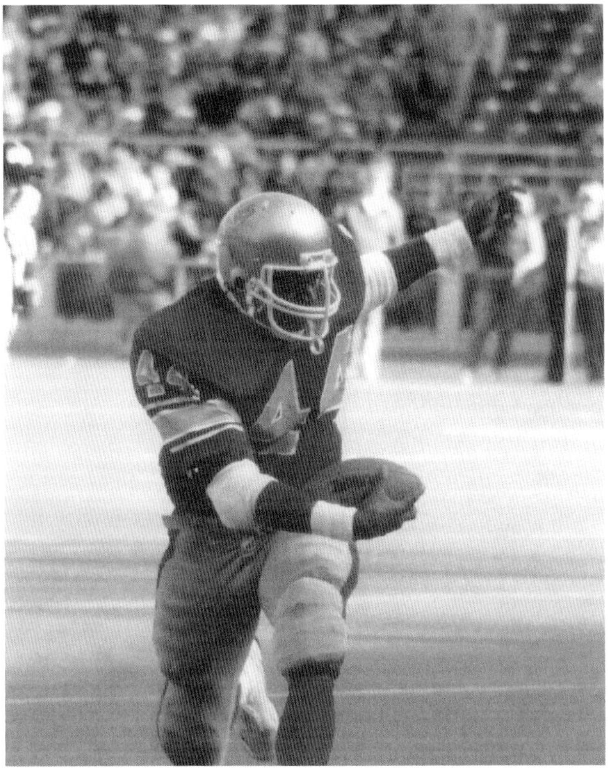

Kelvin Leroy Bryant
An all-round athlete, Bryant (TCHOF 2008) played basketball, football, and baseball and also ran track at Tarboro High School. At UNC, he was called "the finest back in college football" and was a Heisman candidate in 1981. Bryant was drafted to the US Football League and played for the Philadelphia Stars. He was recognized as the league's "Player of the Year" and MVP in 1983. As a Washington Redskin, Kelvin scored 20 touchdowns over the course of 46 games. (Courtesy Kelvin Leroy Bryant.)

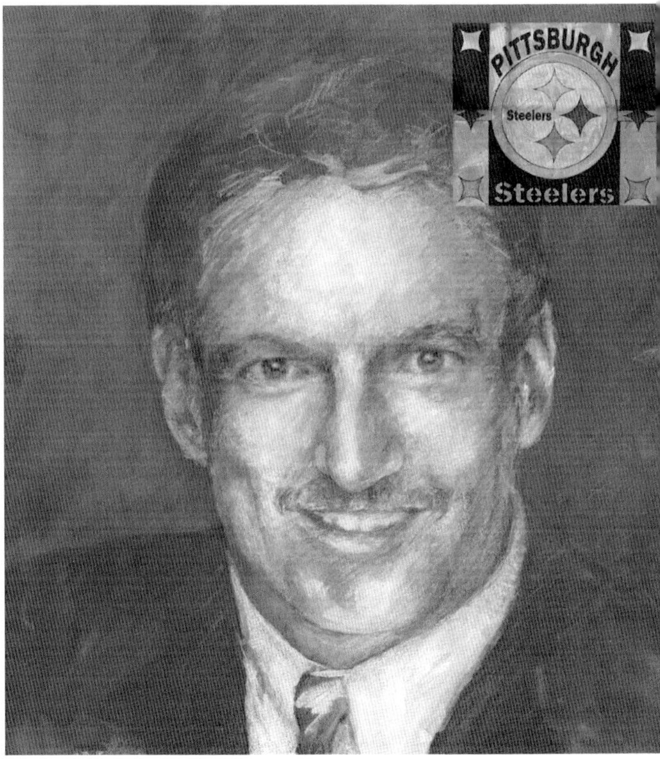

James T. "Jimmy" Clack
Jimmy Clack (TCHOF 2007) played football and basketball at Rocky Mount Senior High and represented the school in the 1964 Shrine Bowl. He earned a degree in history and political science from Wake Forest University in 1969 while playing football and basketball there. He spent 13 years in the NFL (nine as a Pittsburgh Steeler and four as a New York Giant), during which time he played in 146 games and earned two Super Bowl rings. He was president and chief executive officer of Impact International in Greensboro and was active in his community, serving on the board or as a volunteer for area chapters of the American Heart Association, Multiple Sclerosis Foundation, American Lung Society, local hospice, YMCA, and Boys and Girls Club. Clack died on April 7, 2006. (Portrait by Susan Fecho.)

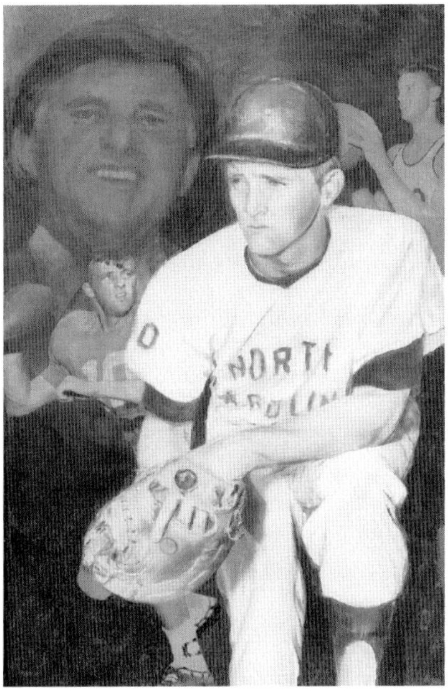

Joseph Daniel "Danny" Talbott
North Carolina Sports Hall of Fame 2004 inductee Talbott (TCHOF 2004) led the Rocky Mount Blackbirds to state championships in baseball, basketball, and football in his senior year in 1963. Talbott was all-conference and all-state in all three sports both his junior and senior years. He was the ACC "Football Player of the Year" in 1965 and ACC "Athlete of the Year" in 1966. Talbott was a two-sport star at the University of North Carolina and went on to play professional football and baseball. (Portrait by Susan Fecho.)

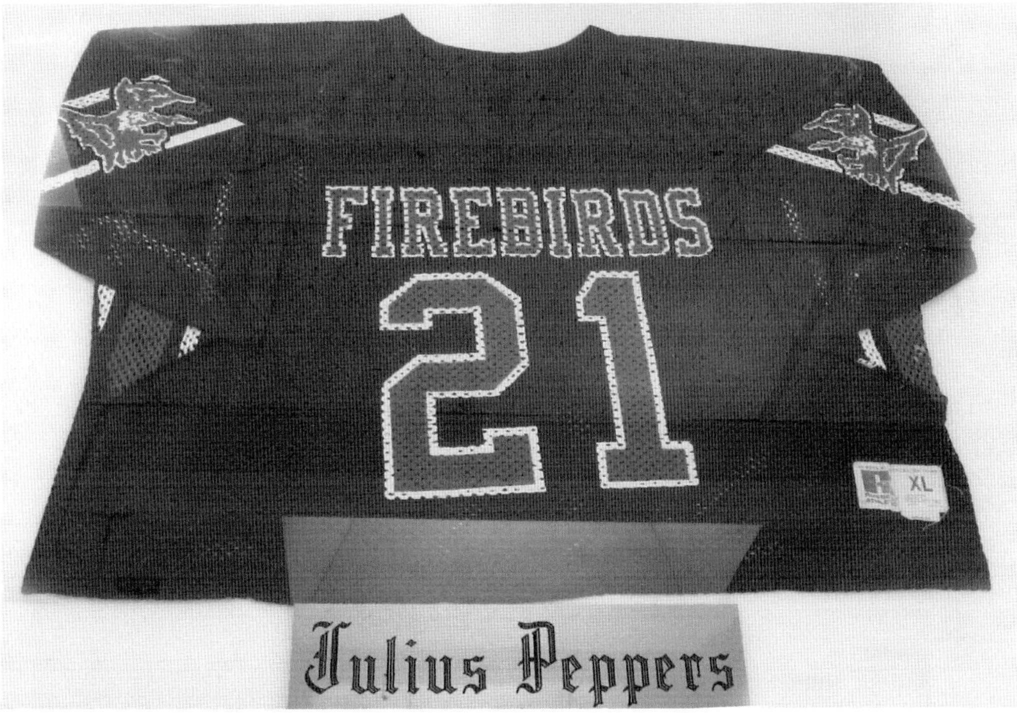

Julius Frazier Peppers
The North Carolina High School "Athlete of the Year" in 1998, Peppers played football and basketball at Southern Nash High School. He was all-conference for four years in basketball and a member of the state-championship relay team in track. Peppers attended UNC, where he played both basketball and football. He was drafted in 2002 by the Carolina Panthers and played in the Super Bowl. He is currently playing with the Chicago Bears. (Photograph by the author with permission from Southern Nash High School.)

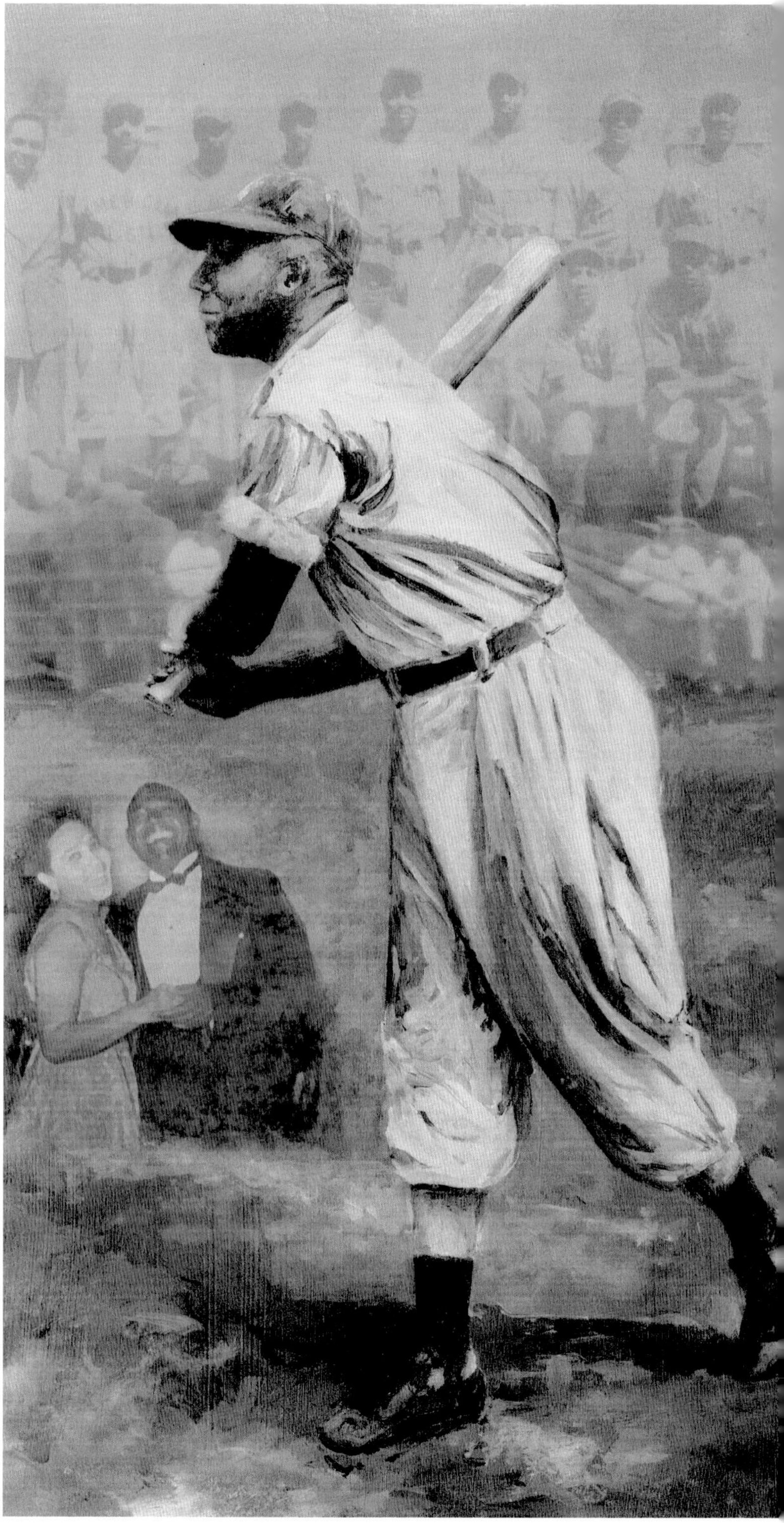

Walter Fenner "Buck" Leonard
Baseball great Buck Leonard (TCHOF 2004) was inducted into the National Baseball Hall of Fame in 1972. He is also remembered as a community leader and motivator, especially of young people. Leonard was born in Rocky Mount on September 8, 1907, and attended Lincoln Elementary School. After quitting school in the eighth grade to help care for his family, he worked in the mill and shined shoes at the railroad station; he later worked for the ACL Railroad. Leonard played minor-league baseball in Rocky Mount and subsequently became a star in the Negro Leagues. A first baseman, he was often called "the black Lou Gehrig." Leonard played for the Brooklyn Royal Giants, but for most of his career he wore the uniform of the Pittsburgh Homestead Grays and played with Josh Gibson. Both were inducted into the Baseball Hall of Fame the same year. Leonard had a .320 batting average, 60 home runs, 275 RBIs, and scored 352 runs. After his baseball career, Leonard was a truancy officer in Rocky Mount schools, where he became widely known as a disciplinarian and a motivator of students. (Portrait by Susan Fecho.)

Charlie Edward "Chuck" Hinton
At Booker T. Washington High School, Hinton (TCHOF 2008) played in the band and also played basketball and football for one year each. He played semiprofessional football before accepting an athletic scholarship to play baseball, football, and basketball at Shaw University. After his Army service, Hinton joined the Orioles and, in 1959, was "Rookie of the Year" in the minor-league farm team. He played in the 1964 all-star game and spent 11 years in the majors. After retiring from professional ball, Hinton coached at Howard University for 28 years. In 2002, he wrote *My Time at Bat*. (Portrait by Susan Fecho.)

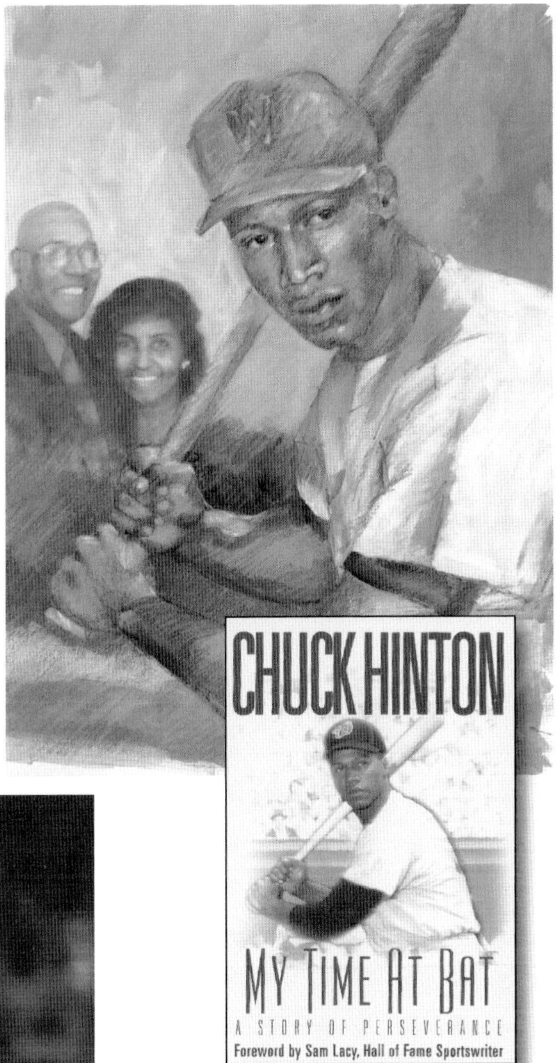

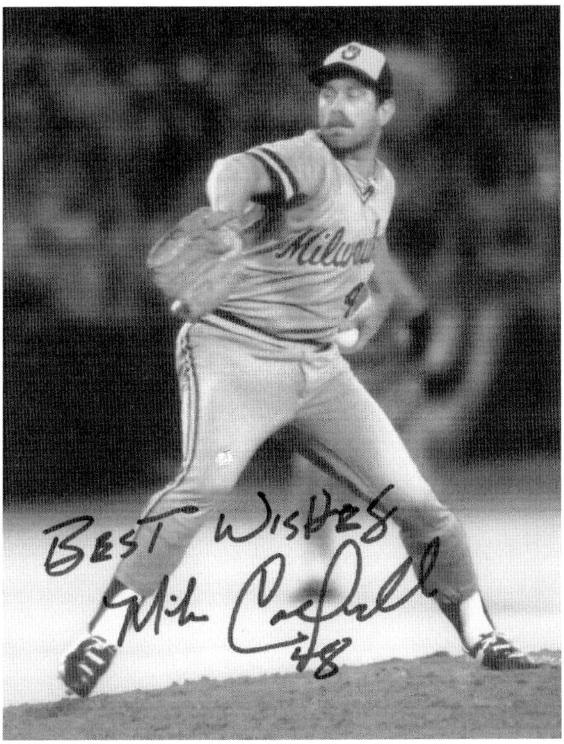

Michael Caldwell
Tarboro native Caldwell pitched two no-hitters in high school and took NC State to its first competition in the College World Series after the team won the ACC championship that season. He was drafted by the San Diego Padres. He also played for the San Francisco Giants and Cincinnati Reds before finding a home with the Milwaukee Brewers. He pitched for 14 seasons and in the 1982 World Series. He ended with a career 3.81 ERA. (Courtesy Michael Caldwell.)

Edward "Harvie" Ward Jr.
Ward (TCHOF 2008) was born in Tarboro in 1925 and learned to play golf on the sand greens of Hilma Country Club. Ward won his first tournament, the Linville Invitational, at age 14. He then won the 1948 North and South Amateur Championship at Pinehurst and the NCAA Championship in 1949. In 1952, he won the British Amateur. Ward was one of only nine to win consecutive US championships (in 1955 and 1956), and in 1956, he won the Canadian Amateur. He played on three Walker Cup teams and was undefeated in six matches. Ward finished fourth in the Masters in 1957. He beat Jack Nicklaus in the 1958 US Amateur. (Portrait by Susan Fecho.)

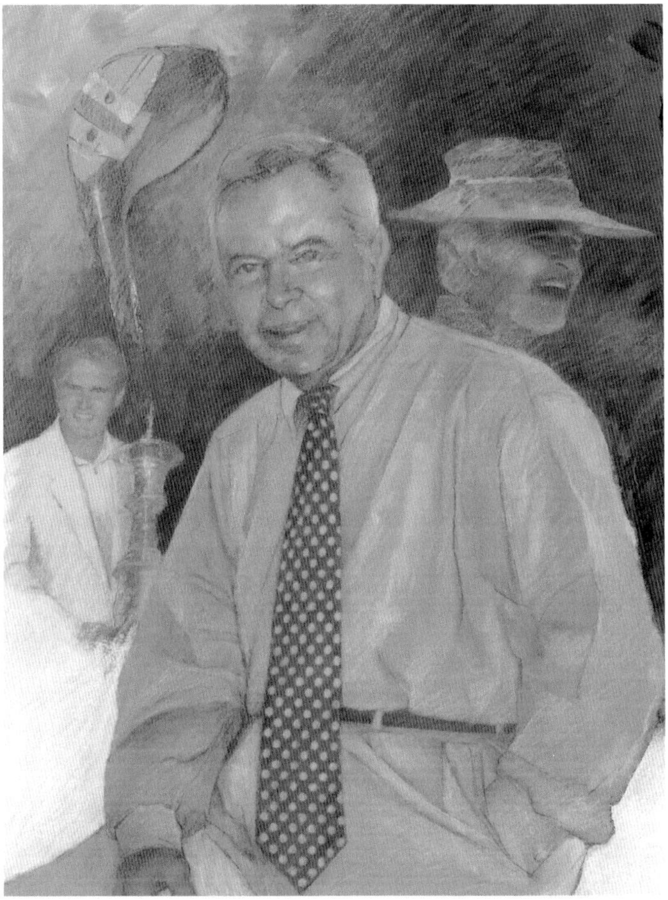

Michael Stokes
Stokes (right) wrestled four years at Tarboro High with a record of 96-4. He was a three-time North Carolina state champion in high school and went to NC State University where he had a record of 68-8. He was the ACC's Most Valuable Wrestler. He finished second to Kendall Cross (who would go on to win Olympic gold) in a 1989 national collegiate competition. Today, the Michael Stokes Award is presented annually to an outstanding wrestler in eastern North Carolina. (Photograph by the author.)

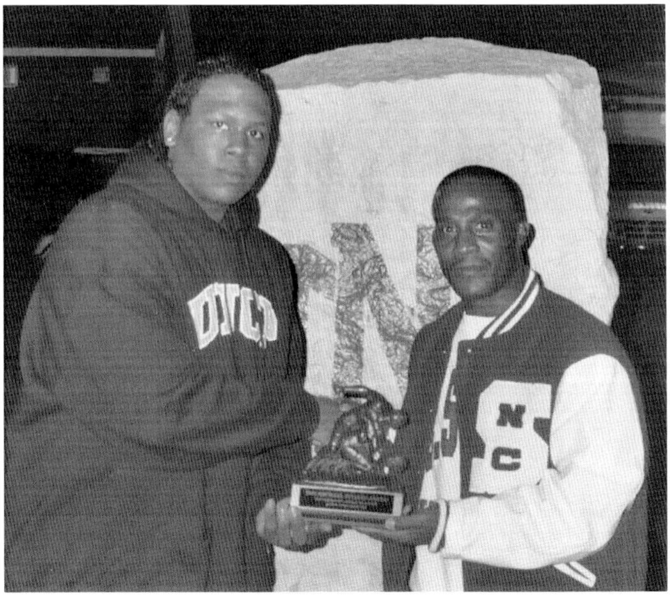

BIBLIOGRAPHY

Barringer, Bugs, Dot Barringer and Lela Chesson. *A Pictorial History of Rocky Mount.* Rocky Mount, NC: Donning Company Publishers, 1977.

Bridgers, Henry Clark, Jr. *The East Carolina Railway: Route of the Yellowhammer.* Tarboro, NC: T&E Publishers of Louisville, 1973.

"Honoring Our Veterans." *Tarboro Daily Southerner.* Special insert. March 31, 2008.

Pace, Lee. *Blackbirds: The Glory Days of Rocky Mount Athletics.* Chapel Hill, NC: Pace Enterprises, 2007.

Rocky Mount: Gateway of Eastern North Carolina, Rocky Mount, NC: Rocky Mount Chamber of Commerce, 1911.

Taylor, Roland, ed. *Mabrey Bass's Tarboro from 1950–1990.* Fuquay-Varina, NC: Research Triangle Publishing, 1997.

INDEX

INDEX

Consistent with our mission to preserve history on a local level, this book was printed in South Carolina on American-made paper and manufactured entirely in the United States. Products carrying the accredited Forest Stewardship Council (FSC) label are printed on 100 percent FSC-certified paper.

MADE IN THE USA